Dead in the Water Endorsements

"Ever wonder what it's like to investigate a murder a hundred miles offshore? Farrell's eye for detail shines through, as does a great New England vibe. You'll feel like you're sitting in a salty old Cape Cod bar, having a couple of beers, and listening to an ancient sea yarn. Fantastic!"

—Michael Harvey, creator of A&E's
Cold Case Files and bestselling author of *Brighton*

"Nathan Carman and his insurer headed to court in Providence, Rhode Island, battling it out in what would be Nathan's biggest legal challenge yet."

—Deborah Roberts, anchor,
ABC News *20/20* "Family Lies"

"A fascinating deep dive into the intricacies of one of New England's most compelling nautical mysteries, with a warning to all would-be criminals of the high seas."

—Susan Zalkind, *Vice*

DEAD IN THE WATER

THE REAL STORY OF NATHAN CARMAN

David J. Farrell, Jr.

A POST HILL PRESS BOOK
ISBN: 979-8-89565-350-0
ISBN (eBook): 979-8-89565-351-7

Dead in the Water:
The Real Story of Nathan Carman

Cover design by Jim Villaflores
Cover photo credit: Michael Dwyer/AP

Note: Images printed in this book and others can be viewed at davidjfarrelljr.com.

Post Hill Press
New York • Nashville
posthillpress.com

Published in the United States of America
1 2 3 4 5 6 7 8 9 10

For My Dear Amelia…
who lived through ANAT.
Twice.

CONTENTS

2018

2019

2020–2023

LOOMINGS

You might say we gave Nathan Carman enough rope to hang himself.

A routine pretrial technique, especially with witnesses who you know going in have credibility problems, is to just let them talk and talk. And make mistakes. But Nathan was a control freak, and it was hard getting him to open up. So our strategy instead was to patiently chum him in closer and closer, and catch him by surprise.

Before law school I first learned how on the thirty-foot F/V *Eddie Boy* out of Chatham. After a codfishing trip "down below" to the Great South Channel, while dressing off our catch, we'd save the guts in a big plastic barrel and then go tuna fishing east of Cape Cod. I would ladle codfish livers or chunks of herring and mackerel overboard as chum, creating an oily slick to attract bluefins. Somewhere in the slick was a hook baited with an entrée of innards—or, even better, a live wiggling whiting.

You can overdo the chum, though. Offering too much gives tuna fish too much to eat and they might skip the hook altogether as blue sharks, and even a mako or great white, will get drawn into a too-generous slick, disrupting everything.

But if all was right and good, a bluefin would bite—then off we'd go on a modern Nantucket sleighride. Eddie Reid was a human reel, fighting the bluefin with gloved hands and rope line. I'd run the boat up on the line as Eddie hauled in, or yelled at me to slow down or back down, and the fish would run, repeat…repeat…repeat…for up to an hour or more, with us trying to get closer each time.

The battle continued as our warm-blooded prey, maybe more than one thousand pounds, was finally so tired that we'd be near enough for me to throw the harpoon, its sharpened bronze dart slicing into the crimson flesh. *Stuck!* Then, as I withdrew the harpoon, the dart toggled 90° onto its long convex axis, and now flat, unlike an arrow, it would probably not pull out. Eye spliced to the dart, stout three-sixteenths-inch ground line exiting the entrance wound, I would cleat down our catch. Then we'd tail wrap and tie it off on the side of the boat for the trip in, where a truck would meet us to take it to Boston for its flight to Tokyo.

It took a while to catch Nathan too. He presented some sort of serious mental disorder spliced into a purported genius IQ. But he was not nearly as smart as he liked to convey. Any knucklehead knows that after blowing someone's head off, you pick up the spent shells and get rid of the firearm to preclude ballistics testing. But Nathan was in over his head three years later when trying to get away with what he did at sea.

After we hooked him, Nathan Carman desperately tried to run free, but I stuck him good. Twice.

***

Before getting underway, let's take a quick look toward the end of the story.

After the lawyers' closing arguments in our 2019 civil trial denying Nathan Carman's marine insurance claim for his sunken boat, he exited the Federal Courthouse in Providence, Rhode Island, and addressed the media waiting on the steps below.

> Firstly, we don't know what caused the boat to sink.
>
> Secondly, this isn't about money. It's an eighty-five-thousand-dollar claim; it's a contingency fee. I get a fraction of that if I win—and I've put lots of time, effort, and, frankly, a lot of misery into this.

After a Hollywood pause, he pulled himself together, continuing:

> I almost feel like I have a responsibility to my mom to make sure that the truth comes out, and Mr. Farrell and the insurers...have made claims against me that are so tremendous I don't feel like I can walk away from them. That's why I'm here. I'm not here about the money. And I just wanted to clarify that.
>
> That's all I have to say.[1]

True to his word, for once, Nathan did not have much more to say in public, only a couple of words later on. Yet one of his lawyers erroneously said this about his reclusive client: "The real story of Nathan Carman may never be told."

Objection.

This book, I respectfully submit, is *The Real Story of Nathan Carman*. It will be presented chronologically, just as Liam O'Connell, my law partner, and our team discovered facts through our investigation and our lawsuit against Nathan Carman for marine insurance fraud. Court proceedings and testimony will be extensively presented verbatim (with only minimal editing for readability, omitting "ums" and "ahs"

---

1 WPRI.com video published on Facebook, September 4, 2019. https://www.facebook.com/WPRI12/videos/nathan-carman-just-spoke-outside-court-saying-this-isnt-about-money-but-rather-m/2118086531834476/.

and other such non-substantive clutter), and the reader should be ready to dive down into the seaweed of nautical evidence, which is how we solved the case.

Please note our law firm does not as a rule talk on the record with the media about our cases beyond "No comment" or "You can quote me on what I say in court and in our court filings." But since Nathan's insurance trial is well astern, and there was never anything remotely embarrassing reflecting on our insurance company clients, our public statements here have few professional restrictions, with three caveats. First, Nathan's pretrial discovery depositions are sealed by court protective orders; however, his essential deposition testimony will be discussed and quoted from his other publicly available statements, and there are no restrictions on his trial testimony, which is extensively quoted. Second, there is one witness whose name and depositions are also protected by court orders, but her involvement is otherwise public knowledge. And third, our insurance clients do not want their names used in this book. So even though their actions throughout were laudatory, I will simply call them the "Insurer."

Our real story is based on the full investigation that Liam and I were able to conduct only because Nathan made an insurance claim for his sunken boat. That gave the Insurer, under the contractual terms of Nathan's insurance policy, the exclusive right—which law enforcement lacked—to require him to give me a recorded examination under oath (EUO), which lasted five hours and occurred just three months after he and his mother departed on their fateful voyage. It was the foundation of the case against Nathan, and this book is the first to address it and our exclusive access to its exhibits.

Based on his sworn EUO testimony, the following month we filed a federal court civil lawsuit against Nathan Carman in Providence to enforce the Insurer's denial of his marine insurance claim. Through formal litigation procedures I further interrogated him in three separate deposition sessions, totaling another ten hours over the course of 2018, chumming, hooking, and harpooning him, respectively.

We subpoenaed otherwise reluctant witnesses to fill in evidentiary gaps. Our expert witnesses studied all the evidence and convincingly detailed their opinions on what really happened versus what Nathan testified happened.

Old-fashioned gumshoe work paid off too, in stunning ways. Routine digging around New England rifled Nathan's story, setting him up to assert his Fifth Amendment refusal to answer my targeted deposition questions. And there was Liam's chase around the world for critical maritime evidence, which placed his life and limb in imminent jeopardy in anything but a harbor of refuge—a recurring theme in this case.

Just shy of three years after the sinking, we went to trial, with United States District Court, District of Rhode Island Chief Judge John J. McConnell, Jr. skillfully keeping the lid on a media circus. We got zero help—*zero*—from law enforcement. And all our work was funded by the Insurer because it was quickly convinced that it would be morally wrong to let Nathan get away with murder. Again.

As will be described, in our marine insurance fraud trial we were prepared to present the whole story behind Nathan's greedy, creepy scheme—the amassing of a family fortune from nursing homes, Nathan's written road map for accelerating his inheritance, the sultry phone call that triggered one murder, the disappearance at sea for another, and the startling similarities between the two. Unveiling this tragedy was based on hard evidence, the kind admissible in a court of law, not speculation from self-appointed experts on social media or mere interviews. No, it is our adversarial litigation system that best ferrets out the truth. We had gotten the go-ahead from one judge to present the whole saga, but Judge McConnell reined us in, focusing on just one clause in Nathan's insurance policy. At trial, we won on that clause, and stuck Nathan a second time.

And now, "the rest of the story."[2]

---

2 "Paul Harvey Famous Quotes," Quotesanity. https://quotesanity.com/paul-harvey-famous-quotes/.

2016

1

"HAVE YOU FOUND HER?"

"Thanks for the heads-up," said the Insurer's on-call adjuster.

I had telephoned to report there were news reports of an overdue Rhode Island recreational boat with a Nathan and Linda Carman aboard. The adjuster then checked the Insurer's list of current boating policies, and it turned out that Mr. Carman was indeed one of its insured customers.

Was I ambulance chasing, like a personal injury lawyer handing out business cards in a hospital emergency room? Sure, I'd probably get the legal work if something developed—but I'd worked thirty years for that insurance company. The smart ones have a network of maritime lawyers around the country and around the world as their eyes and ears to gather local intel.

After all, it's a big ocean. Any number of things can go wrong, and the marine insurer, on behalf of its insured vessel owner, is often the first responder. In this situation, the Insurer might have to hire a salvor to find the missing Carman boat and bring it back to port. There might be a need to deal with fatalities, arrange for medical care, clean up a fuel spill, maybe deal with the United States Coast Guard or law enforcement, and who knows what else? Often that means the insurance company needs someone on scene, usually a trusted local maritime attorney, for serious problems. Best to be ready for whatever might develop.

But who would have ever guessed that seven days later one of the missing boaters would be so fortunate as to get plucked from his life raft by a 653-foot Chinese bulker named *Orient Lucky*? That happened one day after the Coast Guard's search and rescue (SAR) operation was suspended—suspended because the chances of survival were statistically futile. Right away, we had to ask, "Was this suspicious or a miracle?"

On one hand, the Coast Guard has SAR down to a science. With whatever known information there is, Coast Guard cutters, helicopters, and fixed-wing assets (Coast Guard-speak for airplanes and jets) with state-of-the-art radar, infrared night vision, and heat sensors expand their focused search area as days go by, extrapolating from weather and current conditions. According to Coast Guard records, multiple search patterns were conducted along the continental shelf from Hudson Canyon, seventy-five miles south of Long Island, to Nygren Canyon, two hundred miles east-southeast of Nantucket. One helicopter had to make an emergency landing due to mechanical issues. Any debris found on the surface was checked out. An "unknown radar contact" that appeared to be dead in the water turned out to be just a "slow-moving" fishing boat, underway with no way on (not anchored, just drifting).[3]

Ever since I got my USCG unlimited radar observer endorsement in 1990, I've thought "dead in the water" was a very descriptive salty term.

For the overdue Carman boat, the search eventually covered sixty-two thousand square miles, an area bigger than the state of Georgia. Radio broadcasts to mariners alerted vessels in an even larger area to be on the look-out for any sign of the missing vessel or POB (people on board). But after six days, all hope was lost.[4]

---

[3] The records, photos, and graphics discussed in this book come from our investigation and litigation. Most ended up as exhibits in our marine insurance trial and are cited and abbreviated as is this Case Report from the USCG Freedom of Information Act response, Tr. Ex. 18.2.

[4] Tr. Ex. 18.2.

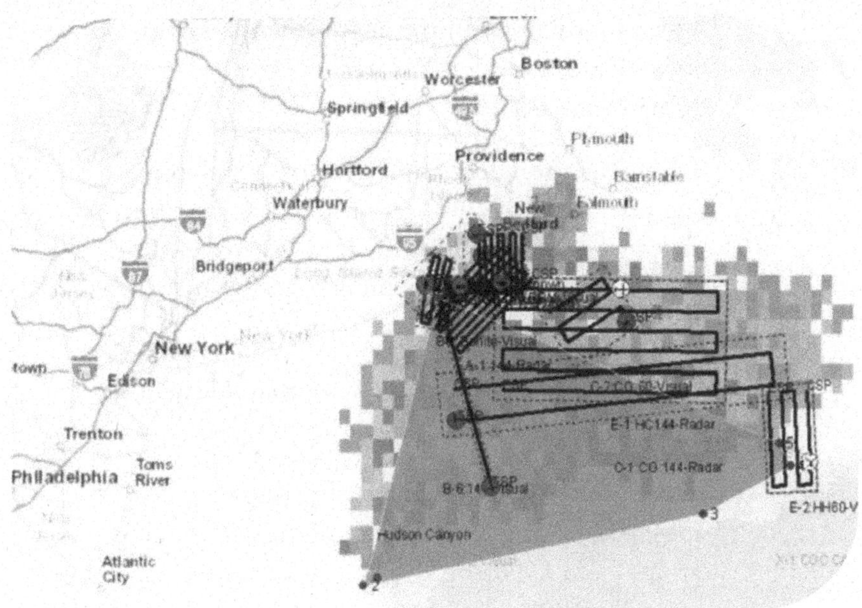

Yet lo and behold, here we had Mr. Carman unexpectedly surface on Sunday, September 25, 2016 inside the search area, appearing outwardly healthy, seven days after he was reported missing. *Orient Lucky* Captain Zhao Hengdong emailed his remarkable find to the Coast Guard in Boston, providing the latitude and longitude of the rescue location, 106 miles south of Martha's Vineyard.

A flat, curiously unemotional interview by radio between Coast Guard Operations Specialist Richard Arsenault and Nathan from the *Orient Lucky* bridge[5] was soon widely played by the news media.

> **USCG**: Nathan, this is United States Coast Guard, Boston. I need to understand what happened. Over.
>
> **Carman**: Mom and I—two people—myself and my mom, were fishing in Block Canyon, and there

5 Evan Lubofsky, "A Son Is Rescued at Sea. But What Happened to His Mother?" *Wired,* July 13, 2021. https://www.wired.com/story/a-son-is-rescued-at-sea-but-what-happened-to-his-mother/.

was a funny noise in the engine compartment. I looked and saw a lot of water.... I had my mom bring in the reel.

I brought the safety stuff forward. I was bringing one of the safety bags forward. The boat just dropped out from under my feet. When I saw the life raft, I did not see my mom—have you found her?

USCG: No, we...uh...no, we haven't been able to find her yet.

Carman: So I got to the life raft after I got my bearings, and I was whistling and calling and looking around and I didn't see her.... It was a week ago today.[6]

After sailing east around Nantucket, then north in the Great South Channel shipping lanes around Cape Cod, *Orient Lucky* dropped Nathan off at Coast Guard Station Boston for a face-to-face survivor debriefing. That night, Nathan spoke to the media from his Vermont home.

> I would just like to thank the public for their prayers and for their concern for both my mother and for myself. Emotionally I have been through a huge amount and my request is just to be allowed to mourn naturally.[7]

The next day Nathan's photo in the Coast Guard launch arriving in Boston (the source for this book's cover) appeared in newspapers across the US, the UK, and Australia.

---

6 US Coast Guard radio interview with Nathan Carman. https://soundcloud.com/cassandra-day-460949382/coast-guard-audio-with-nathan-carman-rescued-at-sea.

7 "Lost at Sea," ABC News *20/20*, February 3, 2017. https://www.youtube.com/watch?v=-GHRWC9jY3M.

Michael Dwyer/AP

First impression, best impression. Nathan Carman went viral, his name on its way to becoming onomatopoeic for evil and greed.

Two days later, even wilder news broke: Nathan had been the primary suspect in the Connecticut shooting death of his grandfather, John Chakalos, three years before. If true, that meant Nathan was the last person to see both his grandfather and his mother alive. *WTF?*

The old adage that motive, means, and opportunity add up to guilt was doubly tied together by a *Hartford Courant* article:[8] "Records show Chakalos' estate was worth about $40 million, and his four daughters, including Linda Carman, were beneficiaries."

Motive, check.

The article further reported the "details of the slaying of Carman's grandfather, John Chakalos, at his home on Overlook Drive in Windsor are contained in the warrant application to search Carman's apartment

[8] Dave Altimari, David Owens, Mikaela Porter, and Shawn R. Beals, "Nathan Carman: Grandfather Was 'Like a Father to Me,'" *Hartford Courant*, September 28, 2016. https://www.courant.com/2016/09/28/nathan-carman-grandfather-was-like-a-father-to-me/.

in 2014." According to the application, "Carman was the last known person to see Chakalos alive" when they had dinner together on December 19, 2013. The next morning, "one of Chakalos' daughters found 87-year-old Chakalos dead in his home—shot three times in the head and torso."

Opportunity, check.

Also, according to the article, "Carman told police he had experience shooting guns at shooting ranges."

Means, check.

The *Hartford Courant* article noted, "[I]n July 2014, Windsor police submitted an arrest warrant for Carman on a murder charge, but the warrant was returned by the prosecutor unsigned the next day…with a 'request for further information.' Carman was not charged. The chief state's attorney's cold case unit is assisting Windsor police in the investigation, but no arrests have been made in the murder, authorities said."

This brings us to Linda Carman. With the same multimillion-dollar inheritance for a motive, a sunken boat providing the means for her death, and Nathan's opportunity with her alone at sea, his guilt seemed like it could add up twice.

The *Hartford Courant* article also reported that the South Kingstown, Rhode Island, police had just conducted a search of Nathan's home in Vernon, Vermont, "seeking documents, maps, global positioning devices, computers, hand-held electronic devices and books that would provide information about the Carmans' location or destination. Police were also seeking receipts for purchases of boat parts or equipment for repairs to Carman's boat."

According to the South Kingstown PD search warrant, their investigation found that "Nathan's boat was in need of mechanical repair and that Nathan had been conducting a portion of these repairs upon his own volition which could have potentially rendered the boat unsafe for operation," to "support a charge of 'operating so as to endanger, resulting in death.'" A "witness told police that Carman removed the trim tabs from his boat and patched the holes with a marine sealant…."

"...South Kingstown police said a friend of Linda Carman told police that she had refused to fish any farther than Block Island and that she believed their destination was Striper Rock near Block Island."

However, a "woman whose boat was docked next to Carman's told police that he told her he intended to fish at the 'Canyons,' about 100 miles offshore, according to the warrant. Carman told the Coast Guard the boat sank at Block Canyon."

Significantly, according to the Coast Guard's Nicole Groll, "Nathan Carman did not see any of [our] planes or ships that searched for six days, including the area where he said the boat went down and where he was found." She continued, "[W]hy he didn't see us and we didn't see him is still unclear." The Coast Guard "did everything we could to find Nathan Carman."

This was Nathan's response to the reporter in a telephone interview also quoted in the *Hartford Courant* article:

> All I'm going to say right now to you is that a terrible tragedy happened.... I'm lucky to be alive, I lost my mother and very, very difficult people, especially the *Hartford Courant,* are...raking up the time when I lost my grandfather. [He] was like a father to me and [they're] casting that in just a very, very wrong light.

2

UNKNOWN UNKNOWNS

That was certainly a lot of information packed into one *Hartford Courant* news article. But what were observers able to know "for sure"[9] about the sinking based on early media reports?

First and foremost, Nathan's mother, Linda Carman, unfortunately didn't make it. Then again, there are always those stories of people vanishing at sea ending up alive and well years later in some far-off land. There's a guy I know whose brother was suspected of something like that. Maybe Linda wasn't even onboard. Pure speculation, but maybe she knew Nathan did it, or maybe she shot her father and needed to get away.

It took less imagination to consider that if Nathan had indeed shot his grandfather and had now just offed his mother at sea, he clearly was proactive in the pursuit of his inheritance.

Or was his *Orient Lucky* rescue the exception, with Nathan otherwise plain unlucky to have innocently lost both his grandfather and mother in such tragic yet different ways?

---

9 "Q: What do you know today…for sure? A: Not a damn thing," Keith Warren Jennison, *Vermont is Where You Find It,* chapter 12 (Countryman Press, 1954).

Borrowing from late Defense Secretary Donald H. Rumsfeld, there were a lot of "known unknowns." And "unknown unknowns."[10]

Second, we knew—at least according to Nathan's Coast Guard radio interview—that his boat sank something like one hundred miles offshore in Block Canyon, due south of Rhode Island, where the continental shelf drops off toward the deep ocean abyssal plain.

Assuming the boat did sink in Block Canyon, Nathan's life raft then must have drifted to the south and east where *Orient Lucky* picked him up, shown below.[11] Wind and current would be the two natural variables affecting Nathan's drift, varying with their respective directions and velocities. What did he do for food and water over that week? Why hadn't the Coast Guard found him?

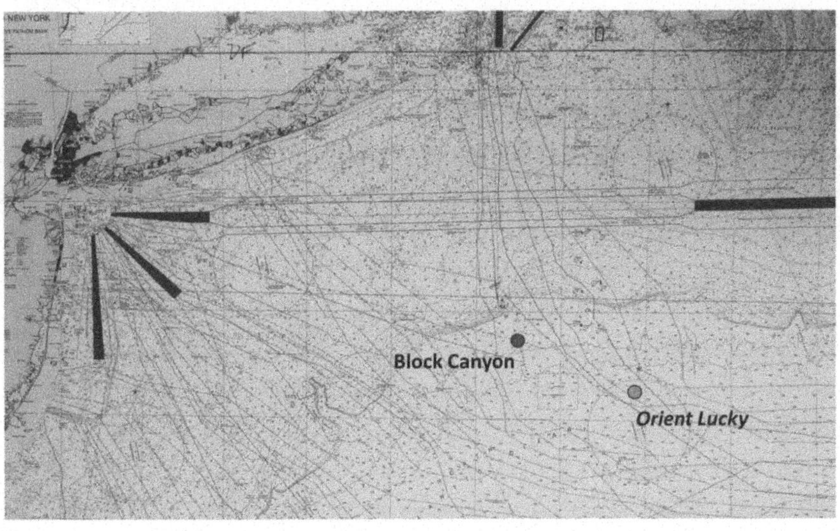

In short, there was not much known for sure at this early point about Nathan's and Linda's final voyage and aftermath, other than he was

[10] Dan Zak, "'Nothing ever ends': Sorting through Rumsfeld's knowns and unknowns," *The Washington Post*, July 1, 2022. https://www.washingtonpost.com/lifestyle/style/rumsfeld-dead-words-known-unknowns/2021/07/01/831175c2-d9df-11eb-bb9e-70fda8c37057_story.html.

[11] Tr. Ex. 39. https://www.rid.uscourts.gov/sites/rid/files/documents/17cv38/082219/P-39.pdf.

alive. It was only his unsubstantiated story that the boat sank September 18 somewhere in Block Canyon. And it was only the *Orient Lucky*'s unsubstantiated report that it rescued him a week later, 106 miles south of Martha's Vineyard. That all added up to a lot of unknown unknowns.

***

Before we go any further, an introduction to some basic nautical concepts will be helpful, with some quick tutorials interspersed later. It shouldn't be too complicated if your author does his job of teaching.[12]

Let's start with winds and currents, very important in this story. Wind directions are named for the compass direction from which the wind blows. Most know from TV weather that a south wind blows toward the north. In contrast, ocean currents are named for the direction toward which the current flows.

Thus, wind and current directions use opposite naming conventions. An east wind and a west current work in unison, both going the same direction (west), whereas an east wind and an east current oppose each other and can cause choppy seas, commonly "wind against the tide," where there are inshore tidal currents driven by the rise and fall of tides, something saltwater boaters can appreciate.

But in the open ocean there are other, nontidal currents, and the Gulf Stream immediately comes to mind. Nathan was so far offshore that maybe he got dragged into it as it curves south of New England and northeast toward northern Europe. Or maybe the cold Labrador Current's New England spurs coming off the clockwise gyre of Georges Bank would have pushed him in a westerly direction. With no hurricanes in the northwest Atlantic during the time Nathan was missing, normal surface winds would have tended to push him downwind. The combined effect of all these wind and current forces on his life raft's drift presented unknown knowns—data that might be researched and retrieved to determine the meteorological and oceanic conditions

---

12 Trial lawyers "are teachers. That's what it means to be a lawyer," Hon. William G. Young, *Reflections of a Trial Judge* (Massachusetts Continuing Legal Education, 1998), 40.

present while Nathan was missing, to see if his story about being adrift for seven days added up.

Maybe it would. Maybe the *Orient Lucky* rescue was prearranged. Maybe another vessel was involved. Or maybe something else.

***

Nearly as big as "poor little Rhode Island"[13] itself, Block Canyon is a deep gorge created by the last Ice Age's retreating meltwaters flooding toward sea level, which was much lower than it is now. Narrow at its north and shallower end, the Block Canyon headwall is a ragged horseshoe-shaped sinkhole in the continental slope, precipitously dropping from fifty fathoms to more than one hundred fathoms deep. With six feet in every fathom, the one-hundred-fathom, or six-hundred-foot, bathymetric (contour) line on a chart (the maritime word for map) depicting the headwall's geography has three or four adjacent lobes, roughly shaped like its sometimes name, the Fishtails. South of there, Block Canyon widens and drops into a broad valley descending the continental rise, running down toward mile-and-a-half depths.

South of New England along the continental slope there are several similar canyons. To the west, the biggest, Hudson Canyon, gouged by the prehistoric Hudson River, which formerly extended 100 miles southeast of Manhattan; to the east, Corsair Canyon (actually in Canadian waters), 230 miles east of Nantucket. It must have been quite a Michenerian sight fifteen thousand years ago for a North American Noah with a boatload of saber-toothed tiger, woolly mammoth, and giant beaver couples during the Great Flood to sail below a dozen huger-than-Niagara waterfalls.

With continuous ice melt, sea level kept rising worldwide, submerging the canyons. Gulf Stream-influenced warmer waters, upwelling in swirling eddies into a canyon gorge, deliver diverse nutrients, which

---

13 "Poor Little Rhode Island," Guy Lombardo and His Royal Canadians, 1945. Although the smallest of the forty-eight states, it had the longest name until 2020, when voters bifurcated The State of Rhode Island and Providence Plantations and jettisoned the second half.

feed microcosms, which feed bait, which feed bigger fish. In the 1970s some Chatham commercial tub trawl boats (using longlines on the bottom with hundreds of baited hooks) fished the canyons for tilefish, a chameleon-colored bottom fish. That was a long trip on a slow boat.

These days a quick canyon trip in an expensive, multi-engine, offshore fishing machine offers sport fishers the lure of topwater tropical game fish excitement. Catches can include a variety of tuna fish, mahi-mahi, wahoo, and even billfish like blue marlin.

Determining whether Nathan's boat sank in Block Canyon or elsewhere would be essential for anyone investigating Nathan's story. It would be optimal, of course, to recover the boat and examine its condition, which would hinge on knowing exactly where it sank.

Even if the boat was never found, Nathan's identification of where he said it sank would be essential in attempting to re-create his claimed drift to the *Orient Lucky*. But what if Nathan's navigation was mistaken, or he was flat-out lying and his boat sank somewhere other than Block Canyon, such that his life raft drift started at another location, or at another time? What if the Chinese-owned *Orient Lucky*, for whatever reason, misreported the rescue location? How near were instruments measuring wind and current directions and velocities? More unknowns. One known known is that it's a big ocean. If those instruments were far from Block Canyon, how accurately could they project Nathan's life raft drift to re-create its course?

***

With more certainty and immediacy, interested observers were able to see news photos and TV video with our own eyes that upon Nathan's disembarking in Boston, awkward though he appeared, he must have had food and water during his time missing at sea because he looked physically okay. That conclusion was further bolstered by photos and video posted by the *Hartford Courant,* taken by the *Orient Lucky* crew, and obtained from the captain by investigative reporter Dave Altimari, who met the ship in Halifax, Nova Scotia, after it departed Boston.

The *Orient Lucky* rescue photos and video showed Nathan climbing step-by-step up the steep gangway and walking on deck, in no apparent distress—apparently after getting knocked around in his life raft for a week. Indeed, *Orient Lucky*'s documentation of the rescue[14] showed the conditions Nathan apparently endured, at least that day, apparently 106 miles from shore, with choppy, eight-foot seas and upwards of a twenty-five-plus-knot north-northeast breeze. Yet there he was, standing up in his bobbing float…on seven days of sea legs.

As you have likely gathered, perhaps to your dismay, "apparently" is a big word for maritime casualty lawyers. In our peculiar field of expertise, we take the apparent maritime story and facts as alleged to us by an opposing party and dissect them in an effort to get to the truth. Commonly it's a fascinating puzzle we are tasked to solve, employing nautical skills built up over a lifetime and professionally honed interrogation techniques, which explains why we enjoy doing it (begrudgingly) at lower hourly rates than, say, slick divorce lawyers.

It certainly seemed appropriate that law enforcement was onto Nathan as soon as *Orient Lucky* dropped him off in Boston. But there was nothing for the Insurer to do unless someone made a claim.

Nathan didn't wait very long.

[14] Tr. Ex. 32.11.

3

"THEN I MADE MYSELF TAKE REST"

Claims adjuster Martha Charlesworth, a lawyer, took Nathan's call on October 7, 2016, noting he was surprised that the Insurer had already opened a file on him. He requested payment of his boat's $85,000 insured value and told Martha, "the boat sank very far off shore and would not likely be recovered."[15]

Sympathetic for his mother's loss, Martha was cordial and professional, but of course she needed more information. Already aware that the Insurer had paid a $33,489.33 insurance claim submitted by Nathan for his boat's overheated diesel engine a few months earlier, she promptly assigned marine surveyor Dexter Holaday to review the replacement engine's installation by Point Judith Marina and assess whether the boat was seaworthy when it departed on its final trip. Martha also appointed our office to investigate and determine whether the sinking claim was legally covered under the terms of Nathan's marine insurance policy.

[15] Tr. Ex. 17.2 at P159.

Our beginning point was the written report of another marine surveyor Nathan had hired to evaluate the boat before he decided to purchase it. Akin to an inspection report when purchasing a house, the same survey report is commonly submitted by the new boat owner to a marine insurer as part of the insurance application process, so it knows what it is being asked to underwrite. Marine insurers don't want to insure something full of holes and destined to sink. Martha sent us a copy.

While anybody might claim to be a marine surveyor, Nathan chose Bernie Feeney of Kingston, Massachusetts, a member of the respected Society of Accredited Marine Surveyors (SAMS). Although I had never run across him previously, Feeney conducted a thorough inspection detailed in thirty-eight well-presented pages, referencing Coast Guard regulations and American Boat and Yacht Council standards. Here's Feeney's essential finding of the thirty-one-foot-long JC Plug No. 1:

> VESSEL DESCRIPTION
>
> 1973 JC 31, it was indicated that this vessel was the hull "plug" constructed for the fabrication of the original hull mold of the JC 31. The "plug" was covered both outer and inner surfaces with FRP [fiber-reinforced plastic] laminates and finished as a lobster boat. The current owner bought the vessel and completely gutted the hull and cabin structures as well as a major refit was performed over a three year period. With a replacement used engine, new running gear, rebuilt internal structures and decking of wood, FRP and aluminum components, the vessel was sighted to be in serviceable condition...suitable for its intended use and an acceptable risk.[16]

As Feeney described it, this was no ordinary mass-production recreational boat resembling a Clorox jug. As the original "plug," it was the mold for dozens of fiberglass-hull JC commercial lobster boats. Much

[16] EUO, Ex. 2 at P334.

more solid than its offspring, the stout plug had a durable internal structure of mahogany over which a fiberglass slab had been laid on both the inboard and outboard sides.

Brian Woods, who sold the boat to Nathan, had creatively refurbished it. Instead of a traditional lobster boat, which has its steering and engine controls forward with a cuddy and bunks below, Woods had fabricated an enclosed center-console wheelhouse (or pilothouse) of aluminum, enabling a 360-degree walk-around deck from bow to stern. The foredeck and topsides were also aluminum, making this a very rugged workboat. The result was the marriage of a strong and sea-kindly hull widely used in New England waters for decades, with a center-console helm favored by many sportfishing boat designs. Even better, this center-console was completely enclosed and weathertight.

Feeney's report included multiple photos of the diesel engine and mechanical equipment below deck, such as two automatic bilge pumps (to pump accumulated water overboard) and a bird's-eye diagram of the boat. He conducted moisture readings of the hull in various spots and found none so high as to question its structural integrity.

Feeney reported to Nathan that everything seemed shipshape. So the two of them and Woods took the boat for a sea trial on Plymouth Harbor, where the Pilgrims had settled almost four hundred years before, looking for a new life of freedom, just like Nathan.

After a cooling hose initially let go and was reattached (a minor problem, easily remedied by Woods), the boat ran well. Among the things Feeney tested while underway were the hydraulic trim tabs on the transom, the very stern of the boat. Picture the ailerons on a fixed-wing aircraft—the adjustable flaps that go up and down on the back edge of the wing, to direct the plane up or down. The same technology is sometimes employed on boats, to assist in properly trimming the boat fore and aft, with the bow up, giving it a little extra lift, so the rest of the hull can slide through the water with less resistance.

Unlike some triple-outboard 1,275-horsepower Contender, the JC 31 with its 300-horsepower Cummins diesel would never be considered a speedboat flying over the waves. Instead, with a semi-displacement hull, in normal sea conditions the JC 31 was later tested by a Cummins dealer and got up to its maximum speed of twenty knots at 2,950 RPMs to ride partially up out of the water to reduce drag while much of the hull remains in the water to provide stability. Backing off the throttle by 300 RPMs then achieves maximum fuel economy and efficient cruising at fifteen to sixteen knots, not just plowing through and displacing the water ahead like a plodding tugboat.

Missing from Feeney's report were an overall photo of the boat and its name, but it's not unusual for a smaller vessel to have had its prior name removed when put up for sale.

***

With a slew of questions and suspicions, Martha sent Nathan a quite routine letter on October 12 requesting a full description of what happened and documentation.

> To assist us with our investigation, please provide us with your detailed written account of the loss along with a copy of any repair estimate or invoices. Also provide any other documents (photos, drawings, a written statement of how the damages occurred) that you think will help us to fully understand your claim and the extent of damages incurred.[17]

A week later, on October 19 (one month after he was missing at sea), Nathan emailed his articulate written response to Martha. We immediately began dissecting it line by line, but one phrase was especially curious. Upon concluding from his life raft that his mother was lost, Nathan wrote "then I made myself take rest."

What a strange choice of words. Martha and Liam and I latched onto it, chuckling throughout the case whenever it was time to knock off for the day, as in "Very nice having dinner with you, but now I must make myself take rest." As a fascinating insight into Nathan's mind,

---

[17] Tr. Ex. 5.4.8.

the following is his typewritten descriptive statement to Martha,[18] in its entirety.

> My mom, Linda Carman, and I, Nathan Carman, were the only two persons onboard my 1974 JC 31 boat when it left Ram Point Marina beween 11:00 pm September 17th and 12:30 am September 18th 2016 with all required safety supplies onboard. We went to a spot southwest of Block Island relatively close to Block Island, I do not know exactly how far, and after fishing at that spot for about an hour we proceeded to Block Canyon where we arrived around the time of sun rise on the morning of September 18th. After arriving at Block Canyon we set out lines and began to troll with the boat on auto pilot. We continued to troll in a northerly direction until around mid-day, I do not know exactly what time, when I perceived that the engine sounded different from normal. Upon perceiving this I opened the hatch in the deck immediately in front of the engine and upon doing so observed that a very large amount of water was present in the bilge. Seeing that the engine was partially underwater I immediately turned off the engine then asked my mom to bring in the lines while I opened a different hatch in the cockpit deck in order to check to see if any of the thru hull fittings had failed. Upon opening the hatch, I was not able to see the through hull fittings because they were under water with the water level in that space being to just below the level of the deck. The water was the color of engine oil and I could not see through it to observe the through hull fittings. Before attempting to further diagnose the problem I began moving the safety gear that was stored in the pilot house, forward so that

[18] Tr. Ex. D-42.

it would be more accessible in the event that the boat sank. I did not realize that the boat was going to sink, but I thought that moving the safety gear forward was an advisable precaution which I proceeded to take. As I was carrying forward the third of the three containers of safety supplies that were stored onboard, the boat sank suddenly and I found myself in the water holding the bag I had been carrying which was a water tight bag containing two of the life vests that had been onboard the vessel as well as other saftey gear.

Once I got my bearings in the water I observed the life raft, which had deployed automatically from its deck mounted cradle, nearby and I was able to collect the other two containers of survival gear, one of which contained the flares, and swim to the raft. I did not see my mom after the boat sank, though I looked around and called out for her while I was in the water and after getting onboard the life raft. I continued to try to locate my mom by looking for her and calling out and listening for a reply until dark, then I made myself take rest.

Immediately after the boat sank there was a brown slick on the surface of the water that was the color of engine oil and there was a small amount of floating debris which included Plano tackle boxes that had been in the cockpit when my mom and I were fishing and a resuable shopping bag of my mom's. Within an hour after the sinking the slick and debris were no longer present around the life raft. The time that elapsed from when I heard that the engine sounded funny and I observed water in the bilge to when the boat sank and I was in the water was very brief, I am not sure exactly how long it was, but I would estimate three to five minutes.

> The boat had seemed to be running normally from the time we left the dock until the time that I heard the unusual sound of the engine and then observed water in the bilge.

***

Just shy of a week later came news of a funeral Nathan held for his mother in Hartford on October 26. Only a half dozen or so mourners attended—far outnumbered by news reporters.

The resounding absence of the Chakalos family at Linda Carman's funeral, staged by her only son, had to be taken most seriously as confirmation that those close to her thought Nathan had been responsible for her death. Nathan arrived at the Hartford church in his huge Ford F-450 pickup, clad in earth tones but carrying a flat of colorful lilies, and his arrogance spawned amazed comments on his chutzpah, gall—you choose the term.

Media attempts to get a few words from Nathan as he departed the church were met with a controlling "I need to close my door" as he drove off, with his father, Clark, in the shotgun seat.[19]

That's the last time we saw Clark Carman. But with his departure and return to obscurity in California, the lawyers came out of the woodwork.

Attorney Dan Small of the multinational Holland & Knight firm, who had been hired by Linda's three sisters—Nathan's aunts—issued a statement, studiously avoiding the word "funeral."

> Linda's friends and family want to make clear that they are not involved in this event. They believe that it is premature and inappropriate to stage this kind of

[19] "Lost at Sea," n. 7.

> an event when there is an ongoing investigation into Linda's disappearance.[20]

I hadn't known Small previously but I had a couple of good friends in his firm's New York City office who were top maritime attorneys. After some quick checking I learned Small was big time too, having successfully defended former Virginia Governor Bob McDonnell in the US Supreme Court over a Rolex watch he received as a gift from a CEO in Virginia.

Nathan also had a mouthpiece, Connecticut Attorney Hubert Santos, who said

> Nathan has not given up hope for his mother's rescue. However, he also understands the difficult realities of the situation and that the Coast Guard stopped search-and-rescue operations last month. He believes that now is an appropriate time to begin the mourning process, and asks that the public and press respect his privacy during this trying time.[21]

"Buckle your seat belt," I told Liam. "These guys are going try it in the press." But we definitely would not and intended to stay out of the limelight as much as possible to do our job, per usual. So, armed with Nathan's written statement, Feeney's survey, and news reports as a lead, Liam went to Narragansett, Rhode Island for a couple of days to find out whatever he could.

He concentrated on Ram Point Marina, where Nathan kept his boat. Liam spoke with the manager, who reported that Nathan's boat was always at the dock, and with other boaters, including the Niejadliks, who kept their boat in a slip next to Nathan's.

---

20 Dave Altimari, "Nathan Carman Planning Memorial For His Mother, Upsetting Her Sisters," *Hartford Courant*, October 22, 2016. https://www.courant.com/2016/10/22/nathan-carman-planning-memorial-for-his-mother-upsetting-her-sisters/.

21 Altimari, "Nathan Carman Planning Memorial."

A sense of community among boat owners is common at marinas. Helpful suggestions, cautionary notes, and food get exchanged in a friendly way. Nathan kept mostly to himself, and when urged, the only things he would ever eat or drink were meatballs and Newman's Own Iced Tea, no bread. He stuck out. People perceived him as odd.

The older Niejadliks had tried to take Nathan under their wings but found him resistant to sage advice, yet they were sympathetic, knowing something was off. And after pressing them, Liam learned they had never seen Nathan's mother at the marina, they never saw any fishing rods, and upon hearing his plans to fish the canyons the next day, they tried to dissuade him due to rough seas they had just encountered on their trip back from Martha's Vineyard.

The Niejadliks also confirmed that a Mike Iozzi, who had a boat at a neighboring marina, had been present at Ram Point Marina the afternoon before Nathan's fateful voyage. They were aware that Iozzi had given media interviews about incredulously watching Nathan drill holes in his transom using an electric drill. Iozzi had been visiting that afternoon with another couple, the Ferreiras, who had a slip two over from Nathan's, and the Niejadliks gave Liam contact information for that couple, who had Iozzi's telephone number.

This was the kind of firsthand witness observations we were looking for, not simply news reports, which are hearsay and often inaccurate and insufficient for determining whether insurance coverage should or should not be available for the loss of Nathan's boat. We needed hard, admissible evidence, not gossip.

Liam promptly emailed a summary of his findings to Martha late October 31, 2016. He recommended that our investigation continue because more questions kept coming up, and we were just scratching the surface with shoreside witnesses.

But looking back, what transpired that Halloween was almost spooky. Nathan nearly pulled it off. He was close to getting his $85,000 hull insurance payment approved, and if he had, he would never have been subjected to our further investigation. That Halloween his trick was nearly his treat, his trophy fish at the boat, only to spit the hook at the very last second. That fish, we would later learn, was pure karma in return for Nathan's earlier Halloween treats.

Indeed, things really were looking up for Nathan during the daylight hours before Liam sent his email as darkness descended. Holaday, operating independently of our office, had not come up with much from Point Judith Marina, where Nathan's overheated engine had been replaced. Its management, tired of pestering by reporters, was afraid of getting sucked into litigation or bad press coverage, and was not cooperative. So, on Halloween morning Holaday reported to Martha that "the prior work performed by Point Judith Marina shows no negligence," with "no proof that the vessel was not seaworthy when it left port."[22] Based on that, Martha shortly emailed Nathan his Happy Halloween news that she was going to start the paperwork to process his claim but would "need ownership documents"[23] from him, and so was short of her promise to pay it.

But on subsequent receipt of Liam's email, Martha emailed Nathan back the next morning, clarifying, "I neglected the fact that my supervisor has to review the documents prior to me sending them to you. The documents are with him for review. Once I have more information I will let you know."[24] That was all true, even if it wasn't the entire reason she was pumping the brakes.

Things did not skid out of control for Martha because Nathan quickly told her he was "not comfortable"[25] sending her the boat's title unless he was assured he would receive an $85,000 insurance check for the loss of his boat. That may sound like chicken-or-egg bickering between a consumer and a big bad insurance company, but contractually, as stated in the marine insurance policy, Nathan was obligated to sign legal title to the boat over to the Insurer before getting paid $85,000 for his claim that the boat was a total loss. What good was it for Nathan to hold onto the title if the boat really "would not likely be recovered," as he had initially reported?

---

22 Tr. Ex. 17.2 at P161.
23 Tr. Ex. 17.2 at P161.
24 Tr. Ex. D-45.
25 Tr. Ex. 17.2 at P161.

His less than forthcoming approach, coupled with Liam's leads and additional information that trickled in, made it easy for the Insurer to take the next step. In a November 11, 2016 letter to Nathan, Martha invoked the insurance policy clause giving the Insurer the contractual right to take his examination under oath. After one postponement, it took place in our Salem, Massachusetts office on December 16, 2016, not even three months after the fateful voyage began.

What is an EUO, which became the foundation of our investigation into the sinking of Nathan's boat? Regrettably, for perspective, we have to address something everyone agrees is stultifyingly dull.

The starting point is insurance. Behind virtually every accident, every time property gets damaged, every time someone gets injured, every claim that someone else is liable, there's insurance—from a fender bender in a shopping mall parking lot to the 9/11 collapse of the World Trade Center Twin Towers. We all hate the way insurance adjusters nitpick, hiding behind clauses in their insurance policies that no one bothers reading, denying coverage for the leak in your roof, and then the next thing you know, you get hit with a higher homeowner's premium bill.

What's not so readily recognized, though, is that in most lawsuits where the plaintiff claims injury by the defendant wrongdoer, the jury award or settlement monies plus the attorneys' fees to defend the case in court are all paid for by the defendant's insurance company. If you rear-end someone who then sues you for whiplash, you thank your lucky stars you have insurance to deal with it.

Insurance cannot, however, cover every casualty under the sun. Not when the loss was intentional. Not when the damage was criminally or fraudulently motivated. Not when the insured improperly withholds critical information about the risk of a casualty. Not when the insurance contract proscribes coverage for certain unacceptably high risks.

If those sorts of claims were insured, two bad things would happen societally. First, there would be less reason for insureds to be careful, and there might even be an incentive to engage in bad acts and get paid for them. Second, everyone's insurance premiums would have to skyrocket to cover those losses. Therefore, sometimes insurers need to take a stand

and say no, this is not a covered loss. Otherwise, there are bad public policy ramifications.

But insurance companies need to be very careful that they act in good faith when denying coverage, because consumer advocates are very skeptical watchdogs. The insurance company better have solid factual and legal reasons before telling its paying customer "no dice." And that's why insurance policies often provide for an insured's examination under oath, permitting an in-person investigation if there's a red flag—like the one Nathan waved at *Orient Lucky* from his life raft.

Another red flag appeared a couple of days before the EUO, right after I first had contact with Nathan's Attorney Santos. We had learned he, too, was big time, a respected Connecticut criminal defense lawyer, known best for getting Michael "Kennedy cousin" Skakel out of jail for the 1975 murder of fifteen-year-old Martha Moxley.

I had asked Martha Charlesworth in her November 11 letter[26] to Nathan to request documents for him to bring with him to the EUO.

> Please bring with you to your Examination Under Oath all documents related to the sunken boat during your ownership of it, including but not limited to your original purchase records; all records, invoices, receipts, and credit card and bank statements reflecting repairs to your boat and purchases for items used on your boat during your ownership of it; all marine survey reports concerning your boat; and all insurance applications you submitted for your boat during your ownership of it. As well, please bring with you copies of all documents provided to *The Hartford Courant* following the sinking and any documents you have provided to law enforcement following the sinking.

As requested above from Nathan, Attorney Santos obligingly emailed me the day before the EUO a copy of an October 12, 2016 letter he sent to the Connecticut US Attorney and State of Connecticut's

[26] Tr. Ex. 46.

Attorney General's office. Attorney Santos had provided that letter to the *Hartford Courant,* which had reported on his disclosure of repairs Nathan had made the day before the boat sank. But notably absent in Attorney Santos's email to me were any attached "records, invoices, receipts, and credit card and bank statements reflecting repairs to [Nathan's] boat and purchase for items used on your boat during your ownership," as Martha had requested.

Our review of Attorney Santos's October 12 letter now made it clear there was another part of Nathan's story he did not tell Martha in his October 19 description. His insurance claim immediately raised concerns, based on his own statements alone, independent of witness observations. Comparing the two documents about the same incident, with all information provided only by Nathan, they were two ships passing in the night—Attorney Santos's letter addressing boat repairs but not the voyage, and Nathan's subsequent report to Martha discussing the voyage but not the repairs.

4

A WITCH CITY WICKED COLD DAY IN HELL

I had spoken to our unflappable managing partner Dave Smith about possibly paying for a police detail at our Salem, Massachusetts office in case Nathan aimed on doing us all in during his EUO.

But we concluded that if the media somehow caught on that we were awaiting Nathan Carman's arrival with a police presence, and cameras showed up to film his arrival, he'd probably run away. It also weighed heavily that Nathan seemed committed to pressing forward with his insurance claim with reputable Attorney Santos, who, we learned, had represented Nathan regarding his grandfather's murder.

Attorney Santos arrived alone. I'd gathered that everyone called him Hubie, but I never reached that level of familiarity with him. Frankly, he was underwhelming. With a self-deprecating smile, he was a tad unkempt. His ample torso substantially spilled over the arms of our sparse waiting room chair, and he seemed old and tired, snoozing off and on while we waited for the late Mr. Carman. There was no cell phone fiddling or request for our Wi-Fi password.

Some lawyers hope you will take them for granted as they wait for the right second to ambush you, a strategy I well know both as ambusher and ambushee. I also considered the possibility that Attorney Santos was just running interference to make sure the coast was clear for his purposely tardy client.

When asked if he'd like some coffee, Attorney Santos politely declined, instead pulling out peanut butter crackers from his old-fashioned, battered brown briefcase. Not politely averting my eyes, I saw it was completely empty. While munching, he asked Liam if he could have a legal pad. Neither of us saw our esteemed opposing counsel write anything on it the rest of the day.

We all wondered, or so we enunciated, whether Nathan might be having car trouble since it was hovering around 0°F in Salem and must have been 15° below overnight at his Vermont home. Just when it was time for me to start griping that Nathan was in breach of his duty as an insured to cooperate with the Insurer, our increasingly infamous insured arrived at 11:30 a.m., one and a half hours late.

Thus, our first in-person contact with Nathan Carman was a wicked cold day in hell, in the Witch City no less. He toted his own identical beat-up briefcase, probably a Hubie spare, which Liam and I eyed warily. Dressed in a faded yellow plaid suit he no doubt found in a church consignment shop, with a short tie à la Oliver Hardy that truly popped, Nathan bore a scruffier goatee than seen on the news, plus long fingers caked with grease under his nails, and furry teeth to match his suit. On introductions in our conference room, Liam and I shook Nathan's dead fish of a hand linked loosely like a marionette's to his arm, slumped shoulders, and forward-bent neck.

As a team, neither Nathan nor his lawyer nor their matching weathered briefcases looked particularly imposing.

When I routinely asked for Nathan's driver's license for identification, he said he'd forgotten his wallet. Seriously? On a two-state drive, through the Commonwealth of Massachusetts with our notoriously ubiquitous, unregulated, unapologetic state troopers salivating for any reason to harass citizens, good and bad alike? I wanted to know what state had issued it and then run a background check. But Attorney

Santos vouched for him, so Liam and I nonverbally agreed, since there was no doubt this was the one and only Nathan Carman, that we would march ahead with the examination.

Although Nathan's tardy arrival sans wallet indicated his level of planning, requiring us to be on top of our game to extract information from him, I was nevertheless optimistic we'd be able to do just that by juxtaposing his written statement to Martha with his attorney's letter to the Connecticut prosecutors. They were two different road maps, which together gave us traction to learn a lot more. And I'll admit, I was pumped, feeling this was the start of something big—which it turned out to be, eventually yielding a third road map a few years later.

I've had to write summaries of witness interviews and depositions hundreds of times over the decades. These include reports from seafarers shocked by the horrific personal injuries they witnessed; from licensed ship officers, eliciting navigational errors and misread radar screens that led to tragic collisions, sinkings, and multiple deaths; and from highly paid professional expert witnesses with MD board certifications or engineering PhDs, all the while looking for one or two logical inconsistencies to scuttle their opinions.

From a pilot boat I've climbed the Jacob's ladder thrown over the side of an arriving 632-foot oil tanker to unravel what the hell happened before Coast Guard investigators got aboard, only to be swept up in a case where all hell broke loose.[27] I've crawled around empty tanks and compartments to see machinery failures and dead seafarers.[28] I've battled slippery lawyers representing rough-and-tumble fishermen out of the Dutch Harbor, Alaska frontier. Deposed heroin-addled New Bedford, Massachusetts fishermen fakes and severely injured recreational boaters completely at fault for their accidents. Cross-examined steroidal long-

---

27 John F. Meadows, *Memories of a Maritime Lawyer,* "Disappearance of the *Jack Jr.,*" (Dorrance Publishing, 2019); Eric Nalder, *Tankers Full of Trouble,* (Grove Press, 1994), 181–5.

28 Maritime casualty lawyers are like television district attorneys who go to the crime scene at the beginning of the show. We have to look at the evidence, no matter what time of day or night, to decide how best to preserve it before it sails away or floats away with an outgoing tide.

shore union crane operators and hangers-on who would drink piss out of a sneaker if that's all there was.

While most of the people we deal with are truly the salt of the earth, we maritime lawyers commonly conduct fascinating anthropological studies of our species' amphibious variants. A common trait is their watered-down view of the rule of law. From teenage jet skiers to international shipping magnates, most vessel owners think they are masters of their universe. But trying to understand Nathan and summarize his EUO testimony in a readable and interesting way for public consumption is a whole new kettle of fish.

His facial demeanor, gangliness, and hygienic shortcomings presented a personality composite with which I am familiar only through limited, involuntary interactions with street people. From my prior observations of Nathan on TV, my gut instinct on seeing this probable serial family murderer in the flesh was to be on guard, ready to defend myself from attack if needed. A world-class triathlete, now staying in shape herding his active kids, I knew Liam could take care of himself too. Unless…

We had no ethical obligation as civil attorneys to consider Nathan innocent until proven guilty. As representatives of our clients, we're entitled to think what we think so long as we assess the evidence fairly wherever it leads us. But getting there meant reckoning with such an overwhelmingly sad sack that it hit me I was going to have to treat Nathan with kid gloves, pull my punches, and not beat up on him other than in a most professional way.

It's like schools teach about bullying. We had to avoid coming across as mean insurance company lawyers intent on abusing a misunderstood paying customer with a mental health diagnosis that would likely come to light and be viewed with sympathy by many. Otherwise, we would end up in big trouble ourselves with the court (the principal), the Board of Bar Overseers (the student council), and our client (the parents), exposing them to maritime punitive damages or big penalties for violating state consumer protection statutes intended to protect innocent insureds.

Accordingly, Liam and I had previously discussed—and quickly reaffirmed on assessing Nathan in person—that we could not be seen as using Nathan's uncharged crime of murdering his grandfather as a scapegoat to deny him boat insurance. We huddled. *Don't go overboard, keep it respectful and strictly professional, concentrate just on the boat because that's why he's here. No need for a fight. Wonder what he's got in that briefcase?*

5

"I CAN BE GIVEN TO SPEAKING SOFTLY"

No surprise, some of the phrases out of Nathan's mouth were just as peculiar as "I made myself take rest" was on paper.

Sworn in by Lauren, our stenographer, who was very professional but visibly a little nervous, Nathan meekly commenced his EUO testimony, saying, "Sometimes I can be given to speaking softly. So if you pick up on that, just point it out and I'll speak up."[29]

What twenty-two-year-old purrs like that? A young Hannibal Lecter lacking any twinkle in his eyes was all I could conjure.

A little later, Nathan described why he had increased the hull (property) coverage of his insurance policy's initial dollar amount by $19,000 to $85,000. "I increased the hull value to reflect the extensive

[29] Because the Nathan Carman's examination under oath is a pre-litigation statement, it was not obtained from him pursuant to discovery obligations set forth in Rules 26-36 of the Federal Rules of Civil Procedure but rather was provided by him as a contractual obligation under his All Risk policy. It is not subject to any discovery protective order.

money that I had spent investing in the boat in electronics and other equipment."

Clearly, this young man was whacked. We'd had our lay suspicions, hardly professional, that Nathan was "on the spectrum," as suggested in media reports. Yet we could not let any preconceptions fog our development of hard facts and the application of law to them. We were in the middle of a deep dive into Nathan Carman, whatever his mental condition. There were numerous theoretical possibilities concerning what happened that needed to be evaluated, the known unknowns and unknown unknowns that needed to be prospected and mined.

There is but one tried-and-true way to net what we needed at this point: Get Nathan to tell his story of what happened in his own words. I wasn't going to argue with him, push him into a corner that I thought was untenable, or make him sweat under hot lights. The examination was a Joe Friday fact-finding mission but with the evidentiary strength of sworn testimony—much more than just penciled names in a notebook. For what looked like $85,000 at stake, we couldn't beat around the bush and then insist the two out-of-staters stay overnight so we could resume the next morning. It was time to get right down to business and get the details down on paper and under oath.

A couple of things became obvious.

As no doubt routinely instructed by capable Attorney Santos, Nathan answered my questions—and only answered them—without volunteering additional information. Usually.

When I asked, "Where do you live, sir?" Nathan answered, "I currently live in Vernon, Vermont, at 3043 Fort Bridgman Road." Only later did we learn he had twice falsely claimed New Hampshire residency.

When I asked, "Did you graduate from high school?" he answered, "Yes, I was—I did receive a high school diploma" from Middletown High School in Connecticut. Figuring he was just being weird again, in retrospect I should have followed up. It was only later that we learned Nathan was not allowed to attend school his senior year.

When I asked about his "schooling after that," he answered that he "took courses" at "Northwestern Connecticut Community College." Turns out that, too, was completely truthful. Only later did we learn that Nathan's grandfather paid the tuition, room and board, and credit card bills, yet Nathan's report card came home with four big Fs for those courses.

Regarding the manatee in the room, during the EUO we barely touched on the grandfather's murder beyond some background questions on how a twenty-two-year-old managed to own a house, a nice boat, and a Ford F-450—hitting the trifecta for many a male retiree, which young Nathan seemed to be.

Employed? No, fixing up the house full time. Last job? Loading Fed Ex trucks at the warehouse. Home mortgage? No, paid cash. Boat? Paid cash. Other vehicles? Yes, also a Ford F-350, paid cash, but it "is currently in the possession of law enforcement."

> Q: And where did the cash come from?
>
> A: I inherited moneys from my grandfather.

This sort of initial Q&A between lawyer and interrogee is instructive for a couple of reasons. It shows the witness can be completely truthful and at the same time hide damaging secrets. Yet the lawyer wants to avoid going down rabbit holes, wasting time and expense on tangents, and frustrating opposing counsel, inviting valid objections of irrelevance and harassment. So on basic things, like background or education or work, we normally just stow the answers away for later follow-up as needed. In contrast, on important substantive subjects, the interrogating lawyer needs to bear down when the opportunity presents itself or lose out on learning something that can make, or break, your case.

Liam and I had identified that Nathan clearly had not come clean on important parts of his story to date, as only partly expressed in Attorney Santos's letter to prosecutors and as only partly expressed in Nathan's written description to Martha. And while Nathan quickly established that he was just as articulate and precise orally as in his writings, it was critical for us to consider what he didn't say or when he wasn't precise. We took those voids as a clear invitation to dive in to flesh out his version of the facts and try to find out what he was hiding and why.

6

HOLES, HOLES, HOLES

Nathan's testimony during his examination under oath laid the groundwork for doing himself in on the murder of his mother with big holes in big parts of his story—the boat repairs, the fateful voyage, and the sinking.

During the EUO we pressed him on each of these issues and filled in his holes, obtaining more facts, or alleged facts, from him, to his great detriment. Throughout the insurance case we held him to his full, sworn story even if we did not believe big portions of it.

Note that Nathan's testimony in the topical summaries that follow was not gathered in a chronological question-and-answer sequence. That's often appropriate with a run-of-the-mill eyewitness, but with critical witnesses, a seasoned litigator will usually hop around from topic to topic and mix up time frames. That keeps witnesses from getting on a roll by testifying sequentially like they had practiced beforehand. Sometimes, if you shake up their testimony, they'll make mistakes, saying something inconsistent without realizing it. Especially with what I perceive to be a very smart witness, this bob-and-weave litigation technique works well, but it is contraindicated for the unsophisticated witness, who just gets confused, producing an unusable record.

In Nathan's case, we absolutely perceived him to be highly intelligent, primarily because he had evaded the Coast Guard for a week and apparently positioned himself so that the *Orient Lucky* would stumble upon him. Liam also noted that if Nathan was on the spectrum, his lack of emotion was probably coupled with very linear thinking, a further reason to bounce around a lot with my questioning.

But there's a big risk in disjointed interrogation. The questioner, too, may get distracted and space out on asking an important question. I came close to doing just that.

The Four Half-Dollar Transom Holes

Liam and I were obviously focused on boat repair work Nathan conducted the day before the fateful voyage, which he blatantly had not mentioned to Martha in his October 19 written description, but which Attorney Santos had divulged in some detail in his October 12 letter to the Connecticut prosecutors.

Attorney Santos's letter described Nathan's removal of his boat's trim tabs from the transom the day before the sinking: "This created holes above the water line, but none below the water line. There were four holes, about the size of a half dollar."[30]

Nathan also, according to Attorney Santos's letter, had replaced one of the boat's electric bilge pumps.

But Nathan's not even mentioning to Martha in his written description four newly exposed half-dollar-sized holes near the waterline and a bilge pump replacement the day before the boat sank, when Martha had specifically requested repair invoices, opened up a hole in Nathan's defense big enough to drive a container ship through.

He started off his EUO testimony on boat repairs he conducted during his ownership by saying, "I did remove the trim tabs. I had also taken out two bulkheads—not two—I had taken out two halves of the bulkhead that was forward of the engine."

30 EUO Ex. 16.

"Let me stop you there," I said. A previously unknown unknown, absent from Attorney Santos's letter, this tantalizing first mention of a structural alteration to the boat needed Nathan's explanation right now. We'd get to the trim tabs later.

> A: And I removed those two pieces of plywood, one to port of the fish box and one to starboard, in order to gain space to store the rods in that area beside the fish box.
>
> Q: Under deck?
>
> A: Yes.
>
> Q: And how did you access those under-deck compartments?
>
> A: From the engine compartment. So immediately forward of wheelhouse, there was a hatch that could be picked up.

This was definitely something to discuss with Brian Woods, the refurbisher and seller of the JC 31 to Nathan. There was friction between the two of them. Nathan described a dispute he'd had with Woods over a "petty dollar amount," which Nathan reported to the police. We suspected Brian Woods was going to be a knowledgeable witness, adding expertise on the boat's construction, and maybe, since Nathan had gone whining to the cops, Woods might be more than happy to cooperate.

Nathan also said the boat's hoses had frozen the prior winter, leading me into a couple of time-consuming dead ends, but also revealing recurring bilge pump problems prior to his replacement of one of the boat's two bilge pumps the day before it sank. He tested the new replacement, which he said worked fine, but he never confirmed the other bilge pump actually pumped water overboard. He even admitted that neither was "functioning correctly" at the time of the sinking—just twenty-four hours later.

He testified that he placed the old bilge pump he took out in the boat's fish box to have a spare aboard.

Like a spare tire? This sounded like malarkey. At sea in a thirty-one-foot boat, if you need to dewater the bilge but your electric pumps fail, you don't take the time to wire in a new one. You grab a five-gallon bucket or a hand pump and bail like your life depends on it. But Nathan's story was a good way to keep anyone from inspecting the old bilge pump to see if there really had been anything wrong with it. Maybe it was as good as new and Nathan was just trying to send us on a wild goose chase. A good marine surveyor can perform a variety of forensic analyses yielding valuable insights. Oh well, not on Nathan's old pump. Time to move on and see later where this bilge pump story might lead.

We still had to find out about Nathan's removal of the trim tabs and how he filled the four half-dollar holes that were thereby exposed on the transom at the waterline. It was tedious but ended up as essential testimony.

Even with simple, low-tech vessel repairs, oral testimony alone is usually confusing without props for a better understanding of what the witness is describing. Since Feeney's survey referenced Bennett trim tabs, we had gotten specification sheets[31] online in preparing for the EUO. Nathan identified his as the BXT model, which helped greatly in our understanding of what he said he did.

Nathan testified that the boat had two of these BXT trim tabs at the transom, just below the waterline. He confirmed that the trim tabs were controlled from the pilothouse and were designed to assist in trimming the boat. Essentially a piece of sheet metal, each trim tab was maneuvered up and down by the two diagonal hydraulic actuators. The actuators' top ends were screwed into the vertical rise of the transom; the actuators' lower ends attached to the trim tabs themselves. The actuators' rams would extend to push the trim tabs down or shorten to pull the trim tabs up.

We also had a photograph from Feeney's survey report which was a great help in understanding Nathan's testimony about his missing boat.

[31] EUO Ex. 5.

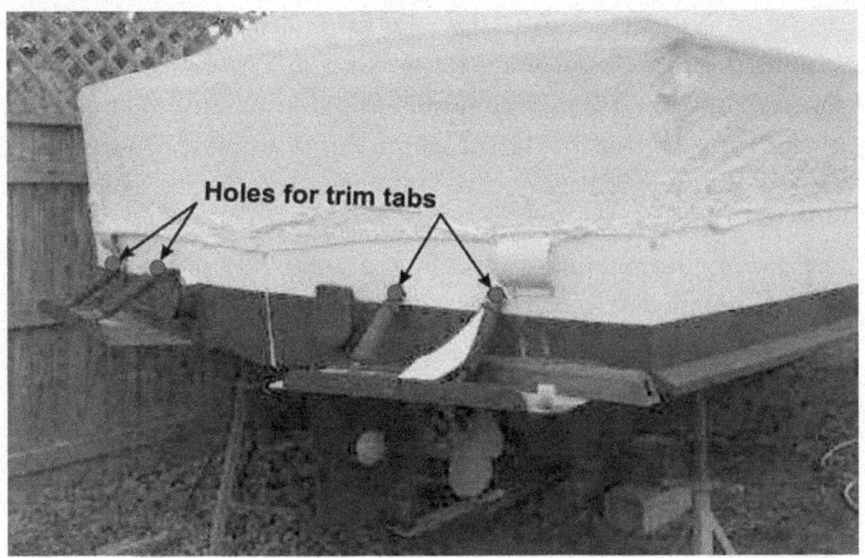

Nathan didn't think the trim tabs were effective, sensing they were a drag, "probably reducing performance, reducing speed, making it harder to get up onto plane and reducing fuel efficiency." Yet he had not collected any data to conclude this or discussed it with any marine professional or conducted any research online or otherwise.

Rather than take on this involved removal job while the boat was hauled out during its recent engine replacement, "on the hard" as yacht people say, or from the floating dock the boat was then backed into, Nathan stood on the deck of his boat and bent from his waist over the transom. Just about the hardest way to go about it. Was he going out of his way to be noticed?

While rolling around on his belly on the top of the transom, he had to reach down toward the water to detach the four actuators from the transom. After unscrewing three screws securing the upper end of an actuator to the transom, a half-dollar hole was exposed in the transom, he testified. Running through the middle of each half-dollar hole was a rubber hydraulic line connecting the upper end of the actuator to a hydraulic pump in the bilge. He then cut each of the hydraulic lines with shears and pulled the lines into the bilge. So that left a total of twelve small screw holes and four half-dollar holes.

Next, Nathan detached the trim tabs themselves by repeatedly striking the sheet metal outboard with a hammer (outwardly hitting the starboard trim tab on its inboard edge, to starboard, and outwardly hitting the port trim tab on its inboard edge, to port), slowly sliding them out of their respective brackets' hinges, and thereby freeing them from the transom.

Ever try hammering something that's partially in the water? We knew from Liam's interviews that this all created quite a spectacle for marina onlookers, and Nathan's testimony gave further proof of that.

After removal, he placed the trim tab gear in the back of his pickup. In contrast to the bilge pump that he hid on the boat, this seemed like an invitation to later inspect the actual trim tabs, actuators, and hydraulic hoses the South Kingstown police had taken into custody.

The crux of the insurance case, though, was the four half-dollar holes Nathan exposed in removing the trim tabs. I had him confirm that the tops of the half-dollar holes were no more than 4 inches above the water, so of course the bottom of the holes were lower and closer to the water. And I got him to acknowledge that even without the trim tabs, while underway his boat's bow would go up and the stern would go down, bringing the holes, as he said, "downwards" and "closer to the water."

I also had Nathan describe the starboard scupper, or "deck drain" as he called it, with its horizontal outboard PVC baffle, on the Feeney photo of the transom. The same deck drain arrangement was at the port side of the transom but covered up by the shrink wrap. The baffles help keep seawater at the stern from washing through the open drain and onto the deck, particularly at slow forward speeds, neutral, or backing.

Because the deck drain holes in the hull are routinely subject to seawater incursion and are a couple inches higher than the four half-dollar holes, the half-dollar holes would be even more susceptible to water incursion. And they were below the deck level, so water getting in through the half-dollar holes would go straight into the bilge, below deck.

This negated the point Attorney Santos tried to make in his letter that the four half-dollar holes were not "below the water line" when the boat was in its slip as Nathan worked on it. To the contrary, the four half-dollar holes so near the waterline were dangerously unseaworthy, pure and simple. A waterline on a boat at rest in its slip does not remain static when the boat is underway, with seawater lapping the exterior hull frequently, including at the stern, above the at-rest waterline.

Continuing his description of the trim tabs removal, still on his belly, Nathan couldn't see into the half-dollar holes whilst bent over the transom (he would have had to stick the top of his head into the water to achieve a line of sight), but he could feel with his finger that all four holes went straight into the bilge through the transom, which he said was around ¾ to 1¼ inches thick. To me, that seemed thin for a boat this size. But the important piece of testimony I then got was that the holes had no backing on the inside, essentially creating four hollow "cylinders" straight into the bilge.

Leaving those four half-dollar holes exposed, less than 4 inches above the water and subjected to rocking from the minor wakes of passing boats, Nathan said he then went to the nearby Narragansett West Marine store. There he purchased a tube of 3M 5200 Marine Sealant, a West Marine Epoxy Putty Stick, and a West System Fiberglass Boat Repair Kit.

He used the 5200 to fill the twelve small screw holes exposed after detaching the four actuators from the transom.

While it was not a big deal, one piece of Nathan's testimony struck me as oddly forgetful. Just three months after rolling around on his stomach filling the twelve screw holes, he could not remember whether he had used a squeeze tube of 5200 (which could be done with one hand) or applied the 5200 with a push gun (which likely would require both hands and make the repair even more awkward). I couldn't see doing much with this but it fueled my skepticism on anything and everything coming out of Nathan's mouth.

In his effort to plug the four half-dollar holes—a much bigger problem—Nathan first tried pouring fiberglass resin into them. But with no backing, the resin just spilled out of the bottom of the holes, and he gave up after fifteen to thirty minutes. To me, that seemed beyond stupid. He then resorted to the epoxy putty stick, which he described as similar to a commonly available J-B Weld product that he'd used before. After reading the fiberglass kit's instructions, he decided to roll up some paper towels into balls and stick them inside the half-dollar holes. "I didn't see how it could hurt," he said. *Or help*, I thought.

He then rolled the epoxy putty, the consistency of Play-Doh or Silly Putty, into four balls about an inch in diameter and stuffed one into each hole. There was "an inch or two" of the six- to eight-inch stick left over. After a few minutes, Nathan tested the putty, advertised on the package and in the directions as quick to harden, using his fingernail and felt comfortable going to sea several hours later.

Now I had to make a decision. Should I ask Nathan specifically about things he might have done, going through the possibilities like a checklist, questioning him about the electric drill, or should I just ask an open-ended question, letting Nathan fill in the blanks himself? Situations vary and there is probably no right or wrong approach. My thinking was that Nathan didn't know what Liam had learned from the Niejadliks, but Nathan likely knew about the news reports and assumed we had read them. I decided to give him a wide-open chance to truthfully tell us more, rather than put words in his mouth.

> Q: So, besides the four balled-up pieces of paper towel that you stuck in the holes on the transom and the tube of epoxy that you bought from West Marine and the tube of 5200 and the fiberglass kit that you didn't end up using, you didn't do anything else to try and fill the holes that were on the transom?
>
> A: No, I did not.

And:

> Q: Did you do anything else to secure the four half-dollar-sized holes in the transom before departing?
>
> A: No.

Bingo. That definitely meant that, although Nathan had it available, he had not applied fiberglass cloth matting over the epoxy putty to seal it on the outside of the hull with the fiberglass resin he had been playing with earlier. Doing exactly that would have been essential to achieving watertight integrity and a seaworthy repair.

Liam reminded me to make sure to have Nathan acknowledge that all the information in Attorney Santos's letter had come from Nathan himself. He did, and that went a long way toward excluding him from insurance under the policy, which does not cover "any loss…caused directly or indirectly by incomplete, improper, or faulty repair…."[32]

Specifically, Nathan's repair of the four half-dollar holes was atrocious and amateurish. Our best guess about Attorney Santos's letter was that he was hoping to get Nathan off with nothing worse than a negligent manslaughter plea. Prosecutors hadn't nailed Nathan for his grandfather's murder, and he could eat crow on this one, probably avoid jail time due to sloppy stupidity and spectral sympathy, and ultimately inherit big bucks.

The full picture that emerged of the September 2016 weekend as Nathan worked on the boat before its nighttime departure from Ram Point Marina was helter-skelter. Having slept in his truck, he first filled up with diesel fuel at another marina several miles away and came back to his Ram Point Marina slip. Then he went to the nearby West Marine store in Narragansett to look for a bilge pump but had to drive ninety miles round trip to another West Marine store in Middletown, Rhode Island to buy the pump he wanted. Then he had to install it. In the late afternoon he started his convoluted removal of the trim tabs and went back to the Narragansett West Marine to buy the 5200 sealant, the fiberglass kit, and the epoxy putty stick.

Nathan's testimony about the Middletown West Marine trip struck us at the time as odd too.

> A: I bought the bilge pump at—I went to the Narragansett West Marine to look for a bilge

[32] Tr. Ex. 25.3 at 3 of 9.

pump and then I also went to the West Marine in—what do you call it? Newport, Rhode Island—or in…or near…

MR. O'CONNELL: Middletown?

A: Middletown, Rhode Island. To look for a bilge pump. I think I bought the bilge pump at the West Marine in Middletown, Rhode Island.

Q: You grew up in Middletown, Connecticut, right?

A: Yes, Connecticut.

Liam and I both thought Nathan's hesitancy on Middletown was contrived. I made a note to find out later what else he might have bought at the Middletown and Narragansett West Marine stores and planned to canvass other marine stores in the area too. Nathan claimed he did not keep receipts and often paid cash when purchasing items for the boat. But as we would find out later, he was trying to obfuscate his Middletown West Marine purchases.

With each new product purchase mentioned by Nathan, Liam jumped on his laptop to access West Marine's and other online catalogues, from which he was able to get stock numbers and specifications, and he then printed each item so we could make them exhibits to the EUO transcript. We had Nathan confirm everything from the epoxy putty stick to the life raft as his exact purchases.

This all was a pretty formal proceeding. With Nathan's flat affect and our poker faces, it was hard to tell if he realized we had skewered him on his pitiful repair of the four half-dollar holes. Then again, maybe that's what he wanted. When it seemed like time to wrap up our repair inquiries, I referenced Attorney Santos's letter to the prosecutors one last time.

Q: Is there anything factually incorrect that's stated in that letter?

> A: Do you mind if I take out my copy of this letter where I highlighted what I'd like to point out?

As Nathan reached for his battered briefcase, the conference room's barometric pressure tanked as at least three of us gasped deeply. I slid my chair back three feet and rolled onto the balls of my feet, ready to dive toward Lauren and shield us behind Attorney Santos's girth. Hands spreading apart, Liam grabbed the edge of the large table ready to lift and flip it toward Nathan.

Nathan opened the briefcase...then brought out the letter (exhales all round), making trivial—dare I say anal—clarifications like:

> Q: On the last paragraph of page two, the last bullet under the heading Repairs, it says, "The weekend before the sinking of the boat, Carman arrived on the evening of Friday, September 16th."

> A: Well, yes, I arrived on the evening of September 16th, which was not a day of the weekend and it was not the weekend before, it was the weekend of.

Thanks for the clarification. It did nothing to contradict Nathan's various weekend repairs adding up to a poorly planned, poorly executed rush job that in no way should have been undertaken just before a nighttime offshore trip.

He wasn't that stupid.

The Ninety-Minute Departure Hole

Nathan's October 19 written description to Martha reported they had arrived at Block Canyon "around the time of sun rise" on Sunday, September 18, and then sank "around mid-day."

Witness time estimates like that are hardly uncommon, even from fastidious people, and their estimates can often be metamorphized into solid evidentiary facts. On his departure time, in contrast, Nathan had tried to create imprecision at the very start of his voyage story, telling

Martha that he and his mother "left Ram Point Marina between 11:00 pm September 17th and 12:30 am September 18th 2016." That's a ninety-minute hole.

In any maritime casualty case, the time of the vessel's departure and arrival, precise routes taken, speeds, course times, compass headings, and other navigational facts are critical. That's how we start reconstructing what happened—or what purportedly happened—where and when it occurred, and the important events before and afterward. Often at sea there are few witnesses. Since Nathan was most likely the sole living witness, learning his story was especially critical.

Maritime lawyers try hard to gather the facts ASAP. That avoids getting surprised and flustered at trial years in the future. Typically, in the modern era, after a vessel collision or allision,[33] a fire, or a grounding, there is a treasure trove of electronic data to preserve in order to re-create the incident. With radar and chartplotters and GPS and engine RPMs and oil pressure and rudder angles all so high-tech-integrated these days, almost any vessel in essence has its own black box of electronic data that can be downloaded onto a thumb drive for preservation, analysis, and even digitized re-creation of events leading up to the casualty. But here we had no boat, no electronics, no one but Nathan. And no body.

A central part of the navigation investigation is typically focused on reconstructing a vessel's course of travel, concentrating on three variables in a simple middle school equation: Distance = Speed x Time, or D = ST.[34] We could still do that with Nathan, even lacking a black box. Establishing two of the variables allows a seventh grader to solve for the third, quite simply, for example, S = D/T.

---

33 The term *allision* "is used only in a special context in reference to ships in admiralty law. When two ships allide, one of them is stationary; ships collide when both are moving before impact," from Bryan A. Garner, *A Dictionary of Modern Legal Usage*, 2nd ed. (Oxford University Press, 1995), 44. That definition is too limited. A ship can also allide with a pier or a bridge, for example.

34 *See* John V. Noel Jr., *Knight's Modern Seamanship* (John Wiley & Sons, 1989), 202.

But Nathan the Desperado was trying to confuse the posse by giving himself a ninety-minute Time variable window, building slop into his story from the outset. It wasn't clear why, but we suspected he thought he could avoid getting pinned down on Distance and Speed and the rest of his navigation and whereabouts, at least giving himself wiggle room to later testify to his advantage, as needed.

We wouldn't let him. It was inconceivable that one month after the fateful voyage Nathan could not be more precise about his departure time when writing to Martha. It was hard to believe that a serious salt-water fisherman, typically focused on the time of slack (which occurs as tidal currents subside and have a six-hour cycle, the cycle itself advancing an hour each day)[35] when fish often feed, could be so cavalier about the time he got underway for arrival on time at his planned fishing spot off Block Island. And with everything we had gleaned so far about Nathan's precision, his ninety-minute gap was just plain not credible. Having written "around sun rise" and "around mid-day," why wasn't he true to form with "around midnight" for his departure time? It was an invitation to get something more precise out of his mouth right now.

During his EUO, though, he initially stuck to his guns. Sort of.

> Q: What time did you depart the dock on the trip that the boat sank?
>
> A: We departed the dock somewhere between eleven p.m. on Saturday the 17th and twelve, maybe twelve thirty a.m. on the 18th.
>
> Q: Okay. And you first went fishing off of Block Island?
>
> A: That's correct.
>
> Q: Where?
>
> A: Southeast. Let me picture a map in my head here.

---

[35] Typical of East Coast semidiurnal tides. *See*, e.g., Jonathan Eaton et al., *Chapman Piloting & Seamanship* (Hearst Books, 2017), 611.

MR. SANTOS: On the 18th?

Sleepy Hubie, who had almost nothing to say on the EUO record, was sharp as a tack and perked right up on hearing "southeast," because Nathan had written to Martha that they first stopped to fish southwest of Block Island. Attempted navigational obfuscation number two—so obviously a flashing neon sign of the Desperado trying to send us in another direction that we did not need to call him out on it now. Was he suggesting dyslexia with the "Let me picture a map in my head here"? Better, I thought, to stow the whole "which way did he go" and digest it after we gathered more information and bear down on finding out what his story was today while under oath.

When Nathan could not give coordinates for the location southeast of Block Island where he now said they first went fishing, for about one hour—which we never expected he would, that would be too precise—we pulled out the nautical charts to pin his story down.

Information from official National Oceanic and Atmospheric Administration (NOAA) charts are now electronically displayed on the screens of even twenty-foot boats' helms, but paper versions are still commercially available. Either format contains a wealth of well-presented and easy-to-understand information on lighthouses and channels, rocks and shoals, depths and bottom contours, adjacent land topography, North-South-East-West "compass roses," and distance scales.

My family had an old chart of "Chatham Roads" (not a street map) on the wall and around fourth grade I started studying it, incorporating its detail of buoyed channels, depths, occasional rocks, and shifting sandbars into my three-horsepower underway domain awareness (a term I didn't hear until years later). I also received a great tutorial from our friends the Wests, who sailed their forty-foot Concordia yawl, exotically named *Sumatra*, from Nonquitt off-Cape to Stage Harbor for a visit.

A quick navigation lesson: A nautical mile (6,076 feet) is a little longer than a land mile (5,280 feet) because the former is based on latitude, the imaginary horizontal, parallel lines running from the Equator (0°) to the North Pole (90° N) and to the South Pole (90° S), which we were taught about in the European Age of Discovery in fifth grade. Remember? These are precisely marked on the west (left) and east (right) side of any paper chart, with the distance of each minute of latitude equal to one nautical mile.

Since each degree is comprised of sixty minutes, one degree of latitude (for example, 39° N to 40° N shown below) on the chart's sides amounts to sixty miles, which allows for easy distance measuring over adjacent areas while using a simple set of adjustable dividers.

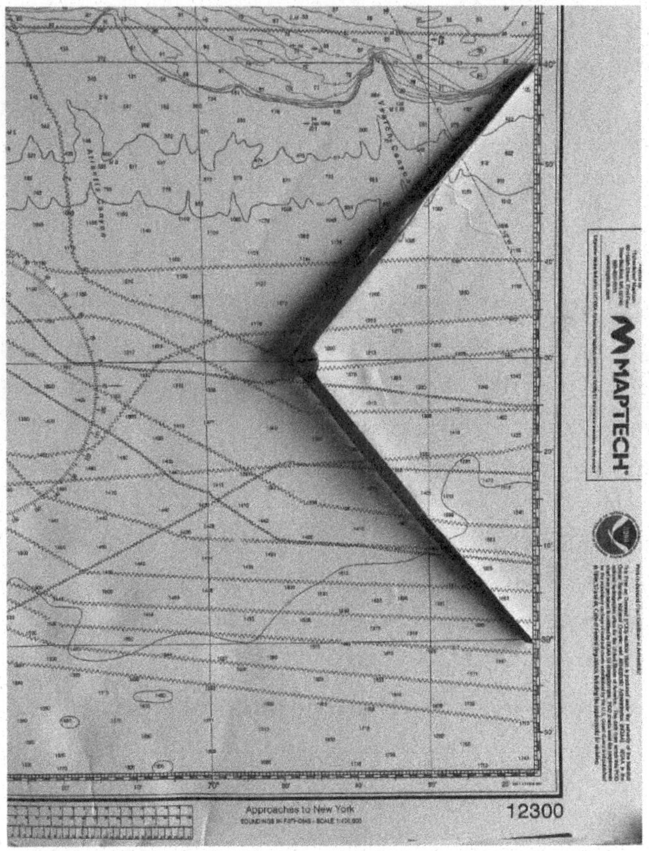

Recall graphing on the Cartesian Coordinate X-axis and Y-axis from high school? X is longitude, which at the prime meridian in Greenwich, England is 0°, and to the west on our side of the Atlantic is 70° and upwards, as shown above; Y is latitude. Don't worry that Y latitude comes first and then X longitude. Together the two coordinates provide a specific location.[36] The best way to remember which goes which way is that latitude, like a ladder, climbs up from the Equator to the North Pole.

Here's the significance of latitude/longitude in this case: First, as a unit of measure for Nathan's navigation, one minute of latitude equals one nautical mile; second, to geographically position the *Orient Lucky* rescue. In contrast, Nathan's geographic positioning would be based on his chart drawings and D = ST.

Relatedly, a vessel's speed is not stated in land miles per hour but rather in "knots," which are nautical miles per hour. Henceforth, whenever we refer to distances, they are nautical miles, and whenever we refer to speeds, they are knots.

NOAA charts can cover big areas, like Chart 12300 "Approaches to New York" for the waters between Nantucket and the Jersey Shore,[37] or with more detail, harbor areas, like Chart 13219 "Point Judith Harbor."[38] With Nathan we started in the middle range, Chart 13215 "Block Island Sound,"[39] which covers Point Judith to the area south of the five-turbine Rhode Island wind farm, and west to Montauk Point on Long Island, with Block Island as its centerpiece. We made all three charts exhibits.

Incidentally, well not really, NOAA Chart 13215 below also shows in the northeast (upper right) corner the very-close-to-shore Point Judith Harbor of Refuge protected by V-shaped jetties. That's where Nathan had taken his boat for a test drive in April 2016 without opening the saltwater cooling seacock, cooking his diesel engine, with the Insurer

---

36 Dava Sobel, *Longitude: The True Story of a Lone Genius Who Solved the Greatest Scientific Problem of His Time* (Walker & Co., 1995), explains the history of the elegant methodology developed to determine longitude at sea.

37 Tr. Ex. 39. https://www.rid.uscourts.gov/sites/rid/files/documents/17cv38/082219/P-39.pdf.

38 Tr. Ex. 41. https://www.rid.uscourts.gov/sites/rid/files/documents/17cv38/082219/P-5.4.6.pdf.

39 Tr. Ex. 40. https://www.rid.uscourts.gov/sites/rid/files/documents/17cv38/082219/P-1.2.12.pdf.

replacing it a few weeks before the fateful voyage. We did not realize just how important that overheat in the Harbor of Refuge was until later.

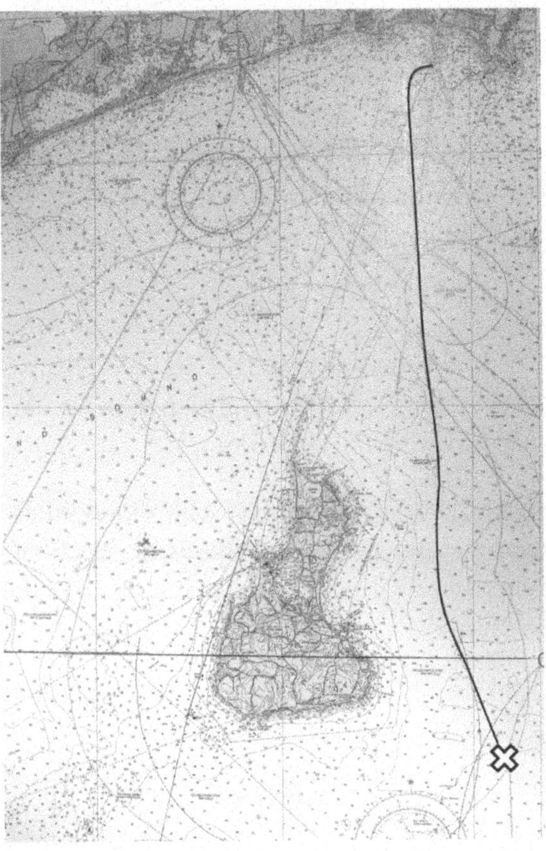

Back now to the fateful voyage. On the chart above I had Nathan take a pen to draw his course out of the Harbor of Refuge and mark with an X the location he testified he and his mother first fished, southeast of Block Island (in that day's version of "which way did he go?"), which he said he was comfortable doing with reasonable precision. To me, that was even better than providing latitude and longitude coordinates since it was graphic. He called that location Striper Rock, his own name for it, with nothing on the chart (or any nautical publications or the internet) to suggest a rock there. Just a flat plain with no bottom structure to hold fish, and at ninety feet deep, it was no place for stripers. He said they fished with live eels. Unsurprisingly, if they in fact even tried, they caught nothing there.

But we did, because there's more than one way to skin a catfish.

> Q: What time did you depart the X area for Block Canyon?
>
> A: I don't know. I'd be deducing based on how long we spent there and how long it would have taken us to get there.
>
> Q: Go ahead and deduce....
>
> A: Well, if we left at midnight and we departed the X three hours after midnight, then we would have departed the X at 3:00 a.m.

Now we were getting somewhere. His ninety-minute departure window was closing, and in fact, all things navigational fell in place from that bit of testimony, even if Nathan tried again to obfuscate, as he did next when I asked:

> Q: And then how long did it take you to get to Block Canyon?
>
> A: It took approximately five hours.
>
> Q: And so you arrived there approximately what time?
>
> A: So, 3:00 a.m. plus—approximately 7:00 a.m. based on that math.

Whoa, a common litigator's word.

> Q: Three plus four is seven. Three plus five is eight.
>
> A: 7:00 a.m. is—because I remember we were getting there shortly after the sun came up, and so I know the sun would have been up by 8:00.

> Q: Okay. So it was around 7:00, you were at your southern terminus?
>
> A: That's my best guess, yes.

With apologies for quoting big chunks of the EUO transcript, which is going to continue because it is Nathan's testimony, this was vital testimony in pinning down his navigational story that we would ride for the rest of the case.

For a mother and son who typically fished for striped bass close to shore, their first and only trip south one hundred miles to the canyons had suspicion written all over it. Nathan testified he'd always dreamed of fishing the canyons, but he hadn't heard of any bite there this year. Liam had learned from the Niejadliks that Nathan said that's where he was heading and cautioned him against it, but why was Nathan so determined?

> A: My mom and I had intended to go striped bass fishing, we had inshore fishing rods onboard the boat, we had eels and so forth. My mom also had expressed concern in the past about me going out on the boat. She's a mother, that's the basis of her concern. And I had given her—I had agreed with her that I would never go out on the boat alone, but that any time I was planning to go out, I would offer her an opportunity to join me. And that was the compromise that we had struck.
>
> So on the way out, I told her that I was planning on going out to the canyons in the coming days and that if she wanted to go with me, that she could. She was working that week and we agreed that I would—that we would go out that evening and—that day, rather than me going out alone later in the week.

This guy will come up with an explanation for everything, I thought.

Any vessel traffic on the way? "None," he answered.

We got him to draw with a pen on smaller-scale Chart 12300 "Approaches to New York"[40] his course south from so-called Striper Rock and then another X for the voyage's southern terminus in Block Canyon, where they turned around, started fishing, and headed north toward home. This allowed us to graphically establish from Nathan's sworn testimony the critical D, S, and T variables, which we could later, if need be, always point out to him as fresher in his mind and more reliable during his EUO than any testimony later on that he might try to alter.

Specifically, we now had him pinned down:

1. The boat headed south for Block Canyon from the Block Island Striper Rock X about three hours after departing Ram Point Marina.
2. The farthest south they got in Block Canyon, marked by another X on Chart 12300, was reached around 7:00 a.m., just after sunrise.
3. It took five hours to go farther south from the Block Island Striper Rock X to the Block Canyon X.
4. So the departure time from the Block Island Striper Rock X had to be around 2:00 a.m., five hours before.
5. Meaning the departure time from Ram Point Marina had to be around 11:00 p.m., three hours before that.

We also had Nathan clearly identify on NOAA Chart 12300 where in Block Canyon the boat sank, which he placed at the north end, near the head of the canyon, testifying it was at the 140-fathom depth mark. In the middle of the Fishtails. He was definitely in over his head.

---

[40] Tr. Ex. 39.

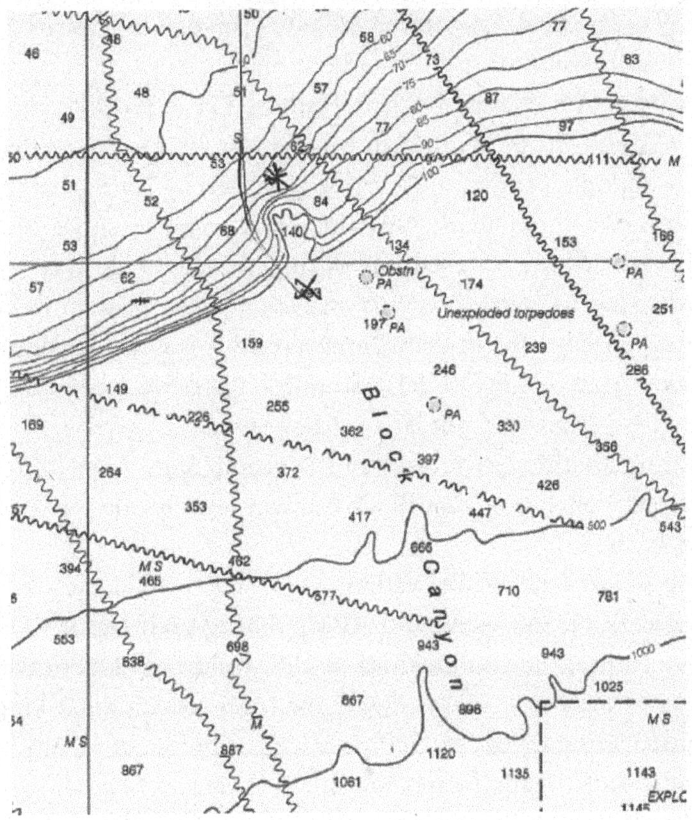

Still, something did not add up. Nathan testified that they trolled north toward home, in the direction of the asterisk he'd marked on the chart, at a varying 4 to 6 knots from the most southern X point that they reached in Block Canyon, for another 5 hours, sinking around midday. That provided additional, helpful D = ST information, but the distance between his southernmost point in Block Canyon, the X where they turned around and headed back north, to the 140-fathom sinking location looked too short to my eyeballs.

During a break, with Nathan and Attorney Santos out of the conference room, Liam and I quickly played with the dividers and confirmed. Trolling north for 5 hours at an average of 5 knots of course meant those start and finish locations would be 25 miles apart. Instead, the location where Nathan drew the X for the Block Canyon turnaround was only about 3 miles south of the 140-fathom mark.

Back on the record, I asked Nathan, "Is it possible your Block Canyon X was further south than you marked it?" He agreed that it was.

The sinking location, now well established by Nathan as the Block Canyon 140-fathom mark, was the single most essential geographic position we set out to establish during the EUO. It was a definite location, what we needed to start analyzing where Nathan went on his alleged seven-day life raft drift. Importantly, it was also a definite location, supported by his D = ST testimony. These were essential, central facts that Nathan could not later credibly evade.

During another quick break in the proceedings, Liam and I agreed we were fast concluding that Block Canyon was the one place the wreck was *not* located.

The diligent navigator reading along may well suggest additional interrogation on the speed and RPMs during each leg of the voyage, compass courses, and so on. And in fact, I did bob and weave and in the heat of the battle space myself out from specifically asking about Nathan's cruising speeds and RPMs. This was potentially a serious error.

But it didn't really matter too much because I had covered myself with the elegant D = ST equation. My gut told me that from Nathan's testimony so far, combined with his chart drawings of his route and both X's and the 140-fathom mark, we had a solid, clear, and concise record reflecting his version of his voyage to Block Canyon, and that we should not give him the chance to muddy the waters by injecting any new slop into his story. When the testimony has gone well and big surprises have been eliminated, it is time to have the witness shut up.

Besides, no one would ever call him Nathan the Navigator. "Dead Reckoning," the underway use of paper charts and "plotting of a vessel's position using courses and distances from the last known position," [41]

---

41 *Knight's Modern Seamanship*, 205 (Dead reckoning—"the most fundamental procedure common to all types of marine navigation"), n. 34; *Chapman Piloting & Seamanship*, 49, 555 ("The term is said to have evolved from *deduced* reckoning, often abbreviated 'de'ed' reckoning in old ships' logs"), n. 35, which is what I told Nathan to do.

could never be the title of a book or movie on Nathan Carman. He wouldn't know how to do that on his own. Astoundingly, he testified he'd removed the marine compass Brian Woods had installed in the wheelhouse—the single most important navigational tool any mariner would choose if allowed just one. It's hard to think of a more unforgivable nautical sin than throwing away your compass. Except in this case.

Back to the point here, Nathan instead exclusively relied on his electronic autopilot for steering and on his touchscreen chartplotter, both interfaced with GPS, to get to his destination. The GPS system for boats is technologically the same as apps utilizing satellites on car dashboards or cell phones. GPS works smartly on land surfaces, with streets and landmarks displayed and driving directions announced in whatever foreign accent you choose. But with the expanse of the sea, the competent mariner has to input "waypoints," or latitude/longitude coordinates, for a particular offshore location. Or, by using the touchscreen, a location can be selected by fingertip, and with the autopilot steering, you will be taken there.

GPS unquestionably makes ocean navigation much easier but heightens operator complacency by delegating course decisions to electronics. AI is changing that, with fully autonomous vessels projected to arrive in the near future, but Nathan did not have that luxury. Say our intrepid Nathan in 2016 wanted to go from Point Judith to fish a mile south of Block Island. If he merely selected a destination on his touchscreen and let the autopilot steer him there without keeping a visual look-out, he would run aground on Block Island, which popped up in the way. It's surprising how often these sorts of incidents actually happen.

***

Graceful dolphins and larger pilot whales, aka blackfish, have had this problem with Cape Cod since the last glaciation created it. A pod in Cape Cod Bay as fall cold fronts pass will suddenly realize they dillydallied too long and should have earlier repositioned southeast to warmer waters well offshore in the Atlantic. So, with all deliberate speed, the pod heads in that direction using their internal GPS but, on the way, runs aground on the inside forearm of the Cape, beaching in Eastham or Wellfleet's Blackfish Creek. This has been happening for thousands of years, a windfall for earlier Cape Codders,[42] and now for IFAW, the International Fund for Animal Welfare.

IFAW set up its world headquarters on the Cape, where its camera crews are the first responders, videoing as many marine mammal groundings as humanly possible, to fundraise around the globe. But off-camera, IFAW historically euthanized many of the washashores, trying recently to preempt that critique by opening a one-patient ER in Orleans.

Speaking of marine mammals, what's up with pinnipeds? Because they eat boatloads of fish, the Commonwealth of Massachusetts' historic five-dollar seal-nose bounty led to virtual extinction from these waters, so the 1972 Federal Marine Mammal Protection Act was passed and the seal population slowly started to recover. But the Act's fecund criminal penalties have completely backfired, with gray and harbor seal populations exploding to a combined one hundred thousand over the last two decades, even down to Rhode Island and Connecticut. That's quick.

Hundreds of great white sharks moved in just as fast. Before the bounties, the Monomoyicks and Nausets would have more sustainably culled the seal herd, with sharks less prevalent than now, so the current situation is unprecedented and askew. Surfing on the Outer Cape, in a black wetsuit, on a board that from below looks like a sleek seal, is a death wish. Always liked to have sides on my vessel.

Digressing logically once more before we get back to Nathan, this crooked arm arguably should be renamed Cape Shark, not just for the great whites but also for the little dogfish many in the local commercial fishing fleet now target, sadly. Codfish, so abundant when Bartholomew Gosnold named the Cape in 1602, are gone.[43]

Worse, codfish habitat was destroyed at the end of the twentieth century. In the early Cold War years, huge Soviet factory trawlers lurked

---

[42] *See* Phil Schwind, *Cape Cod Fisherman*, chapter 10 (International Marine Publishing, 1974).

[43] A tin codfish hangs from the ceiling of Cape Cod's Barnstable County Superior Courtroom. It would be in poor taste to replace it with a shark.

just offshore and scoured the ocean bottom while also spying. Spoken Russian could be heard into the 1970s in the background of Cape radio broadcasts and on fuzzy TV, especially Providence/Fall River Channel 6. "That's right, Choo Choo!"[44]

After the 1976 Magnuson-Stevens Fishery Conservation and Management Act made fishing in the two-hundred-mile US Exclusive Economic Zone available only to US-flag fishing vessels, the soviet of New Bedford largely took over, with big powerful diesels towing heavy, indiscriminate fishing gear over the bottom, clear-cutting and strip-mining old growth like "lemons" and "clay pipes" in the nooks and crannies and nurseries of fishing grounds with those names. Larger areas like the Great South Channel's hard-bottom fjord were likewise injuriously harvested. All flora and fauna—not just the targeted species—hauled up on deck died, a waste known as bycatch, or more accurately, bykill. Compounded now by warming waters in the Gulf of Maine due to climate change, recovery is hard to envision.

Under the Magnuson Act, the federal government's regulation of the New England groundfish industry, codfish in particular, was an unmitigated disaster. In a misguided effort at grassroots democracy by delegating to fishermen the formulation of fishing regulations, Congress let the foxes control the henhouse, typically rubber-stamped by the National Marine Fisheries Service. Severe overfishing was the result. I well remember one 1981 trip with our freshest, best cared-for, sustainably hooked codfish yielding only thirteen cents per pound from the wholesale buyer. At the same retail store for Christmas Eve forty-three years later, we paid $22.49 per pound for codfish imported from Iceland.

***

Back now to Nathan and his version of GPS navigation. Like a video gamer in an automated cartoon world, he didn't even use other nautical devices available to him. Or so he said.

He didn't use his VHF radio, which he could not remember last testing. We concluded that Nathan wanted to avoid broadcasting anything

[44] Railroad Salvage Stores ad, also annoyingly on Channel 6.

that might be used to track his location, like the sickos who make false SOS calls but end up getting pinpointed and prosecuted by the Coast Guard and local US Attorney's Office. But that did not mean Nathan couldn't just listen to his radio and make good use of its high-tech automatic identification system (AIS) so he could monitor on his integrated chartplotter screen other vessels' movements by virtue of their unique AIS call signs—while not transmitting his. Kind of like spying.

Nor did he use his radar, which was turned off, he said. Radar emissions also can be detected by vessels with specialized equipment, which Nathan would not want. So he chose to forgo the collision-avoidance benefits and navigational assistance of radar, which could be used to confirm his boat's position while passing by Coast Guard buoys, accurately maintained on station. Like a vessel with no way on, an anchored buoy is also dead in the water.

One hundred per cent reliant on his electronic chartplotter and autopilot, that is how Nathan traveled around Block Island on several fishing trips allegedly with his mother, how he would have gotten to his imaginary Block Island Striper Rock X in the dark, and how he would have gotten to the Block Canyon southern turnaround five hours after that. There was no need for him to factor in winds, waves, or currents in steering toward his destinations. The electronic devices did it all for him, with the autopilot adjusting the rudder in response to any surface conditions that might push the bow slightly one way or another, keeping it straight on its course to his GPS-designated destination. Wherever it might be.

That's right, who knows where he really went? Who knows if his electronics were properly working? That's the reason professional mariners today still use the compass and dead reckoning to independently confirm where they are, as a backup to electronic failures. That does sometimes happen, like a laptop that loses Wi-Fi, or when a car's Check Engine light comes on and computer diagnostics are required for troubleshooting. When that sort of failure occurs in the open sea without a road to follow, if you have not been independently keeping track of where you've been, have fun figuring out where you are now so you can try to find your way home. Especially if you threw away your magnetic compass.

Nevertheless, Nathan's testimony gave no indication he had any problems with unreliable navigational electronics or malfunctions, and I wanted to rule that out so he wouldn't try to claim it later. His chartplotter was working fine, showing he was inside the walls of Block Canyon as labeled, he testified. He was confident in his course descriptions and drawings. He could easily have practiced using all his fancy navigational electronics on his home computer. We just wanted to make sure his testimony and chart markings plausibly fit together as a whole, to make sure we had it locked down and to ensure that he would not be able to slither out later. One change in just one of his D, S, or T variables would throw the other two off, if we didn't nail them down now. Afterward we would assess whether the story he was telling was truthful or whether it was for some reason still full of holes.

Nathan may not have realized it, but he assisted greatly in tying down his story with something else our species—virtually all mobile species—have used for eons in their travels. Even if his boat was miraculously recovered, we knew that saltwater incursion minimized the chances of conducting a forensic data analysis on the marine electronics to re-create his course. Yet certain natural phenomena would never get lost, would never corrode, and could not be put on autopilot.

Sunrise. That's when they reached the southernmost point of their trip, as Nathan told Martha and confirmed during his EUO. The exact time of sunrise and sunset on any given day varies surprisingly both north to south and east to west within the same time zone. I had checked September 18, 2016 for the area of Block Canyon. The "first tip of Sun at Sunrise" was about 6:35 a.m., according to the sunrise/sunset tables in my trusty *Eldridge Tide and Pilot Book.* So Nathan was right, the sun would have been up by 7:00 a.m.

Besides giving us an independent time reference, his sunrise testimony gave our voyage investigation an outside anchor, an outer boundary. It meant that no matter where Nathan actually went, according to his testimony, he did not go any further than when the sun rose, no matter how mistaken his electronics or his calculations or any subsequent changes to his testimony might be. He had established a 7:00 a.m. "sunrise arc"—the maximum distance he could have traveled on his five-hour trip from the Block Island Striper Rock X, and he was boxed in to so testify in the future.

This was his story, his sworn testimony. It very well might not be true, but his testimony about his trip was triangularly constrained by the inescapable time of sunrise, by his Distance = Speed x Time testimony, and his chart markings. We would scrutinize it all later, but he was never going to get away with changing it appreciably. And if he tried to change one variable, the others would have to change too, and he would get himself all fouled up—we would see to that.

In sum, we had Nathan Carman tied down on his navigation story, under oath, three short months after he sank. Sorry to beat a dead horse on this, but it gave us solid evidence on the two apparent end points of his life raft drift, which we increasingly felt did not happen: (1) his starting point at the 140-fathom mark in Block Canyon and (2) his "rescue" by *Orient Lucky* forty miles away and seven days later.

The Wholly Incredible Sinking

Nathan's October 19 written description to Martha about the sinking, now about thirteen hours after leaving the dock, also had lots of holes. Again, we needed to get him to fill in this piece of his story under oath.

Describing their fishing as they headed north in Block Canyon, he said, "We were trolling with some deep-running lures, like large Parrish-type lures and we had surface baits, which included a couple daisy chains and a cedar plug daisy chain I had purchased from people on Craigslist." All are artificial lures.

As he had written to Martha, the sinking happened within three to five minutes, which he reiterated under oath.

> A: All I can say is—All I can say is that we started somewhere in the vicinity of the X, trolling north within Block Canyon—within the walls of Block

> Canyon, and that the boat sank after we started trolling north. We started trolling north around 7:00 and the boat sank around midday. We were trolling between 4-6 knots.

This sounded like "that's my story and I'm sticking with it," which was just fine. Nathan had thus made the time estimates he gave Martha solid.

But the rest of his sinking evolution, to use Coast Guard-speak again, then mutated into a wholly incredible species of maritime myth.

As they trolled northward, Nathan said he was unaware of any mechanical or maneuvering issues. The first thing he noticed was a funny engine noise, so he went to the deck hatch just forward of the wheelhouse and lifted it to check the diesel. He saw water up to the engine's plastic battery boxes, which protect the batteries from water and keep them from shorting out.

Concerned that the diesel engine was about to suck in water instead of air, Nathan went to the wheelhouse and brought the engine quickly to idle and shut it down. (Why the boat hadn't felt logy with that amount of water was hard to believe, and so was his concern about engine water ingestion, since the turbo's air intake is much higher than the water level he had just reported.)

Deafening silence then descended on the boat. Not just no more "funny engine noise," but zero engine noise whatsoever, for the first time in thirteen hours. No other vessels anywhere on the horizon. Mother and son all alone, almost one hundred miles at sea, the bilge filling with water. No life jackets grabbed from the wheelhouse or handed out to his passenger, the one person in the whole world he had known the longest.

Then, during all this crisis, the only and very last thing son and mother ever said to each other: "I asked her to start reeling in the lines" and "she responded 'Yes, I will reel in the lines.'" But Nathan never said anything whatsoever to his mother about the water he saw below deck.

He went from the wheelhouse aft to open the port deck hatch, where he had installed the replacement bilge pump the day before, to see if the seacocks had failed. That space was full of "dirty water" and he couldn't see through it, but it did not smell of oil or diesel fuel. I wanted to know how much water, to compare with what he'd just seen at the forward hatch.

Q: How far below the deck?

A: Not very far below the deck.

Q: Inches, please.

A: Three inches.

Nathan then secured that hatch. Six feet away, he never laid eyes on Linda again after wordlessly rising from his hands and knees. As far as he knows, she never moved from that position. He had no idea how the water was getting in, and he never—not then with the boat full of water, or earlier in the day—bothered to check his epoxy-puttied holes on the transom. He just returned to the wheelhouse, "preparing for the possibility" of abandoning ship.

An illustration should help here, just as it helped Liam and me understand and record Nathan's story. I had Nathan amplify his testimony with handwritten drawings on Bernie Feeney's bird's-eye diagram of the boat's components.

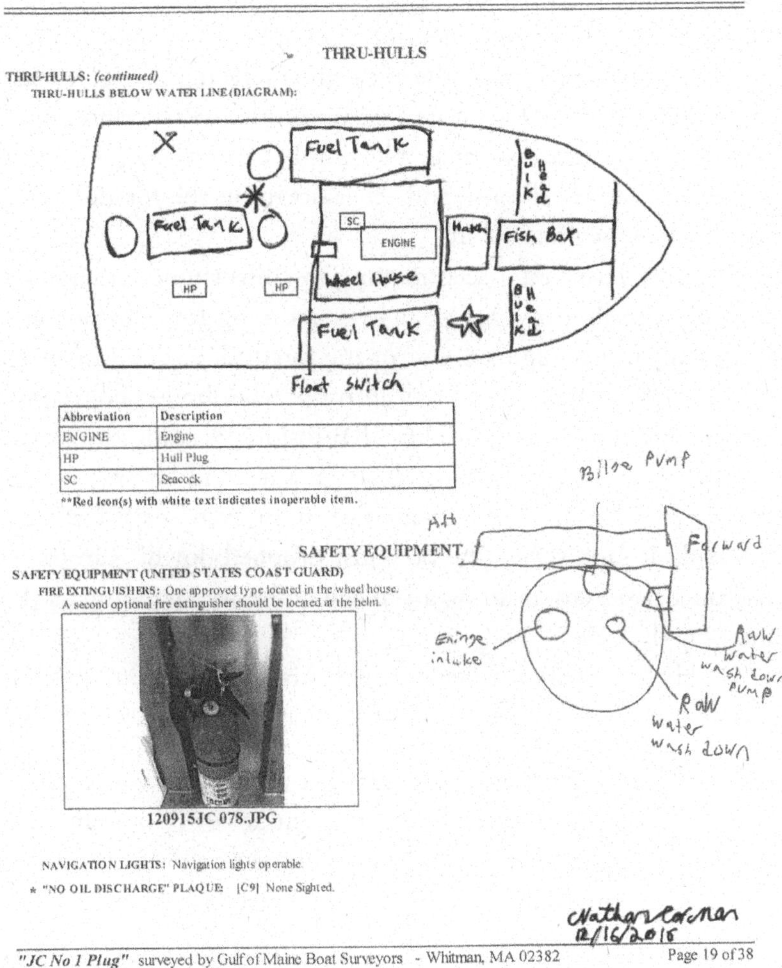

III. SYSTEMS

THRU-HULLS

THRU-HULLS: *(continued)*
THRU-HULLS BELOW WATER LINE (DIAGRAM):

Abbreviation	Description
ENGINE	Engine
HP	Hull Plug
SC	Seacock

**Red Icon(s) with white text indicates inoperable item.

SAFETY EQUIPMENT

SAFETY EQUIPMENT (UNITED STATES COAST GUARD)
FIRE EXTINGUISHERS: One approved type located in the wheel house. A second optional fire extinguisher should be located at the helm.

120915JC 078.JPG

NAVIGATION LIGHTS: Navigation lights operable

* "NO OIL DISCHARGE" PLAQUE: [C9] None Sighted.

Nathan Carman
12/16/2016

"JC No 1 Plug" surveyed by Gulf of Maine Boat Surveyors - Whitman, MA 02382 Page 19 of 38

P00352

The two plywood bulkheads, which Nathan had removed, he drew and labeled to port and starboard of the fish box. Between the fish box and the engine is the hatch just forward of the wheelhouse. The asterisk is where Nathan kneeled to try to see the thru-hull connections below the port circular hatch. The X is Linda's location when he last saw her from that hatch.

Entering the wheelhouse, Nathan gathered emergency gear stowed in waterproof boxes and bags. But while inside the wheelhouse he did not reach for the microphone, only a couple of feet away, to radio for help. Neither did he remove the adjacent emergency position-indicating radio beacon (EPIRB) from its bracket inside the wheelhouse to get it ready to send a distress signal. He simply carried a bag of emergency gear out of the wheelhouse and set it down on the foredeck for easier access in case they needed it.

Then he returned a second time to collect more emergency gear from the wheelhouse—again, neither radioing for help nor grabbing the EPIRB, just going back out to the foredeck to deposit the gear.

And then a third time, back into the wheelhouse, collecting more gear, not radioing, leaving the EPIRB inside. Heading to the foredeck one last time, "the trim of the boat forward and aft was not perceptibly altered" (meaning the boat was on an even keel), but then "the boat sank, it sank very—the bow just dropped down." On the Feeney diagram I had Nathan draw a star where he was standing as the boat sank—by the bow.

It only got worse for Nathan with his testimony on why he didn't send a distress signal during one of those trips into the wheelhouse.

> A: I have it deeply engrained in me that you don't signal for distress unless you are in imminent—your life or limb is in imminent jeopardy. And I didn't realize the boat was sinking until it sank.

Whoa, whoa, whoa. How much more imminent jeopardy of life or limb need Nathan have attained? With a dead in the water boat full of water at the edge of the continental shelf and no other vessels around, all he had to do was activate the EPIRB and wait an hour for a Coast Guard helicopter to take him, and his mother if she was still with him, ashore.

This was damning testimony, and there was no sense in arguing with Nathan. He had stepped in the bight of a line and we would keel-haul him. Yet I couldn't resist a little follow-up:

> Q: And you're actually saying that the vessel sank bow first?
>
> A: Yes.
>
> Q: Now, how can you explain that? You seem like a smart guy. How do you explain that?
>
> A: I feel like I would be speculating if I tried to answer that.
>
> Q: Okay. Well, have you thought through your mind in the time since September 18th, when the boat sank, how did it sink bow first? Have you considered that question?
>
> A: I've considered how it sank, yes.
>
> Q: What possible factors can you come up with that it would sink bow first?
>
> A: The fact that the keel is deeper fore than aft. So, at the very front of the boat, obviously it's sloped, so I don't know how deep the keel would be relative to the cockpit, but it's—The cockpit is shallower than midships and slightly forward of the midships.

This response was nothing but an unconvincing nonanswer that I was glad to have on the record since it was obvious to me the boat would have sunk by the stern, and even faster due to Nathan's removal of the forward bulkheads, which thereby eliminated two air pockets of floatation at the bow.

Contrary to his intentions, Nathan's testimony was a gimme on stern-first sinking, with water coming in his four half-dollar transom holes. We'd have no problem finding a marine expert witness to tap it in. And even better, in the alternative, we had another argument that would come back to haunt Nathan. Assuming for the sake of argument that the boat did sink by the bow, that was only conceivable because he removed Woods's bulkhead, allowing water to flow forward. This is another prime example of Nathan getting in over his head. There would be more.

And if Nathan's Coast Guard radio interview from the *Orient Lucky* seemed flat, his EUO's fuller description of his mother's demise was more chilling in its matter-of-factness.

> Q: How many days were you in the life raft?
>
> A: Seven days....
>
> Q: How did the life raft deploy?
>
> A: It deployed automatically.
>
> Q: And how long were you in the water before you were in the life raft?
>
> A: A brief period of time. I was able to collect the safety gear and get to the life raft. So, minutes....
>
> Q: What happened to your mother?
>
> A: When the boat sank, I did not—I found myself in the water. I wasn't able to locate her.
>
> Q: Did she go down with the vessel?
>
> A: I know she was a strong swimmer.... I don't know if she—if when the bow dropped, she either struck her head or struck a limb such that she was either unconscious or unable to swim. I don't know if she got tangled in the fishing line or got a hook

caught on her, which would have connected her to an 80-pound-test rod, or if she got tangled in the dock lines that were in the cockpit....

Q: And you didn't hear any voice or scream of help from her of any sort?

A: Not that I perceived.... One second I was walking forward, and the next second I'm in the water. I don't know how acute my senses would have been in that fraction of a second, which is also when any call for help would most likely have come, but I did not receive any call from her.

This "fraction of a second" oceanic swallowing of Nathan's boat was even less believable than in *The Odyssey*. Yet his precision immediately continued, with Nathan offering that maybe the reason he didn't see his mother in the water was the swell—a "sine wave" four feet high from trough to crest. So mathematically precise when he wanted to be, but in contrast, so vague when he didn't. Such a smarty-pants on sine waves, but he didn't attempt to swim around in those waves to look for Mom. We would see more of this so very intelligent yet so very ignorant dialectic later.

To sum up, Nathan's sinking story lacked any credibility, as we usually say in court when calling someone a liar. Nathan did not say anything, not one word, to his mother, or hear from her or see her on a water-full, noise-free boat with excellent sight lines during the couple of minutes he readied emergency gear to abandon ship one hundred miles at sea, thrice not sending any distress signal. Then the boat just dropped out from beneath him in "a fraction of a second," bow-first.

Giving Nathan every single benefit of the doubt, there is no way the sinking happened as he outlandishly, landlubberly testified. No reasonable person would ever believe it.

There was more about Nathan's EPIRB testimony that was both revealing and suspicious. He revealed that his mother had purchased the EPIRB and registered it with NOAA under the boat's name, *Chicken*

Pox, which Brian Woods had given it. But Nathan testified that he himself never called his boat *Chicken Pox* and that name on the transom had been completely painted over by Woods before he sold it. Nathan just called it "my boat." It was the media, not us, who promulgated *Chicken Pox*, adding to the hype. We never called it *Chicken Pox* for the time frame after Nathan bought it.

The additional suspicious part of the EPIRB, besides Nathan's not activating it, was his placement of it aboard. He mounted it inside the aluminum wheelhouse, tucked up underneath the aluminum dashboard, in the forward port corner, after consulting with his mother but not any marine professionals. But EPIRBs are properly mounted outside, so if a vessel sinks, when the EPIRB hits the water it will release from its hydrostatic bracket, floating free of the wreckage to emit radio distress signals to dedicated satellites without interference. Inside the phone booth that was Nathan's wheelhouse, when the boat sank (wherever and whenever that happened) by the stern, the EPIRB's radio waves were enveloped by aluminum and submerged before they were able to transmit anywhere.

Nathan essentially confirmed this by testifying that the EPIRB "was in the bracket at the time that the boat sank, so I don't believe it would have gone off." That would have been the last thing he wanted.

A final revealing piece of testimony from the EUO involved a "quite large" cooler, two-by-two-by-five-feet, containing ice, "a bottle of lemonade," plus chopped "mackerel, squid, and maybe some bunker" that his mother kept "a lot" of "frozen in her freezer." Nathan testified he had no plans whatsoever to use the chopped bait to fish Block Canyon: "The reason that was onboard was not for tuna fishing." They had solely trolled his artificial rigs going north.

As with the EPIRB's mounting (since she was never going to be able to testify), Nathan again pointed to his mother as the reason the chopped bait "she brought" was aboard. He had written Martha that after the "boat sank there was a brown slick on the surface of the water that was the color of engine oil" which lasted "an hour."

Something about that made no sense. It was so good, I just left it alone.

***

During his weeklong life raft drift, Nathan said he saw only one ship's lights on the distant horizon and no search aircraft. He had a change of clothes and survival supplies in his emergency gear, including a small compass, but he could not tell what direction he drifted. He agreed that the photo of him climbing up the *Orient Lucky* gangway after seven days as a human bobber was accurate.

I felt we did not need to get much deeper into it now since the boat was gone. That's why we were getting testimony, and I did not want to subject us to criticism for engaging in a too long fishing expedition. So, during another short break, Liam and I agreed we had what we needed and then some, and with a subsequent mutual nod, I soon wrapped up Nathan Carman's examination under oath. It was 5:04 p.m. and felt like snow as we closed in on the darkest evening of the year, with miles to go before we could take rest, miles to go before we could take rest.

Since I had to find a hotel to attend Ma Hester's funeral the next day, and Liam had to get home to his brood, he and I debriefed on the EUO quickly and the tragedy we now had to unravel. "He's one hundred percent a liar," Liam said. I nodded. "Yeah. He really stepped in it."

We were both suspicious of almost everything in Nathan's testimony, which was entirely open to question, but we at least had a concrete record of what Nathan's story was so we could scrutinize it factually and disprove it as needed. I was thinking his testimony had provided at least two and likely more solid legal reasons he should not have insurance coverage for the loss of his boat.

On the way home Saturday afternoon I stopped at the Hyannis West Marine store to check out and purchase all the trim tab repair items Nathan had identified. The West Marine Epoxy Putty Stick was killer. "For fast emergency or permanent repairs on fiberglass, wood, metal and plastic surfaces."[45]

[45] Tr. Ex. 5.4.16.

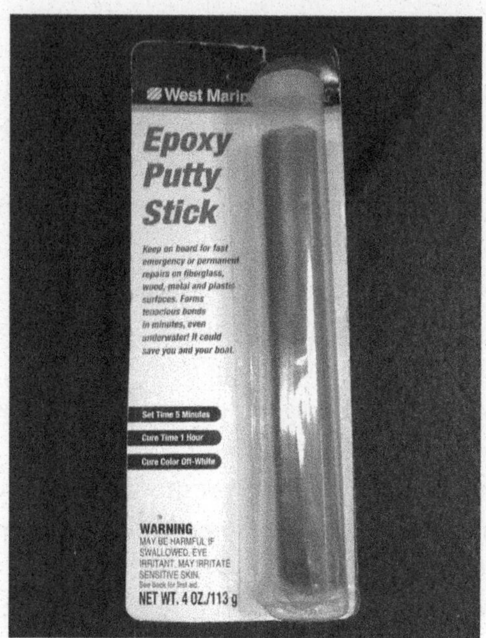

Surfaces. Not holes.

7

"YOU CAN'T MAKE THIS STUFF UP"

My first marine casualty investigation was when I was going into my senior year of high school.

Eldredge Marine employed me the summer Skip Hall bought it from the Gunny Eldredge successors and changed the name to Chatham Yacht Basin. It harbored no real yachts, just outboards in slips. Much of the boatyard's work was on commercial fishing vessels like Paul Lucas's trap boats, which I scraped and bottom-painted in my capacity as chief underwater technician. I got a great out-of-school education from Skip and the old-timers who worked there and along the shore as well as the many who stopped by for gams.

There was Archie Nickerson, a very kind craftsman of few words who served in the Coast Guard after his father was lost on the bar. Born with a pipe between his teeth, an Olde Cape Cod trait, his drawl virtually extinct, Archie masterfully oversaw us move big, heavy fish boats in wooden cradles, employing only jacks, round poles as rollers, and the Dodge Power Wagon.

There was Crayton Nickerson, Sr., a too-old-to-fish-anymore, shanty-based tub trawl bait cutter and manufacturer of three-foot-wide bay scallop dredges for the fall harvest of the single most succulent seafood morsels in the whole world. (If used as chum, tuna fish would jump right into the boat for more.) He shared Yankee ingenuity with me, confirming the wisdom of my saltwater soaks to treat a miserable case of poison ivy, contracted while waiting for a very nice visiting Jersey Girl to come home from work one night. "Lucky that's all you caught boy." Not even close.

There was Ben Buck, a tough blacksmith prone to going on sporadic benders, but not an alcoholic. He just liked drinking. I felt accepted that he'd allow me to joust with him on socioeconomic issues and even lambaste Tricky Dick Nixon—but only if I was unemotional.

There was Ron McVickar, whom I watched while I assembled mooring components as *Banshee* came up Oyster River after a charter fishing trip one day. O'Day Sprites from Stage Harbor Yacht Club sailing school squeaked "Right of way!" at him and Ron barked back, "Rule 9 makes me the stand-on vessel in a narrow channel. Read your Rules of the Road!"[46] And so I did.

There was Frank "Flutie" James, who after an appearance would scratch off in the sand in his red Corvette convertible with a "Custer Had It Coming" bumper sticker, newly famous as Wamsutta for taking a divergent view of Thanksgiving festivities at Plymouth Rock on behalf of the Wampanoags, who eventually received federal recognition.

Last but not least, and the sole survivor, there was tea-drinking Ross Ringheim. Equal parts grump and comedian, a font of wooden-boat-building knowledge from his days up-Cape at Crosby's, he was also an original espouser of the evils of crony capitalism. Years after Skip sold the boatyard and it went all corporate, Ross somehow was still working there, tutoring my son Sam when he followed in my footsteps.

On the day of that 1972 casualty in question, three *Mod Squad*-ish tourists showed up at the boatyard. Skip orally bareboat chartered them

[46] 1972 Convention on the International Regulations for Prevention of Collisions at Sea (COLREGS).

his Mako outboard with appurtenances, which I later learned is legalese for rented it to them to go waterskiing. I was pumping gas on the fuel dock when they came back an hour later, one of the guys absent his right index finger.

Skip freaked out, sure he was going to lose the boatyard before the ink was dry. But the *Squad*'s story had holes of its own. The guy claimed he was holding the wooden handle of the tow rope with one hand when the triangular rope bridle pinched his finger against the handle on a tight turn, severing it. Having water-skied with identical equipment, I whispered to Skip there's no friggin' way that could happen and they must have been screwing around. I could only imagine the victim had wrapped the tow rope around his finger and given a thumbs-up as the operator gunned the outboard to pull him up out of the water when goodbye digit. I pointed out to Skip that an inadvertent clove hitch cinching tighter and tighter would be particularly surgical.

Convinced, and an imposing figure when he wanted to be, Skip let the victim know this was all his problem. The boatyard experts concurred with my forensic analysis, opining it a "good thing that damn hippie didn't wrap that tow line 'round sumin' else," with phlegmy chuckles all 'round. (Not "Ayuhs"; that's Down East and Up Country.) I got good recommendations from Skip for years afterwards, and he taught my sons to sail, although they complained he yelled even more than I do.

It was a privilege to learn from this quahog chowder of characters and visiting blowhards and unnamed Prohibition rumrunners, the predecessors of pot smugglers, which was a big thing in the 1970s, an industry that gave at least one current burgher his start.

Stuck well out in the Atlantic on New England's scenic right elbow, Chatham has always been on the frontier of civilization, including maritime law, with colorful stories of mooncussers luring ships ashore with lanterns in northeasters (which didn't work for Chrissake when the moon was out), and wreckers plundering vessels that ran ashore on our sandy shoals even if there was a full moon. In 1772, Chatham's Ansell Nickerson, while not the region's first seafaring outlaw (he was preceded by Captain Kidd, who may have buried treasure in Pleasant

Bay shortly before his Boston arrest in 1699), was tried for murdering the *Abigail* crew, consisting of three of his family members, with no eyewitnesses—a not uncommon at-sea theme.[47] He was represented by John Adams, Esquire, who got Ansell acquitted. His first examination under oath was at trial. Too late.

And I will confess to occasional barratry during my college years running the Chatham Bars Inn boat, grateful there were no marine casualties among the fifteen thousand passengers I carried by virtue of my Coast Guard passenger-for-hire license. While owner E. R. McMullen, who ran the grand resort in a Humphrey Bogart white dinner jacket, tolerated my off-hours trips to the Pendleton wreck or Monomoy Point and even Nantucket, mostly so guests could fish for stripers and blues, he was understandably hopping mad at me when he had to hire outside landscapers because the Inn's grounds crew was unfit-for-duty the better part of a week.

In breach of management's "no more employees on the boat" order, I had secreted the grounds crew to North Beach for a camp-over. Befuddled by beer and paralyzed by pot, they passed out, feet toward their bonfire. Next morning, soles one big blister, they had to crawl on hands and knees over the sand back to the boat when I went to pick them up. My apology to Mr. McMullen that I transported them because I felt sorry they didn't get tips went over like an anchor. Nevertheless, my job was secure because this was nearly fifty years ago, before commercial exam schools spoon-fed USCG license candidates, and there was no one around who could replace me.

Another, most key mentor was Vince Corteselli, and now we are coming back on course to the Nathan Carman story. Vince started assigning me cases in 1986 for Skuld, a Norwegian insurer of oceangoing ships, which had just jumped into the Bering Sea fisheries, naive to US litigation. Up to four-hundred-foot catcher/processors were targeting pollack, grinding their catch into fake crab surimi in the belowdecks

---

[47] Jeremiah Digges, *A Modern Pilgrim's Guide to Cape Cod* (Modern Pilgrim Press, 1947), 48.

factory chock-full of moving sharp objects. Skuld insured real crab boats too, like those later seen on TV's *Deadliest Catch*.

What could possibly go wrong? Broken backs, mangled legs, degloved hands, sexual assaults, collisions, multiple deaths, sinkings. A lawyer, Vince had seen it all and is the best in the business at handling marine insurance claims and overseeing litigation.

My first big trial was for him in Seattle federal court. A Norwegian immigrant who had learned the American tort system, plaintiff Syvert Biktjorn conceivably needed the cervical surgery he underwent, but he left a wake of incriminating medical records with a dozen distinct versions of how a seven-hundred-pound crab pot supposedly injured him on the *Silver Cloud* in the Aleutians.[48] To boot, I found that Sy had a crooked surgeon and a simultaneous car-crash insurance claim in New York independently resulting in that same condition. Wife Lillian, claiming loss of consortium (forgoing sex as a result of hubby's injury) in both of his cases, had a treasure trove of medical records herself. Colossally constipated, she happily reported to the family physician, "Gave birth to an 8 pounder, Apgar score 10, mother and stool doing fine."

"You can't make this stuff up," Vince and I often howled, or moaned, in unison over the decades. A Brooklyn-trained maestro, although he'd probably prefer puppet master, Vince orchestrates counsel all around the country on his various cases and sometimes asks to be corrected if he is wrong, which I've only rarely experienced. He is also unafraid to speak his mind even when he knows damn well he shouldn't, and so over the years he's developed a propensity for finding new jobs with different marine insurers, eventually landing in the recreational boating field. He barged in and took over the Carman case as only Vince could and kept it alive when other insurers would have caved. He is singularly instrumental in what happened to Nathan.

---

[48] *Biktjorn v. Bendiksen*, 774 F. Supp. 581, 1992 AMC 347 (W.D. Wash. 1991).

2017

8

OUR RACE TO THE COURTHOUSE

A couple of weeks after Nathan's examination under oath, Attorney Santos sent me a letter alleging all sorts of bogus bad faith claims against the Insurer for not paying Nathan his $85,000 for the sunken boat immediately if not sooner.

Vince summoned me to the Insurer's headquarters for a meeting, with instructions to circulate beforehand a draft letter for Martha to send to Nathan denying his insurance claim and a draft lawsuit against Nathan to enforce that denial.

We also contemplated that one of Nathan's aunts might make an insurance claim for Linda's death, triggering liability coverage under the policy of up to $300,000, plus the contractually necessary but distasteful appointment of separate counsel to defend Nathan, which in his case would have cost even more. So really what was at stake from the Insurer's point of view were potential payouts many times exceeding the $85,000 hull claim. It was a much bigger dollar case than the public perceived.

Rather than bore the patient reader with what crusty old maritime lawyers see as the fascinating development of marine insurance concepts over the last several centuries, here, based on his examination under oath, are the three basic reasons we concluded Nathan was not entitled to insurance as we prepared the lawsuit.

First, as already noted, Nathan's policy under a capitalized, bold-type **EXCLUSIONS** heading did not cover "any loss, damage, expense or cost of repair caused directly or indirectly by incomplete, improper or faulty repair," other than by a repair facility preapproved by the Insurer, which Nathan was not.

Second, and this is esoteric but solid, a marine insurance policy becomes null and void under the concept of *uberrimae fidei*, when the insured vessel owner breaches the duty of utmost good faith to disclose to the insurer material information about the risk. One of the lofty treats of practicing maritime law is relying on old US Supreme Court maritime cases for precedent, like *McLanahan v. Universal Insurance Co.*, 26 U.S. 170, 185 (1828), which we quoted in our denial letter to Nathan.

> Where a party orders insurance, and afterwards receives intelligence material to the risk, or has knowledge of a loss; he ought to communicate it to the agent, as soon as, with due and reasonable diligence, it can be communicated.... If he omits so to do... the policy is void.

Here, the Insurer initially provided coverage to Nathan based on the JC 31 as described in Bernie Feeney's prepurchase survey report. However, Nathan then altered the boat, removing the trim tabs, opening up four half-dollar-size holes near the waterline, and inadequately sealing them with epoxy putty. He removed a structural bulkhead and floatation voids. He had problems with a bilge pump he couldn't fix. These were dramatic changes to the boat, unbeknownst to the Insurer, increasing the risk of its sinking in an ever-precarious watery environment. Nathan was unilaterally and secretively changing the odds—before heading one hundred miles offshore for the first time in his life. He failed his legal obligation to update the Insurer on these physical changes to his boat.

Third, insurance does not cover criminal acts, and with good reason. As mentioned earlier, it would be horrible public policy. There are enough bad acts in the world without encouraging them, so the law prohibits insurance policy payouts when the insured intentionally caused the loss or the loss happened while committing a crime. Nathan's policy made this explicit, excluding "any loss, damage or expense caused intentionally by, with the knowledge of, or resulting from criminal wrongdoing by any 'insured.'" Nathan's EUO was so damning in so many ways that we expected law enforcement would soon be charging him with murder or manslaughter, so we confidently included this allegation too. Not to mention, which we did not yet, this all seemed to tie in with his grandfather's murder as well.

Those were the three major arguments included in our denial letter to Nathan and incorporated into our Complaint for Declaratory Judgment, the initiating pleading we would file in the lawsuit. Again, with apologies to the reader for this exciting discussion, please understand that these are the tools of my trade. This book is about how we used them, rare though they may be, to solve double unwitnessed family murders.

And rather than just take Liam's and my word for it, we contacted two marine experts for their initial opinions based on Nathan's EUO testimony.

Eric Greene, a naval architect from Annapolis, provided a letter describing an experiment he performed stuffing West Marine Epoxy Putty Stick balls into half-dollar-sized holes in one-inch-thick plywood and letting them harden. Not only was it difficult to accomplish, with the epoxy putty falling through the unbacked holes when squeezed in, but after hardening, the epoxy plugs were not secure in the holes and could be loosened easily. Greene concluded that with the holes so close to the waterline, water would enter the bilge, eventually weighing the hull down until there was a free flow of water in through the holes, leading to the boat's sinking.

Mike McCook, a marine surveyor who over the years routinely worked for the Insurer, also provided a letter stating that Nathan's removal of the plywood bulkheads jeopardized the integrity of the boat, allowing water accumulating in the bilge to flow forward and accelerate sinking—by the stern. The gimme.

The plan Vince and I hatched was to send Martha's denial letter to Nathan and Attorney Santos with the attached Greene and McCook letters, and that same day file the lawsuit in US District Court for the District of Rhode Island, where Nathan performed his faulty repairs.

We choose federal court whenever we can because its jurisdiction includes admiralty and maritime cases and federal judges are usually very smart and often familiar with maritime law, or at least teachable. Furthermore, federal courts have strict procedural rules that are generally enforced by the judges, which deter lawyer shenanigans, helping to keep everyone focused on the real issues and on schedule.

Another advantage to a marine insurer in bringing suit in federal court rather than state court is that the case will be tried by a judge without a jury. With the exception of personal injury cases, that's generally true for most civil maritime cases. The arcane but historically accurate reason is that English admiralty jurisdiction, which did not have juries, was inherited by the American colonial courts, and in turn by the federal courts through the US Constitution's Article III establishment of our federal judiciary. With someone like Nathan, who some juror might take pity on because of his apparent Asperger's, or who might hate insurance companies, those unknown unknowns can more likely be eliminated with a federal judge making all the decisions. And personally, if the case involves technical maritime engineering or navigation issues, I'd rather try it before a smart judge than a "who knows what you might get" jury.

So there was a race to the courthouse component in our plan. We wanted to file the lawsuit first in federal court before Attorney Santos filed his threatened bad faith suit perhaps in state court in Rhode Island or Vermont, Nathan's apparent state of residence. In state court we would lose the advantages of playing in our own federal sandbox. And with this whole Nathan Carman thing in the news, our strategy of having the Insurer file suit first would be good optics.

When Liam and I had everything put together, I flew down to the big client meeting, where I had to address several questions from top management.

"Are you sure we will win?"

"Yes," I answered.

"Did this guy really kill both his mother and grandfather?"

"Sure looks like it, but we don't need to prove murder to win."

"What if this blows up—are we willing to stay the course?"

"Look," Vince jumped in, "we can't pay this guy and be seen as aiding and abetting his second murder. He'll take the eighty-five-thousand dollars and use it to pay legal fees to fight for his inheritance. We can't roll over on this."

We filed the lawsuit three days later, on January 27, 2017.

9

"LOWEST HANGING FRUIT"

Normally, in a newly filed federal civil lawsuit, things plod along slowly for several months with few developments. Not much happens besides administrative matters on the docket, which is the clerk's online file of the case, where the parties e-file their pleadings and the court posts its orders.

During this lull before the storm nothing regarding the new case goes on in the federal courtroom either. And even contact between the parties' attorneys is minimal, since "discovery" has not begun. That kicks off later, when the parties begin exchanging information about their witnesses, their documents, their claims, and have the opportunity to formally "discover" each other's evidence, typically by taking oral, sworn depositions of key witnesses. In essence, discovery is the means by which the opposing lawyers find out about the other side's case, both its strengths and weaknesses, and that generally starts around the time of the lawyers' first scheduling conference with the judge, some months after the lawsuit is filed.

We weren't anywhere near that information exchange. But we definitely had a leg up on our opposition by way of our pre-litigation testimony obtained from Nathan during his EUO.

Then, only one week after filing our lawsuit, we received a second evidentiary windfall, compliments of Nathan. Further documenting his weaknesses, ABC News aired an hour-long episode, "Lost at Sea," as part of its *20/20* series on February 3, 2017.[49]

None of us were aware that "Lost at Sea" was originally scheduled for broadcast the night we filed the lawsuit. It seems our lawsuit postponed the show a week because Anchors Elizabeth Vargas and David Muir started off with "breaking news" on this "story right out of the movies." In a "major new twist," an insurance company had just filed suit against Nathan Carman for intentionally causing the sinking. The first page of our Complaint for Declaratory Judgment was shown on-screen. Attorney Santos, for Nathan, and Attorney Small, for Nathan's aunts, provided commentary throughout.

Nathan sat for a couple of extensive interviews with Linzie Janis, who did an excellent job pressing Nathan to explain himself. Ms. Janis is a very attractive blonde woman, as is a distinctly different woman who would later surface in this case. Nathan was smitten with both. They made him weak in the knees. He puddled like a puppy around them. But he still had bite.

Nathan started his "Lost at Sea" interview with a prayer: "Lord… help me to accurately and effectively express what I've been through." To the fetching Ms. Janis he whimpered, "I loved my mother. Present tense, I *love* my mother." This was spellbinding reality TV.

For someone purporting to chronicle his saga with the Almighty's help, Nathan refused to answer Ms. Janis's questions more often than an "I can't comment on that" sheriff addressing the press at an active crime scene, which Nathan was.

Several times as Ms. Janis pressed him, Nathan would cut her off.

"I'm not going to go into that now."

"I'm not going to answer that."

"I'm not going to go there."

"I can't answer that question, and we're done with before I turned eighteen."

---

49 "Lost at Sea," n. 7.

Abruptly, "I'm stopping right there with that question."

Then, after Ms. Janis posed a question on our lawsuit's claim that "you sank the boat on purpose," Nathan shut the interview down with a hissy fit. "We're done for this evening, period...we're done here...we're done here," he stated, walking off the set, pointing his finger angrily, oddly shaking his head, waving the cameras away. Controlling his interview. And fate. Voluntarily telling his story but then clamming up when the going got tough.

Nathan came off as a disturbed young man, almost taking aim to shoot himself in the foot. He looked bad on national TV, and his "Lost at Sea" footage would look even worse when later used in court.

Yet he came back for more, willingly succumbing to Ms. Janis.

"Do you think the police have picked on you?" Ms. Janis pressed.

Nathan responded, colorfully for once, "I think that the police saw me as the lowest hanging fruit," in reference to his Asperger's diagnosis, which he admitted on-screen.

That was the single admissible reference to an Asperger's diagnosis that Liam and I were ever able to assemble. Our subsequent formal discovery requests for Nathan's medical records were rebuffed as "irrelevant." Frankly, that was just fine with us. It took any mental health issue Nathan might later claim out of our litigation and along with it any sort of incompetency defense. He took the same approach with Ms. Janis, not allowing her to get "into my personal health records which I'm not going to disclose." Nathan thereby also deflated Attorney Santos's "Lost at Sea" claim that Nathan had a "disability."

Nevertheless, Asperger's and autism were widely discussed in the media whenever Nathan came up. Ms. Janis narrated, "Asperger's syndrome" is "on the autism spectrum, associated with social awkwardness and flat, measured speech patterns." She noted "his mom, Linda, a nurse who worked with autism patients" loved fishing with Nathan, posting on Facebook, there was "No better way to connect" and bond with him.

Ms. Janis also interviewed a psychologist, Rebecca Sachs, PhD, who had never treated Nathan but contended that people with Asperger's "sort of give information in a linear fashion," confirming Liam's earlier prediction, while also claiming that their perceived "need to control things" is "just an impression that comes off." And as Nathan then said on TV, "I'm not someone who understands relationships or who's good about talking about emotions." In his case, was that due to autism or something more sinister? Could it be both? Dr. Sachs has not returned my several phone messages seeking her comment for this book.

Attorney Santos's and Attorney Small's appearances on *20/20* were not the kind of lawyering our firm had any experience with whatsoever. In fact, the extent of both attorneys' televised commentary was the polar opposite of the way we handle our cases. Our corporate shipowner and insurance clients have strict policies prohibiting press statements from their lawyers. Any public statements related to a maritime casualty come from expert public relations firms that the clients have on retainer. You won't hear from our friends representing the *Dali,* which allided with the Francis Scott Key Bridge in Baltimore. The orders from institutional clients are clear—lawyers should stick to lawyering in court proceedings and not try to otherwise shape public opinion.

Granted, neither Nathan nor his aunts were institutional clients. Clearly, though, Attorneys Santos's and Small's interviews were directed to the public and prosecutors, not the courts. But who was benefiting here, client or lawyer? Nathan himself was a loose cannon on "Lost at Sea," shooting off his mouth, then unilaterally calling for a ceasefire, fully sabotaging himself, voluntarily providing audiovisual evidence that could and probably would later be used to point out his inconsistencies and contradictions and to attack his overall credibility, or lack thereof. Attorney Santos, a kindly great-uncle though he appeared, made a huge mistake allowing Nathan to so nakedly expose himself on national TV. Although not yet charged by prosecutors, the Miranda warning that "anything you say can and will be used against you in a court of law" should have been heeded.

Instead, Nathan spoke into the camera, "I did not kill my grandfather. I did not cause my mother's death." Oh really, literally? What a fascinating juxtaposition of verbs. People don't kill grandfathers, guns do? Matricide, by sin of omission?

Little in the broadcast revealed anything new about Linda Carman's disappearance at sea that was not already on our radar screen and, for the most part, had already been extracted in far greater detail from Nathan during his EUO six weeks earlier. However, the "Lost at Sea" backstory on the John Chakalos murder provided us a bounty of information and a jump-start on figuring out how it best fit into our lawsuit.

Through the "Lost at Sea" reporting, additional media coverage, and things we learned on our own over the next year or so, a picture of the Chakalos family's three generations came into focus for Liam and me. Whether the stories reported were wholly accurate, and even if they were, whether they would be admissible at trial seemed questionable since many would be too long ago or too prejudicial to Nathan under the Federal Rules of Evidence, so we would have to pick and choose the items we wanted to pursue.

All the Chakalos family tales made our handling the boat case a lot more interesting, but primarily we had a maritime casualty and marine insurance legal issues that demanded our attention so we couldn't sink a lot of time into tangential human-interest stories. We'll leave that to others who spent more time researching dirty laundry. But here's a nutshell.

John Chakalos, the patriarch, whose parents emigrated from Greece, was a tough World War II machine-gunner in the Pacific and was reported to have a made a fortune in real estate. Perhaps, but he was primarily in the nursing home business. There are people who make big money from low-cost death mills, depleting elderly savings before government subsidies kick in. High demand with frequent patient turnover. In any event, with John's loving wife Rita, stories of his serial side action aside, he amassed at least $44 million which got corralled by the Chakalos Family Dynasty Trust, with each of his four daughters as beneficiaries. According to daughter Valerie's testimony in our case, the girls got along okay growing up, with normal hair-pulling fights and the like. Ouch.

The Chakalos home with John's office was in a modest neighborhood of Windsor, Connecticut. But less than one hundred miles north, on the other side of the Connecticut River, the family had an eighty-eight-acre hillside estate in West Chesterfield, New Hampshire. Here John claimed residence, so he could stop paying Connecticut state income tax since New Hampshire has none. At the top was a Georgian brick mansion, verging on a small castle. Below was a sweeping, bucolic meadow view to the south. At Christmastime the whole place was lit up like Santa's Village, a flatlander's show of opulence mesmerizing Little Helpers but sapping the local electrical supply.

John was a good and active citizen and a philanthropist, too, for causes close to his heart. He was a major donor to the Greek Orthodox Cathedral in Hartford. He donated a fire truck to the West Chesterfield Volunteer Fire Department in the name of his grandson Nathan, his first male descendant. John was also keenly interested in his children and grandchildren getting good educations and working hard. But, as can happen, some will come up short.

Linda may have been one of those. There was talk of her gambling away large sums of money and getting periodic infusions from John. He offered to buy a Dunkin' Donuts franchise for Linda and Clark to get them on a steady path, but that fell through, as did their marriage. With Clark off to Cali, Linda got Nathan, their only child, and a player to be named later. He called me after our trial to report he'd warned Linda that Nathan was going to kill her in her sleep.

By any measure, young Nathan was a troubled kid. Aunt Valerie testified by deposition in our case, when he was "say between 4th and 6th grade" he became "very agitated, angry, he had grabbed an umbrella to use as a weapon, and my parents were trying to go to him to comfort him to see what was wrong. I mean, he was out of control, flailing this umbrella around, not letting anybody near him, and screaming."

Around the same time, when Valerie was in the pool and seven months pregnant, Nathan tried to "dive bomb" her three times with running cannonballs into the deep end.

Valerie related that according to a neighbor's complaint, Nathan grabbed that family's golden retriever by the collar, "beating him with a stick and wouldn't let go." Another time he pulled out a "huge knife" and went after Valerie's well-behaved dog's throat. And he held a girl "down against her will in a play tent that was in the backyard." (Valerie did not mention a knife on that occasion, contrary to other reports.)

There were no "predictors as to what would or would not set him off." Valerie "absolutely" would not leave her kids alone in the same room with their older cousin. He never received any discipline, according to Valerie, who blamed his mostly absent father.

Nathan went off to the Greater Hartford Academy of Math and Science for a couple of years, where he probably studied sine waves, so undulating, so soothing, so formulaic, $y = A \sin(\omega t + \varphi)$. He experimented with things too. Halloween was a special time for Nathan. He gave out frozen fish guts in baggies for Trick or Treat.[50] As earlier noted, what goes around comes around.

When Nathan was attending Middletown High School, Valerie was called to the office to help work with Nathan. "[T]here was a time he was escorted out by ambulance," she testified in her deposition. His troubles in high school continued; outspoken in class and stubborn, it's no surprise he was bullied. But Nathan was no passive victim and understood legal principles. He had run-ins with the vice principal and school secretary, calling them Satan and an agent of the Devil, respectively.[51]

At the end of 2010, Nathan suffered a psychological crisis, apparently stemming from the death of his horse Cruise, which John Chakalos had purchased and boarded for Nathan at Fox Ledge Farm in East Haddam, Connecticut. Nathan was reportedly admitted to Mount Sinai Rehabilitation Hospital in Hartford for a week in April 2011, where a fight broke out between Linda and her father over Nathan's care,[52] and Linda was charged with assault and battery on an elderly person. Charges were eventually dropped at her father's request.

After Nathan got out in August 2011, when he was seventeen years old, he first hit TV news, with broadcast alerts that he had run away and a surveillance photo of the early Desperado at the New Haven bus terminal. He surfaced in Virginia with over $4,000 in cash and a newly

---

[50] James D. Walsh, "Dead Wake," *New York Magazine*, January 22, 2018. https://nymag.com/intelligencer/2018/01/nathan-carman-linda-carman-death-at-sea.html.

[51] Walsh, "Dead Wake."

[52] Shelley Murphy and Evan Allen, "The Lonely Boy She Feared For," *Boston Globe,* October 9, 2016.

purchased moped with 2.5 times the horsepower of Cruise, so Nathan could go further, and faster.[53]

Nathan spoke so eloquently about his love of Cruise on "Lost at Sea," just as he had about his mother, just as he had about his grandfather. After each of those deaths Nathan went missing with more cash available than most adults carry. Cruise apparently suffered from colic, but his precise cause of death has not been uncovered. In retrospect, equinocide needs inquiry. Animal cruelty is not limited to canines.

It has been reported that after Nathan's return from Virginia, his parents sent him out West to a wilderness boot camp.[54] As Nathan had testified in his EUO, he did get his high school diploma, but we learned he was disallowed the formative experience of his senior year, which he spent at home.

Things there weren't rosy either. With idle hands the Devil's workshop, Nathan reportedly stopped taking his medications. Linda was concerned about his "paranoid delusions" and "religious idiocy."[55] Frequently quarrelling, Nathan moved out and went so far as to live in an RV in the driveway. Mother and son called truces to get together for occasional fishing trips, during which a wonderful time no doubt was had by all.

While it was Linda who touted Nathan's alleged 140 genius IQ, he took it to heart. And so did I, because it matched so poetically with his 140-fathom sinking spot. He thought he was smarter than everyone and that his navigation was beyond question. Wrong x 2.

Upon receipt of his high school diploma, Nathan fancied himself as having all the credentials needed to serve as his grandfather's "interlocutor," shadowing him at work, as Nathan testified, but he was really just a chauffeur and hearing aid. He saw himself with a bright future for "personal and professional growth" in the business world as successor to John, so why would he have any motivation to kill the golden goose?

---

53 *See* Walsh, "Dead Wake," n. 50.

54 Walsh, "Dead Wake."

55 Walsh, "Dead Wake."

But with that explanation Nathan ignored that his grandfather so highly valued him that he received no salary.

Yet there were tangible benefits—his own apartment where he could be free of his mother, a credit card, and a Nissan pickup (although Nathan had a tantrum and swore at the old man when he "broke his promise" to give him a nice $50,000 Ford F-150 pickup). Everything for the first male descendent was funded by the spoiling patriarch.[56]

***

On December 14, 2012 something else happened in Connecticut that is unthinkable yet significant for this story. Adam Lanza, another head case, shot his mother and unloaded an assault rifle on twenty mostly first graders and six teachers at Sandy Hook Elementary School in Newtown. Also pertinent here, in response, the state of Connecticut enacted a strict assault rifle ban on April 4, 2013.

A few months later, John Chakalos paid the tuition for Nathan's all-important higher education, with Nathan enrolled for the fall 2013 semester at Northwest Connecticut Community College, taking classes in accounting, management, macroeconomics, and composition,[57] tools that would supplement his innate business skills.

We would learn a lot more about Nathan's 2013 and 2016 murder years through discovery in our lawsuit, but the cherry on top of the "Lost at Sea" sundae was a photo of Nathan getting thrown out of a 2016 Trump rally due to his "odd demeanor." One can reasonably posit that Nathan supported unbridled gun rights, even for the mentally deranged, as a Second Amendment freedom necessary to a well-armed militia.

---

56 Electronic Case File No. 139 at 33; US District Court of Rhode Island Civil Action No. 17-38-JJM-PAS (hereafter docket entries in this case are referred to by ECF number).

57 ECF No. 139 at 33.

10

"DID YOU LEAVE IT AT THE DUNKIN' DONUTS?"

The "Lost at Sea" sweet spot for us was the unsigned arrest warrant for Nathan's murder of John Chakalos, and a related search warrant affidavit,[58] a copy of which we obtained soon after the TV show from Dan Small. It contained a lot of information which Liam and I studied as the most reliable summary of that murder investigation.

And like all of Nathan's stories, it had some gaping holes.

The affidavit detailed how Nathan, age nineteen, "was the last person known to see John Chakalos alive" around 8:30 p.m. on December 19, 2013, after they had dinner together. According to Linda, she was scheduled to meet Nathan at the peculiar hour of 3:00 a.m. the next morning to drive to Rhode Island. It didn't say why. But Nathan was over an hour late, unaccounted for during that time, and did not answer her cell phone calls because he had turned his off. Also, he "discarded both the hard drive of his computer" and his truck's "GPS unit," which were "both integral pieces of evidentiary value."

---

[58] ECF No. 47–4.

Wow.

Another of Nathan's aunts, Elaine Chakalos, found her father shot to death in his bed later that morning, December 20, 2013.

"[I]nvestigators learned from various sources that Nathan Carman was capable of violence when his coping mechanisms were challenged." Citing the school episodes, the affidavit also quoted neighbors who called him a "time bomb waiting to go off" and "Murder boy." Nathan's "family members expressed enough fear that they hired armed private security to protect them in their homes." The police found detailed handwritten notes by Nathan for "making self-propelled Improvised Explosive Devices [IEDs]" and sniper rifles deployed by drone with facial recognition capability.

Our concern about Nathan's brief case that cold day in hell six weeks before was validated.

A forensic psychologist was quoted in the affidavit regarding Nathan's alleged Asperger's syndrome, noting it is consistent for such people to "perseverate on topics and activities that they are involved in. They tend to research topics exhaustively and to minute detail. Because of their difficulty with social reciprocity and ability to identify social cues, they tend to spend an unusual amount of time alone and on their computers."

We took that with a ton of salt. While it seemed on point for Nathan, it also describes plenty of lawyers.

It was the firearms information in the affidavit that was most intriguing. Nathan's seized firearm paraphernalia included:

> Remington 870 Tactical Shotgun
>
> Gamo Whisper Pellet Rifle, Velocity 1200 F.P.S.
>
> (71) 12 Gauge Shotgun Rounds, various types, (1) spent
>
> (50) Remington 12 Gauge Plastic Shotshells
>
> (10) Federal 12 Gauge Buck Shot

> Gamo Rifle Scope
>
> State of CT Ammunition Certificate, 03/20/14–03/20/19

Another gaping hole was that law enforcement did not have custody of a .308 caliber firearm to match with "308 caliber class" bullet fragments that killed John Chakalos. Furthermore, the police found "no bullet shell casings [expended cartridges] at the scene," noting that "cleaning up the crime scene is consistent with the...effort to elude identification and subsequent arrest and prosecution for committing a crime."

The search warrant affidavit discounted World War II "vintage rifles of a 308/762 caliber" in the Chakalos attic since they had not been recently fired. But it was this note in the search warrant that Liam and I laser focused on:

> On 7/17/14 Windsor Sergeant William Freeman learned that Nathan Carman purchased a Sig Sauer 716 Patrol .308 caliber rifle from a gun store in New Hampshire. This is consistent with the same caliber weapon used in the homicide of John Chakalos. Nathan thus far has concealed this info from investigators and failed to disclose this weapon during any interviews with Windsor Police.

The seven-month criminal investigation involved the Windsor Police Department, Connecticut State Police, and FBI. The warrant affidavit summed things up as of July 2014: "Carman has since refused to grant police investigators any further interviews nor submit to a polygraph test."

To our knowledge nothing else had happened. A big billboard with John's face and a reward posted by the Chakalos family yielded no leads.

But the missing Sig Sauer was huge. As Dan Small rhetorically asked of Nathan during an interview,[59] "How do you lose it? Did you leave it at the Dunkin' Donuts?" Since Nathan wasn't going to be able to refuse

[59] Walsh, "Dead Wake," n. 50.

giving me a second interrogation in the context of a formal deposition in our lawsuit if he wanted to continue pressing his insurance claim, I wondered if we might help. Specifically, on googling the model, Liam and I determined it sure would be nice to find out what Nathan did with his "Sig Sauer 716 Patrol .308 caliber rifle."

But I wasn't about to just ask Nathan point-blank. "These things must be done delicately," as Boston-educated Margaret Hamilton schemed back in 1939 in her quest for killer footwear.[60]

[60] "Famous Movie Quotes," Movie-Sounds.org. https://movie-sounds.org/famous-movie-samples/quotes-with-sound-clips-from-the-wizard-of-oz-1939/these-things-must-be-done-delicately-or-you-hurt-the-spell#google_vignette.

11

WATER ALWAYS SEEKS ITS OWN LEVEL

As mentioned above, as of the "Lost at Sea" television broadcast, we hadn't kicked off discovery in our insurance lawsuit yet. Attorney Santos had not even taken the first step of answering our complaint.

Yet in that void of nondevelopment, the tenor of the nascent litigation took a downhill turn on February 16, 2017 when Liam got an email from Attorney David F. Anderson, a Boston maritime personal injury lawyer, advising he was going to be representing Nathan.

My first thought was expletive deleted. My second was that Dave Anderson and Nathan Carman sure are two peas in a pod. I'll make full effort here to neutrally describe my interactions with Attorney Anderson. From prior experience I knew he was a very smart and crafty adversary. I also knew it would be as professionally ugly as it gets.

Predictably, Attorney Anderson's e-filed answer to our complaint included a six-count counterclaim against the Insurer alleging all sorts of contractual breaches and horrendous bad faith malfeasance. In other words, the response to our lawsuit was in essence a Nathan Carman lawsuit against the Insurer. Taken to its logical conclusion, Defendant's argument was that since Nathan's hull insurance was an "All Risk" policy, that meant it covered all and every conceivable property loss including sinking—by whatever means. Any policy clauses purporting to exclude coverage, so the argument went, were unenforceable as contrary to the word "All." That the Insurer was trying to enforce policy language exclusions was nothing but pulling the wool over innocent Nathan's eyes, violating all manner of commercial decency, and requiring the Insurer to pay not only Nathan's $85,000 claim but also his attorneys' fees and punitive damages to discourage such heinous foul play in the future.

However, there was a flaw in Defendant's ginning all that up. Filed as an attachment to Nathan's counterclaim, and thereby adopted by him as authentic and true, there was a document the Insurer sent to Nathan when the insurance policy went into effect. It clearly stated, "This insurance is subject to the terms, conditions, limitations and exclusions of the policy."[61] Specifically, that included no coverage for a boat that sank due to the insured's criminal activity or inadequate repairs. Similar warning language was all over the Insurer's website, which Nathan had seen before, thus sapping Defendant's counterclaims that exclusions in an All Risk policy are nothing but bait and switch.

Like annoying greenheads, Defendant kept buzzing bad faith right through trial, continually coming up with some nuanced iteration of the same grievance. This consumed hundreds of litigation hours, in the hopes the Insurer would just give up and pay the $85,000 sinking claim.

Attempting to wear down the opposition and string out a lawsuit is not uncommon in litigation against cost-conscious insurance companies. After all, Nathan had gotten $33,489.33 from the Insurer for his engine overheat, without any questions, so why not again?

That wasn't going to happen this time. Martha, Vince, Liam, and I just kept swatting each incoming attack, and Judge McConnell squished them once and for all at trial. I'll spare the patient reader most of the boring details.

You will also be spared the bulk of the endless discovery battles that engaged opposing counsel. It's no exaggeration to say that virtually

---

[61] Tr. Ex. D-3.

every important written discovery question, every important request for documents by the Insurer, every important question Liam and I posed in depositions, were opposed by Attorney Anderson with some long-winded objection or at least a time-consuming soliloquy if he couldn't come up with a real objection. That too is not a litigation trait unique to him.

But without doubt, getting substantive responses out of Nathan required filing expensive motions with the court when most opposing maritime counsel typically work things out between themselves—Attorney Anderson and a few others excepted. And in this case, there was way more than $85,000 in insurance proceeds at stake—Attorney Anderson and I both knew it in our bones. If Nathan won, there would be no criminal prosecution and vice versa, if the Insurer won, Nathan would be charged criminally. I also knew that on behalf of the Insurer we needed to stay above the fray, keep our eyes on the ball, and fight clean.

Vince and I had also been through enough death cases before to know that law enforcement usually takes over early on and criminal charges are typically filed in due course. Then witnesses shut up on the instruction of counsel, with the insurer often taking a back seat as the facts slowly unfold. But it didn't appear that criminal charges against Nathan were coming anytime soon. Although we were aware that Brian Woods and marine surveyors Dexter Holaday and Bernie Feeney had been interviewed by the FBI, we were unaware of any serious progress with a federal grand jury that had been convened in Connecticut. While we were occasionally contacted by CGIS (Coast Guard Investigative Services—think NCIS), it always seemed they were looking for leads on things we had already developed, like their request for a copy of the transcript of Nathan's EUO and its charts and other exhibits, which I provided to Eric Gempp of CGIS who drove to Chatham, but for which we got nothing in return.

Liam, who had been a Coastie before law school, knows how the Coast Guard thinks and works and tried to find out how much information they had collected from Nathan during their in-person post-*Orient Lucky* debriefing in Boston, but CGIS would not let on. Neither would the South Kingstown police, who would not even return our calls requesting a chance to inspect the boat parts from Nathan's pickup truck which they had in custody. Cops, ugh. And I recognize the feeling is mutual.

This all had Vince getting perturbed that we were doing the investigative work of the authorities, but there wasn't anything much we could do now to push them into filing criminal charges. So we were relieved that a second front opened up against Nathan with his aunts, Linda's sisters, filing suit against him in July 2017 in New Hampshire.

12

THE SISTERS' SLAYER SUIT

The sisters' New Hampshire probate court suit was premised on two points. First, that John Chakalos was a legal resident of New Hampshire, living at his West Chesterfield estate. Second, on unusual New Hampshire common law equitable principles (judicial decisions, as distinct from statutes passed by the legislature and signed into law by the governor) which would prohibit his slayer from benefitting from the estate.

Simply stated, the sisters in *Valerie C. Santilli et al v. Nathan Carman* sought a New Hampshire probate court decree that, since he killed his grandfather, Nathan was ineligible to receive any inheritance from him. That would be the same result in any other state. Connecticut would be pertinent if Windsor was indeed John's legal residence, but there it would require a full-blown criminal conviction of Nathan first. But the sisters did not want to give Nathan a head start to take the money and run before conviction. So, due to the oddity of New Hampshire common law, the steeper burden of a criminal conviction "beyond a reasonable doubt" was unnecessary there, with the lesser "more likely than not" burden of proof in a civil case applicable for the sisters to try stopping Nathan in his tracks.

Thus the New Hampshire probate proceeding alliteratively became the Sisters' Slayer Suit. It produced good courtroom drama, revealed the Chakalos Family Dynasty Trust as Nathan's major financial motive, and added factual tidbits we were happy to weave into our insurance suit.

The New Hampshire state case also deflected media attention from our Rhode Island federal case, and I was just fine with that, so we could continue to scurry around behind the scenes.

Unlike federal court, New Hampshire probate court allows cameras in the courtroom so the Sisters' Slayer Suit proceedings were streamed live and covered by TV news. After each hearing, the media would descend on the players, with Sisters' Attorney Small lining up behind a microphone array to amplify what had just gone on inside—contrasted with Nathan normally slithering away to the parking lot and driving off without comment. But not always. Liam attended most of the proceedings in person, as an observer. He had some worries about its success on the merits from the start.

Rarely desirable from an opposing counsel's perspective, Nathan decided to represent himself *pro se*—without a lawyer—in the New Hampshire case. He issued a press release[62] firing Attorney Santos, due to growing concerns about his "basic competence."

> This decision does not affect the matter currently pending in Rhode Island Federal District Court where I am being represented by different counsel, and I have no plans to change attorneys in that matter.
>
> Henceforth, I plan to take a responsible but more open approach to managing public relations than my attorneys have permitted me to take to date, and I plan to aggressively pursue all legal avenues available to me for rectifying the injustices which have already been

[62] Bob McGovern, "Nathan Carman fires two lawyers," *Boston Herald*, February 8, 2018. https://www.bostonherald.com/2018/02/08/nathan-carman-fires-two-lawyers/.

> perpetrated and obtaining a just outcome in the matters that are ongoing.
>
> Further questions or requests for comment from media organizations should be forwarded to me directly at the e-mail address, NathanCarman.MediaRelations@Outlook.com....
>
> I did not kill my grandfather or my mother, nor did I engage in the violent behavior in my childhood that has been reported.... It is my aunts who are being driven by malice and greed to make the vexatious, false, and insupportable allegations which form the basis of their probate lawsuit in New Hampshire.... I will be vindicated, and perhaps my grandfather's true murderer will be uncovered.

These are the words of a twenty-four-year-old, who cut just the pitiful figure we had been concerned about when I took his EUO, and now found himself without a lawyer in a probate courtroom that deals daily with sad family episodes of real people torn apart by domestic strife and tragedy, not just who gets how much when someone dies.

Judges always bend over backwards to protect the pro se litigant from opposing attorneys. And opposing poor Nathan was a big law firm, in a *Goliath v. Nathan* battle, and an out-of-state Goliath at that. This predisposed presiding Judge David D. King to some skepticism, as when Dan Small argued that all the media attention demanded judicial intervention, with the judge responding that much of the media attention had been spurred by Small's post-hearing press conferences.

Despite their struggles, we were mostly pleased to cooperate with the Sisters' attorneys at Holland & Knight. We knew we had a strong ally in Dan Small. He announced the Sisters weren't interested in Nathan's "blood money" inheritance for themselves and would give it to charity if they prevailed in keeping him from getting any. And we were very happy to work with his law partner, highly respected Chet Hooper, dean of the maritime defense bar.

Chet told me he was working on the "wet" murder of Nathan's mother, as opposed to the "dry" murder of Nathan's grandfather—a maritime lawyer's inside joke on how London admiralty law firms differentiate casualty from transactional work. Hilarious, right? Chet would know, having been president of The Maritime Law Association of the United States in the 1990s. I trusted him completely and disclose that not long before, he had nominated me for that same esteemed position.

So Chet and I were able to work well together, except for one snag. Someone had convinced the Sisters not to waive any claim they might have against Nathan for the wrongful death of Linda. If he were to actually inherit his millions, the Sisters wanted to be able to go after him in retribution, even though their demonstrable dollar damages in a Death on the High Seas Act suit against Nathan would have been minimal since none of her Sisters was financially dependent on Linda. If we were to lose our case invalidating Nathan's insurance policy, their wrongful death claim would invoke third-party liability coverage, as Vince feared, with the Insurer then exposed up to $300,000 for Linda's death, plus the duty of paying for Nathan's defense of that insurance claim. Vince naturally wanted nothing of it and insisted on the Sisters giving the Insurer a signed waiver in return for our full cooperation. The Sisters refused. So the exchange of information between the lawyers handling the two lawsuits with fundamentally similar goals was much more guarded than it needed to be.

We nonetheless obtained some information through industry contacts that the Sisters had unsuccessfully sunk something like $800,000 in sonar efforts to find Nathan's wreck in the area where *Orient Lucky* picked him up, but it was almost a mile and a half deep there.

We also reviewed a preliminary drift analysis the Sisters commissioned by a private outfit to see if Nathan's life raft could have drifted from Block Canyon to the *Orient Lucky.* But the parameters and data input were imprecise and I did not find the results very compelling. So Liam and I, with Vince and Martha's support, continued to press on mostly by ourselves using our own resources and our own expert witnesses.

13

ADDING THE DRY MURDER TO OUR WET MURDER

Back in our Rhode Island federal court case, the battle lines were clearly drawn on one major issue early on: Was the Insurer's desire to conduct formal discovery into the 2013 murder of the grandfather relevant to the insurance case involving the 2016 sinking of Nathan's boat on which his mother died? This all came to a head at opposing counsels' first court appearance before Magistrate Judge Patricia A. Sullivan at an August 7, 2017 scheduling conference.

We had argued in our pleadings that since the Insurer broadly alleged Nathan breached his policy by engaging in "criminal wrongdoing" that "his actions/inactions regarding his mother's death are within the scope of discovery as 'relevant' to the sinking and 'proportional to the needs of the case,' as is his grandfather's unsolved homicide, potentially similarly motivated by Nathan Carman's possible $11 million inheritance."[63] I admitted we were not ready to make specific accusations of murder

[63] ECF No. 16.

for either death against our client's customer, but we should be able to explore it in discovery and amend our pleadings if appropriate.

Attorney Anderson argued in opposition that if we weren't specifically accusing Nathan of murdering his grandfather, then trying to conduct discovery on that was not relevant to our current claims.

It was a close question. Judge Sullivan generally seemed to agree with us, cautioning quite rightly though, that just because something is discoverable does not make it admissible at trial. So we knew we had our work cut out for us on the dry murder, particularly since Nathan had never been criminally charged for it. We couldn't go off and play private attorney general.

But we as civil lawyers had one thing going for us that the criminal prosecutors did not. We were going to be able to ask Nathan pointed questions about the shooting in writing and during his oral deposition, while under oath, and thereby take the grandfather's murder investigation to a new level.

The prosecutors were never going to be able to do that—Nathan would never agree to talk with them again, and even if he were to be criminally charged, he would not likely take the stand at trial. Nobody was likely to get Nathan to ever talk about his grandfather's murder again after his "Lost at Sea" debacle—except us and maybe Dan Small in the New Hampshire case.

So Liam and I focused on what we could do most cost-effectively on the John Chakalos murder without reinventing the wheel law enforcement started rolling before it all went flat with the unsigned arrest warrant and turned into a cold case. We picked our battle on the big hole—the very missing Sig Sauer the search warrant affidavit alleged Nathan had purchased in New Hampshire.

As the affidavit stated, the Sig Sauer was essential evidence, so forensic ballistic testing could be performed on the bullet fragments that killed Chakalos to see if those bullets were fired by that very Sig Sauer—its whereabouts a known unknown.

That's what we decided to dig into for our efforts to neatly tie together his grandfather's shooting and his mother's death at sea three years later as integral to Nathan's criminal scheme of not only obtaining his $85,000 in hull insurance proceeds but also his multimillion-dollar share of the Chakalos Family Dynasty Trust. Despite Nathan's profession of love for both his grandfather and mother, from Nathan's bottom-line perspective, with his two geese out of the way, his premature golden egg had been doubly laid and was now harvestable.

Our first effort was a written interrogatory to Nathan, with his answer to be signed by him under oath.

> INTERROGATORY NO. 12: Regarding firearms, please identify (a) all federal and state firearm identification cards, permits, or licenses issued to you, the dates issued, and the dates revoked (if any); and (b) all firearms you currently own or possess, formerly owned or possessed, and subsequently own or possess until the termination of this litigation, stating the dates of your ownership or possession, the name and address of the person or entity from whom you obtained the firearm, and what happened to any firearm you no longer own or possess.

Combined with that was a request for documents.

> REQUEST FOR PRODUCTION NO. 5: Please produce copies of all federal and state firearm identification cards, permits, or licenses issued to you or subsequently revoked.

Nathan and Anderson ignored them. We had to go back to court during the fall of 2017 for hearings with Judge Sullivan, who ruled with this limitation: "Defendant must respond to both requests by supplying information about the specific firearm that has been associated with the death of his grandfather."[64]

But soon after that court order Attorney Anderson took the position that there never was a "specific firearm that has been associated with the death of his grandfather," so the mere reference in a search warrant to an

[64] ECF No. 31 at 4.

unknown Sig Sauer was not good enough. And again they ignored our discovery requests.

Rather than push more motion papers without fruit, Vince, Martha, Liam, and I figured it was time to stop the back-and-forth and just interrogate Nathan in person on the Sig Sauer during his upcoming January 2018 deposition. Anderson wasn't going to be able to put us off forever.

14
CHUM

As inviting as the Sig Sauer was, our firm spent far more time during the fall of 2017 doing grunt work to get ready for Nathan's deposition on the wet murder. This included tracking down witnesses and increasing our knowledge base in order to chum Nathan in closer to his demise.

First, we established a good connection with Brian Woods, who provided all sorts of information on his extensive structural work on the JC 31 he sold to Nathan. Second, Liam worked hard on getting testimony from a reluctant Mike Iozzi, the key eyewitness to Nathan's trim tabs removal. And third, we struck life raft pay dirt.

JC 31 Refurbisher Brian Woods

Brian Woods was as adamant that the boat was solidly seaworthy as he was pissed at Nathan for stiffing him on the full purchase price. When Nathan showed up to take delivery of the boat, he was short $600, so Woods let him take it but held onto the title, and they agreed to meet later to finish the deal.

Nathan was so odd, compounded by his insistence to go through the Cape Cod Canal to Rhode Island in December, that Woods drove to the Canal and videoed the transit,[65] because he was just plain suspicious of Nathan's intentions. What a nice-looking boat underway! With a 380-gallon diesel fuel capacity, and an efficient fuel consumption of five gallons per hour at cruising speed, Woods gave it a range of nine hundred miles.

Over the next couple of weeks Nathan went silent and Woods decided to go find the boat in Rhode Island and take back his dock lines and his Massachusetts registration plates. In response, Nathan squawked to the police, who telephoned Woods, and quickly decided they had better things to do.

I asked my son Dave, who was working with us at the time, to see what he could dig up, and he nicely got to the bottom of it. He obtained a publicly available copy of Nathan's Rhode Island boat registration and learned he had previously registered the boat in New Hampshire, using his grandfather's West Chesterfield address. New Hampshire will register boats for a fee even without the registrant proving ownership with a title. Proud of its "Live Free or Die" philosophy but in need of making up for its lack of a state income tax, the Granite State has to grab revenues otherwise, so it runs a monopoly of state-owned liquor stores, and apparently looks the other way when thieves or welchers like Nathan register their boats there without proof of ownership. Nathan then transferred the laundered New Hampshire registration to Rhode

---

65 Tr. Ex. 32.26. https://www.youtube.com/watch?v=fwaAwa8_2GI.

Island, which assumed good title without any inquiry of its own, with Nathan thereby accomplishing an end around to not pay Woods the $600 balance. I reported all this to Woods and, as expected, it was good for our case. Nathan had picked the wrong guy to cheat.

Fully cooperative, and motivated to prove his sound workmanship, Woods met me at a coffee shop in Plymouth and detailed how meticulously he'd restored the 1973 plug turned lobster boat over eight or nine years during slow winter months. In the coming weeks Woods provided dozens of photographs and video, giving us a full picture of the boat's components for the first time. He had photos showing, for example, the careful steps he took to install forward bulkheads at the fish box.[66]

Woods was incredulous that Nathan had deigned to remove those bulkheads, thereby weakening the boat's internal structure at the bow. Woods was also completely dismissive of Nathan's reasoning. Storing fishing rods below would require awkwardly contorting both Nathan

[66] Tr. Ex 12.19.

and the rods down the two-by-three-foot forward hatch framed by the aluminum rectangle in the foreground above, and then bending and banging them around and forward into what were designed as potential insulated storage spaces, which could be made accessible with optional deck hatches, and which doubled as floatation voids.

Instead, Nathan could easily have kept his fishing rods secured under lock and key, easily accessible from the main deck in aluminum storage spaces Woods offered to Nathan as an option adjacent to the wheelhouse, below the port and starboard gunwales.

Woods also walked me through his installation of the trim tabs, which followed the printed Bennett directions, complete with templates for drilling thru-hull holes in the transom for the hydraulic lines to connect to the actuators.[67] He drilled ½ inch diameter holes through the transom and was 100 percent certain that is just what he drilled—four of them, one for each of the four ⅜ inch bronze tubes which screwed into the actuators. And just as absolutely certain, Woods did not and would have had no reason to drill anything bigger and less safe—like half-dollar-sized holes—instead.

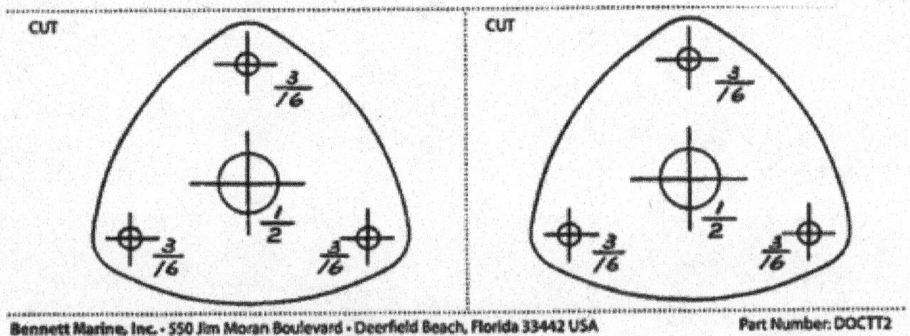

[67] Tr. Ex. 12.39.

Woods was a great help and would continue to be throughout our trial. He was understandably proud of his refurbishment and convinced that Nathan sank the boat on purpose, positive it was no accident. Attorney Anderson took Woods's deposition in December 2017 and received testimony in accordance with what I just described.

Hole Saw Mike Iozzi

Mike Iozzi was helpful too, but Liam had a much harder time massaging a reluctant, elderly witness into testifying about what he observed the afternoon before the fateful voyage as Nathan frenetically worked on his boat. Not that Iozzi was a shrinking violet when he gave early media interviews while Nathan was still missing at sea. But once Nathan was found alive, Iozzi clammed up, fearful for his and his wife's safety.

Liam wooed him hard, with multiple phone calls, two interviews at Dunkin' Donuts, and a visit to Iozzi's home workshop. It took weeks. Liam confirmed that Iozzi was a knowledgeable boat owner and that the afternoon before Nathan went missing, Iozzi had been visiting his friends, the Ferreiras.

Iozzi was sitting in a low-slung beach chair on the dock watching Nathan comically fiddle around onboard, bent and contorted over the transom, struggling with the trim tabs removal, making a sticky mess of himself with the 5200 sealant. But Iozzi became alarmed that Nathan was going to electrocute himself when he pulled out a hole saw driven by an electric drill connected to shore power and ran it at the waterline while dangling over the transom. Iozzi warned Nathan to be careful, but Nathan shrugged it off.

From the vantage point of Iozzi's beach chair, the edge of the dock blocking his view of the waterline on the boat, Iozzi would not now say he saw any holes Nathan drilled into the transom but he told Liam that Nathan "wasn't just polishing around the waterline with a hole saw."

And what was the size of the hole saw Nathan was using? Iozzi was certain it was one and one-half to two inches in diameter. We could not have dreamed up anyone more familiar with hole saws. Iozzi had massive hands and bananas for fingers after decades of manual labor. He ran a steel fence installation business, often working in concrete parking lots, frequently using hole saws on his jobs. His home workshop featured dozens of hole saws of various dimensions. Nathan had picked another bad eyewitness.

Liam and I kicked around how best to get testimony from the reluctant Iozzi and decided, since he was so critical, that Liam should get a written statement from him, just in case he refused to cooperate with us later. But as he was about to notarize Iozzi's signature, it dawned on Liam that his Massachusetts notary stamp wouldn't work in Rhode Island, so he persuaded Iozzi to drive with him a couple of hundred yards over the line back into Massachusetts. Liam got the signature and, knowing Anderson, took some selfies, for good measure, of their location.

Liam then took it a further step and set about taking a video deposition of Iozzi which could be admitted at trial were he unavailable for some reason, including death. Liam coordinated with our local counsel Sean O'Leary, who had helped us get admitted to the District of Rhode Island for this case. Sean was always available to help throughout, and we used his office in Warwick for Iozzi's deposition. He testified about his observations in accordance with what he had earlier told Liam.

These were terrific facts we had collected going into Nathan's deposition. Woods had drilled four ½ inch diameter holes in the transom for the trim tabs; Iozzi had seen Nathan using a larger hole saw on the transom waterline; and on Nathan's own admission, the four holes he exposed were the size of half-dollars.

If we go back to Nathan's Mathematics and Science school days, and get precise, using 3.14 for π (pronounced pi) and r for radius (half the diameter), since the area of a circle = πr^2, the four ½ inch diameter holes Woods originally drilled and would have been exposed immediately on Nathan's removal of the actuators add up to under 0.8 square inches—less than a square inch. However, based on Nathan's admission, with a JFK half-dollar instead, which has a diameter of 1 3⁄16 inches, four holes of that size add up to 4.4 square inches. So, Woods's original transom holes must have been enlarged, and Iozzi saw Nathan using a hole saw to accomplish that. While no one except Nathan knows how many or how big any holes Nathan actually drilled were, just holding him to his four half-dollars admission, he made Woods's original holes more than five times bigger.

"As the transom holes have gotten bigger, Carman's problems in this case have also grown," we wrote in a brief,[68] widely quoted in the news media, including a December 8, 2017 *Boston Globe* article by Travis Andersen with the headline, "Nathan Carman 'enlarged' holes in boat's

[68] ECF No. 30 at 2.

hull, court filing says."[69] Thirty-seven online reader comments followed, pretty much summed up by the first: "creepy." And as the *Boston Herald* announced[70]

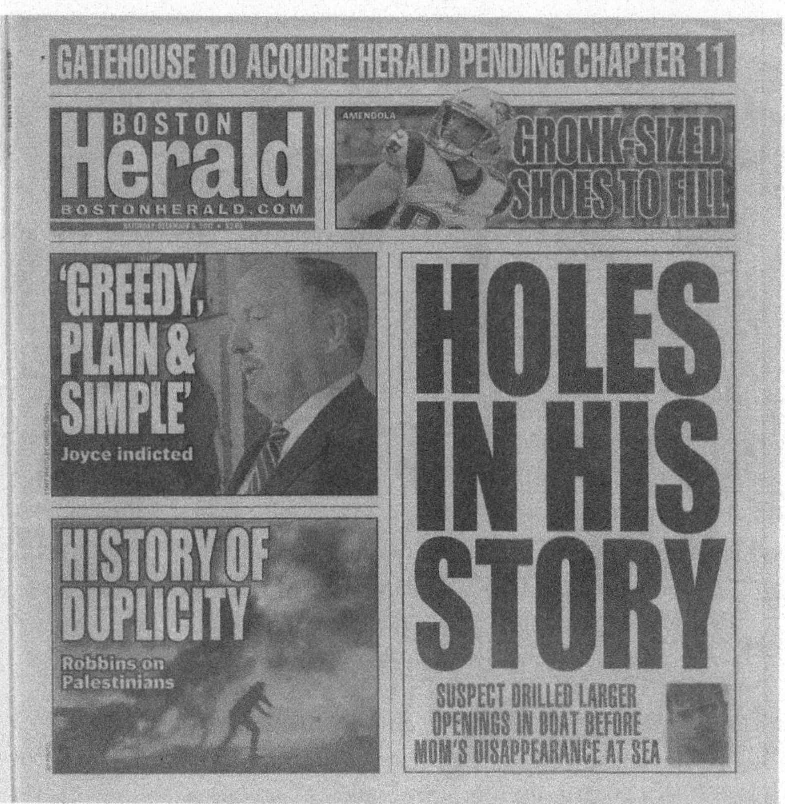

GATEHOUSE TO ACQUIRE HERALD PENDING CHAPTER 11

BOSTON Herald
BOSTONHERALD.COM

AMENDOLA
GRONK-SIZED SHOES TO FILL

'GREEDY, PLAIN & SIMPLE'
Joyce indicted

HOLES IN HIS STORY
SUSPECT DRILLED LARGER OPENINGS IN BOAT BEFORE MOM'S DISAPPEARANCE AT SEA

HISTORY OF DUPLICITY
Robbins on Palestinians

Woods Hole Oceanographer Richard Limeburner

We also blew a hole in Nathan's life raft story but kept it secret for now.

---

[69] Travis Andersen, "Nathan Carman 'enlarged' holes in boat's hull, court filing says," *Boston Globe*, December 8, 2017. https://www.bostonglobe.com/metro/2017/12/08/nathan-carman-enlarged-holes-hull-boat-that-sank-with-mother-board-court-filing-says/rON9pu3xf6dCUmCcApQLqJ/story.html.

[70] Bob McGovern, "Boat Was Full of Holes," *Boston Herald*, December 9, 2017.

Wallowing next to the woodstove after a Sunday Cape Cod Athletic Club road race, I hunted around the internet for some sort of ocean drift scientist. It didn't take long to determine that our expert was right here on Cape Cod, at the world-renowned Woods Hole Oceanographic Institution (WHOI), and I decided to email him right away. I didn't want Dave Anderson retaining him first.

> From: Dave Farrell
> Sent: Sunday, December 17, 2017 2:07 PM
> To: Richard Limeburner
> Subject: Reverse drift analysis
>
> Dear Mr. Limeburner:
>
> I am a maritime lawyer in Chatham. My office is working on a federal court case involving a recreational boat sinking and death off southern New England.
>
> We're interested in obtaining weather and current data during September 2016 and a reverse drift analysis from a known point, back seven days, along the lines of your work on Air France, I would imagine.
>
> I will try to telephone you on Monday.
>
> Kind regards,
> David J. Farrell, Jr.

> From: Richard Limeburner
> Sent: Sunday, December 17, 2017 5:04 PM
> To: Dave Farrell
> Subject: Re: Reverse drift analysis
>
> David,
>
> I will be available Monday to talk about the recreational boat sinking and death off the coast of southern

> New England. I assume this is in reference to the F/V *Chicken Pox*.
>
> From my satellite-tracked drifting buoy research at Woods Hole Oceanographic Institution (WHOI) I know a lot about historical and real-time surface currents on the New England shelf south of Martha's Vineyard and Rhode Island. I see you also have experience with ~30' vessels on the shelf out to 100 nm.
>
> Factual information giving times and positions would be most helpful in estimating the drift of the life raft, especially the USCG accident report.
>
> Cheers,
> Richard

Score! We spoke and emailed over the next week. I sent Limeburner excerpts from the Coast Guard SAR report we had recently obtained, particularly the latitude/longitude of the *Orient Lucky* rescue position. By email dated December 29, 2017, Limeburner advised:

> David,
>
> Attached is an updated draft plot of my latest estimate of the life raft's path 9/18/2016 at 1200 to 9/25/2016... by using real-time data from nearby Woods Hole Oceanographic Institution (WHOI) buoys and from satellite-derived data....
>
> It is very unusual to have real-time data observations when calculating a reverse drift. We are fortunate....
>
> Happy New Year,
> Richard

These were indeed good tidings.

Richard Limeburner's "reverse drift" analysis seemed compelling. Assuming Nathan's life raft drifted seven days, as he testified in his EUO, and ended up at the *Orient Lucky* rescue spot, where would he have needed to be when he started, where the boat sank? Limeburner accessed wind and current data for those seven days from a fortuitously nearby WHOI buoy and backtracked the requisite drift. Where would the life raft have been an hour before the rescue? And an hour before that? And an hour before that? All the way back to midday on Sunday, September 18, 2016 when the ex-*Chicken Pox* fell out from underneath Nathan? And Limeburner's preliminary answer was more than thirty miles *southeast* of the rescue location 106 miles south of Martha's Vineyard.

Yet Nathan's 140-fathom Block Canyon sinking spot was forty miles *northwest* of the *Orient Lucky* rescue location. Thus, on Nathan's story, he would have been drifting against the current to arrive at the *Orient Lucky*, just as I had wondered, consistent with the Georges Bank clockwise gyre. And now it was clear he would have been overall drifting upwind too. Physically impossible x 2.

Over the course of 2018 we would refine Limeburner's analysis to irrefutably sink Nathan's entire at-sea tall tale, based on precise oceanographic buoy data in WHOI's own backyard. Located on the southern New England continental slope, which Limeburner called the Shelf Break, the WHOI buoy was pretty much right in between Nathan's Block Canyon 140-fathom starting spot and the *Orient Lucky* pickup spot.

Nathan had picked just about the worst place in the whole world to jump into his life raft.

2018

15

"GOD IS LIKE LAND WHEN YOU ARE ON A SHIP AT SEA"

Nathan showed up looking like an altar boy for his January 22, 2018 deposition, sporting a cute golf outfit. Below is a photo of him before he was sworn. With his new lawyer's shaping and shopping, gone were the days of Ted Kaczynski. But Nathan was still the same underneath. It was all in the eyes. No window dressing could ever cover up that flat, blank peer, just like when he got discharged at the Coast Guard pier in Boston sixteen months before.

Attorney Anderson, I knew, would be himself too, only more so. His combativeness could try the patience of a saint, or a judge, and certainly all his opposing counsel. But his client in this case didn't just claim a sore back, he was fighting for his life.

Dave Anderson and I had but two things in common—first, a Belmont Hill education, and second, of course, maritime law. His nautical experience was rowing crew, which he continued at the University of Pennsylvania and in Olympic trials before law school at Boston University. He was able to parlay that into a lucrative law practice over the years, concentrating in a very narrow niche representing injured seafarers.

***

In the entire world, there are two types of industrial workers who can sue their employers after getting hurt. For everyone else, if you are physically injured on the job, the best you can do in getting compensation from your employer is by making a workers' compensation claim. You will then automatically receive governmentally set benefits from your employer's insurer, including medical care and partial wages for your time out of work. That's the standard way on-the-job injuries are treated in the United States and much of the industrialized world. The injured victim cannot sue the employer for anything more. Workers' comp is a legislative compromise—injured workers, regardless of fault, have their necessities taken care of by their employers promptly and without question, and in return, employers cannot be sued for whopping dollar damage claims like pain and suffering and emotional distress or for spousal loss of consortium, like the lovely Lillian Biktjorn.

United States railroad workers and seafarers are the world's two exceptions. In the early 1900s, Progressive Era politics tried to right injustices of the Industrial Revolution and our first Gilded Age and with the support of the railroad brotherhoods, a labor union precursor, a federal law was passed giving railroad workers engaged in interstate commerce the right to sue their employers for negligence before a jury. This was just before workers' compensation laws were passed in most states for virtually everyone else—factory workers, hardware store clerks, construction workers, teachers, coal miners, nurses, lumberjacks, florists, firefighters, office staff.

Seafarers, though, because they spent so much time at sea, were slower to organize, but when post-World War I commerce got rolling again, federal legislation was enacted to supplement ancient but meager judicial remedies for injured seafarers too.

The Merchant Marine Act of 1920, better known as the Jones Act, was primarily a protectionist statute intended to boost the US shipping industry, and to achieve that it contained an important management/labor compromise. It required that any ship engaged in our domestic or coastwise trade fly the US flag—meaning the ship must be US-built, -owned, and -crewed. And to entice seafarers to sail those ships, the Jones Act also gave injured seafarers generous remedies paralleling the railroaders'—the right to sue shipowner employers for negligence before a jury.

As it then developed, the Jones Act was liberally interpreted by the courts as merely requiring that the shipowner's negligence have a "featherweight" connection to the injury, making jury awards easier. Later on, the US Supreme Court ruled that any shipboard unseaworthy physical condition causing seafarer personal injury constituted shipowner liability, and that too gets determined by a jury. Plus, the shipowner was contractually obligated to provide, regardless of fault, basic medical care and basic living expenses for the injured seafarer. So, with post-injury necessities assured, the injured seafarer can on top of that claim featherweight negligence and strict liability unseaworthiness in front of a jury in the hopes of hitting the lottery with a big award from the shipowner.[71]

This is not to minimize a dangerous profession and the horrendous injuries that can be experienced at sea, far from medical care. It's best to settle that type of case early, avoiding protracted litigation and putting money into the hands of the victim. But the easy proof of shipowner liability is also subject to abuse, fake claims, and inflated dollar losses.

---

[71] David J. Farrell, Jr., "After 100 Years Has the Jones Act Sunk the Jones Act and Vice Versa?" *Tulane Maritime Law Journal*, vol. 47 (2023), 209.

Together, these three US seafarer legal remedies against the ship-owning employer even go well beyond railroader benefits, with leading scholars noting that the US seafarer is "the most generously treated personal injury victim in American law"[72] and "the beneficiary of a system of accident and health insurance at shipowner's expense more comprehensive than anything yet achieved by shore-bound workers."[73]

Attorney Anderson's law firm has mined this three-ways-to-win personal injury regime over the decades, making a fortune on 40 percent contingency legal fees, often at the expense of New Bedford fish boat owners, directly contributing to the high price of sea scallops.

It's not just commercial fishing that bears the brunt of Jones Act personal injury costs—it's the entire US maritime industry. On top of the uniquely high jury awards and resulting huge insurance premiums facing US-flag shipping, US seafarer wages are much higher than their Indian or Philippine or Ukrainian counterparts. Furthermore, building ships in US shipyards, as required by the Jones Act, dramatically drives up the cost of doing business as a US shipowner. Compared to South Korea, building the same cargo ship in the US is five times more expensive.

With all these protectionist costs imposed by the Jones Act, US-flag shipowners in international trade cannot compete with lower-cost foreign shipping. To that extent the Jones Act has backfired, and US ships have been forced to leave the overseas cargo business in droves since World War II. Everyone should be alarmed that US-flag ships now carry only 1.5 percent of our oceangoing imports and exports. That presents a grave national security threat to our island nation.[74]

The Jones Act thus goes a long way to explaining why Nathan was picked up south of Martha's Vineyard by an *Orient Lucky* and not a *Lady*

---

72 David W. Roberston, Stephen F. Friedell, and Michael F. Sturley, *Admiralty and Maritime Law in the United States*, 3rd ed., (Carolina Academic Press, 2015), 188.

73 Grant Gilmore and Charles L. Black Jr., *The Law of Admiralty*, 2nd ed. (Foundation Press, 1975), 282.

74 Farrell, "After 100 Years," n. 71.

Liberty. We were determined to make that location an insurmountable hurdle for Nathan and his Jones Act attorney.

***

People think from watching TV that trials are won and lost in the crucible of the courtroom. That's where the truth unfolds. Johnnie Cochran's "If it doesn't fit, you must acquit" is a great example (well, not). But in my experience, civil litigation outcomes are determined in pretrial depositions of the plaintiff and defendant. That's where the key evidence and admissions by the parties emerge, forcing settlement or a motion for summary judgment, and if that doesn't work, for use at trial.

In federal court civil cases, a deposition is normally limited to seven hours, which means one day with about an hour lunch break. If you want more than seven hours of testimony, the deposing lawyer will probably need to go to court to get permission from the judge, if there's a good reason.

With Nathan, there was a lot to cover, and Anderson would do his best to run out the seven-hour clock. Liam and I knew we had to keep moving along and not get bogged down on any one question. We had to pick our lines of inquiry strategically, and if I wasn't getting anywhere, I had to just give up and go on to the next question before time ran out.

First thing I did was ask Nathan whether he wanted to change anything about his EUO testimony. These sorts of questions after a year has gone by can be risky—if given the invitation, Nathan might try to fog up what he had earlier said. But quite confident we had him well tied down a year before, I figured we might as well deal with any attempted testimony changes now, right up front, which I fully expected since Nathan now had this new lawyer representing him. But no, Nathan testified, nothing in the EUO transcript "should be changed to better reflect the truth."[75]

This was a great start. It meant half-dollar holes, shabbily filled. Absurd, mythical sinking. Into his life raft at 140 fathoms in Block Canyon. Nathan was doubling down on his incredible tale, and he was going down.

Unfortunately, we next had to get basic exceptions to his All Risk insurance policy out of the way. This took an hour or so of cantankerous challenges from Attorney Anderson.

We then turned to how Nathan had managed to overheat and destroy the original diesel engine Woods had installed in *Chicken Pox*. This incident occurred on April 26, 2016, less than five months before the sinking, inside the Point Judith Harbor of Refuge, where "the V-shaped breakwater affords protected anchorage for small craft."[76]

After Nathan had taken the boat to Point Judith Marina for some minor troubleshooting, he ran his boat out to the Harbor of Refuge for a sea trial, failing to make sure the sea cock for the diesel's saltwater cooling system was open, and the engine cooked, seizing up. He was inside the protective breakwaters, with no whitecaps or fog, very close to shore. He set his anchor where he marked an X on NOAA Chart 13219.[77] There were no flames, just steam and the burning-rubber smell dreaded by any motorist, but he felt the predicament urgent enough to call 911 on his cell phone. He was towed back in by the Coast Guard.

---

[75] Carman's federal court depositions were deemed "Confidential" by Attorney Anderson and also in the Sisters' Slayer Suit, subject to protective orders making them unavailable to the public. However, Carman's key deposition testimony as quoted in this book, as well as other information from the depositions, is otherwise publicly available and in filings on the court's public docket, primarily ECF No. 139.

[76] *United States Coast Pilot 2* (NOAA, 2005), 266.

[77] Tr. Ex. 41.

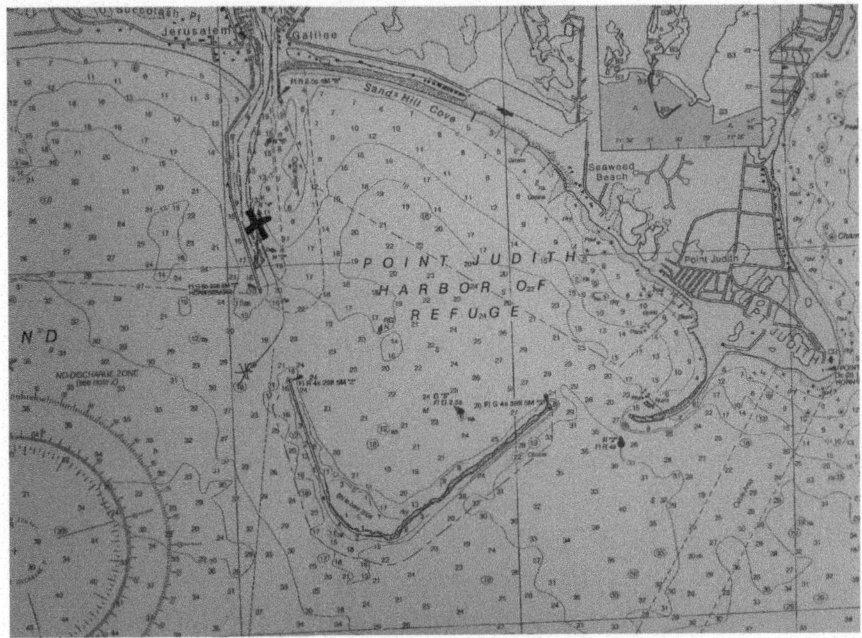

Point Judith Marina replaced the diesel in the coming weeks—with no resistance at all from the Insurer, who paid the $33,489.33 repair bill immediately. An easy touch.

The handle on the sea cock is easy to open on the first sign of overheating—but even easier to just leave closed if that is your intention. Liam and I had been wondering if Nathan closed it on purpose to get a new engine for a longer trip he was planning in the future, in the process also testing the Insurer's willingness to pay claims. Pretty smart, but pretty diabolical, if Nathan had indeed done that. But it would have been time-consuming to explore that theory in the deposition, and we didn't.

Viewed differently, though, Nathan was neither smart nor diabolical. Calling for emergency help seven hundred yards from shore and getting towed in by the Coast Guard could not have contrasted more starkly with his "deeply engrained" EUO testimony not to call for help unless "your life or limb is in imminent jeopardy"—for which his boat full of water one hundred miles offshore did not qualify. *What a crock.*

Thus, Nathan's three failures to radio or activate the EPIRB during his sinking evolution sank him even deeper.

On his trim tabs removal, Nathan came up with a new reason that he had not disclosed in his examination under oath. Now Nathan's testimony was that a charter boat captain had told him a bluefin will dive under the boat and cut the line on the sheet metal edge (a valid concern). That was now why, Nathan testified, he decided to take the trim tabs off before heading to the canyons. Whole new reasons are always suspect, however, especially when I asked Nathan at the beginning of the deposition whether there was any EUO testimony that he wanted to change.

The best new testimony we got from Nathan on the transom holes was that he could not with "absolute confidence" say he did not use a hole saw and had a "vague sense" of using one. Clearly no denial, he wasn't disputing Iozzi's observations.

Around midday, to coin a phrase, we made ourselves take lunch, to coin a phrase. Nathan and Anderson apparently went off to eat meatballs (no bread) and contemplate their dimensions as epoxy putty prototypes, no doubt while drinking Newman's Own Iced Tea, as Liam and I skipped lunch and downed coffee.

Any break in a deposition—to go to the head, to give Lauren's fingers a rest, and especially to go to lunch—is precarious, since it gives the deponent and lawyer a chance to talk in private. With no judge watching the deposition resume in real time, post-lunch changes in testimony are not uncommon.

After lunch, following some quick wrap-up on the overheated engine, I shifted gears and had Nathan testify about the four half-dollar holes "that I opened—I exposed," when he asked to "interject," stating, "I think I got half-dollars and silver dollars confused in the EUO. The holes were slightly larger than a quarter."

Whoa. Now he's saying a quarter or a half-dollar or a silver dollar? Clearly, Nathan was trying again to obfuscate and wiggle out of damaging evidence, trying to change the size of the half-dollar holes which had been central to his story and were memorialized in Attorney Santos's letter dated October 12, 2016—just twenty-five days after Nathan's trim tabs removal.

This is a good example of why Nathan was not a convincing witness to anyone but himself and Attorney Anderson, who thought he was fighting the good fight. He would later be authoritatively told otherwise. Both were in too deep. This post-lunch quarter-hole downsizing seemed like desperation, just too cute. But why, then, did Nathan also say the holes were possibly silver-dollar-sized? They're even bigger. We were short of time, and I decided to leave it alone. Four half-dollars were just fine by me.

When you're in a boat, you want to keep the water on the outside. Any four holes will make it sink. To be precise, the difference in diameters between a half-dollar (1 3⁄16 inches) and a quarter (15⁄16 inch) really didn't matter when both were substantially bigger than Woods's original holes (1⁄2 inch). Nathan's attempt, albeit minimally, to downsize the four holes clearly showed that he realized that four inadequately sealed half-dollar holes in the transom at the waterline were fatal to his insurance case (even if not to Linda, but more on that later). This waffling, volunteered downsizing testimony burnished our litigation position that Nathan had conducted faulty repairs, disentitling him to insurance coverage under the terms of the policy.

After moving onto navigation issues, Liam, and I especially, were buoyed by Nathan's testimony that his boat cruised at 2,600 RPMs, which he said was around 15 to 16 knots. That's exactly what solving for Speed = Distance ÷ Time gave us. He further testified that was the speed for the five-hour Block Island X to Block Canyon X leg. He had to.

And even better, Nathan specifically confirmed that "the sinking spot occurred," as he had marked in the EUO a year earlier on Chart 12300, "between the X and the asterisk," which is "around the 140-fathom mark" and "more or less within the walls of Block Canyon." He sealed that location by further testifying, "I have no reason to change the testimony that I gave at the examination under oath regarding this."

This was huge. No wiggling attempted. Neither Nathan nor his new attorney had come up with any reason to change the 140-fathom testimony. We were going to sink Nathan with Limeburner's oceanographic data showing the life raft could not, given the wind and current conditions present that week, have drifted from Nathan's twice-testified 140-fathom mark in Block Canyon to where *Orient Lucky* picked him up.

Nathan also testified, "I think differently than many people." As lawyers would say, we will stipulate to that. Here's one reason why: On the life raft he had "fifteen days" of provisions "per person for two people."

"Wow," I said, "why so much?"

Because he'd read Nathaniel Philbrick's *In the Heart of the Sea*, a modern telling of the true story of a Nantucket whaler stoved-in by an angry leviathan—the inspiration for Herman Melville's *Moby-Dick*.[78] Eschewing his state-of-the art marine electronics, Nathan instead relied on early nineteenth-century survival tactics, assembling thirty days of food so that he would not "end up like" Philbrick's "very vivid description of starvation at sea" and "gnawing on the bones of shipmates" off South America.

Ososphobia—the fear of cannibalism? Yet three distinct wheelhouse failures to radio or set off his EPIRB? There was a lot I could do with this.

Then there was a shiny nugget that appeared as I was just going through a checklist. Nathan "withdrew $2,000 cash at a local Citizen's Bank" the day before departing on the fateful voyage and fueled up, topping off all three diesel fuel tanks.

I stowed this away, as did Nathan the remaining cash with his thirty days of provisions and a hand-cranked water maker. He had enough that he could stay hydrated and nourished and fly home from Ireland (correction, the Hamptons) if no one rescued him. And otherwise short of money, he surely could use an $85,000 insurance infusion to hold him until his Good Ship *Dynasty Trust* came in.

While it was not part of the deposition, because getting into religion is always going to raise objections, this would be a good time to present

---

78 Herman Melville, *Moby-Dick: Or, The Whale*, chapter 1, "Loomings"; chapter 44, "The Chart"; chapter 53, "The Gam"; chapter 62, "The Dart"; chapter 72, "The Monkey-Rope" (Penguin Classics, 2003).

Nathan's handwritten letter to *Orient Lucky* Captain Zhao.[79] As we lawyers would also say, the document speaks for itself. As his mother would have said, it verges on "religious idiocy."

> Captain Zhao Hengdong,
>
> I want to express my deepest and most sincere appreciation to you and the entire crew of the Orient Lucky for having rescued me from the sea. If my mom is lost, which I fear is likely, I will have no one on earth who will welcome me sincerely into their home. So I appreciate the efforts you and your crew have made to make your ship a home to me while I have been aboard.
>
> If there is ever any way in which I can repay you, or if you ever decide to visit America on holiday and would like for me to show you around, I welcome you to contact me.
>
> Sincerely,
>
> Nathan Carman
>
> P.S. When the world takes everything from you, there are several ways in which you can respond. The best way is to use the experience as an opportunity to see and be grateful for what you do have and what you are given.
>
> God is like land when you are on a ship at sea, from your vantage you cannot see Him, yet not believing in Him does not make Him any less real.

---

79 Dave Altimari, "In Letters to Captain, Nathan Carman Laments Likely Loss of Mother," *Hartford Courant*, December 12, 2018. https://www.courant.com/2016/10/05/in-letters-to-captain-nathan-carman-laments-likely-loss-of-mother/.

Unlike land, however, there are no real hazards or perils on the approach to safe harbor.

In the midst of the darkest and stormiest night of one's life the Lord is not there like jagged rocks on the sea shore waiting to tear apart he who seeks shelter too late. Rather, God the Father is like the keeper of an inn on the coast who waits up on stormy nights ready to welcome shipwrecked sailors into the warmth and safety of His dwelling.

And God the Son, Jesus, is like the volunteer Coast Guardsman who willingly leaves the warmth and safety of His father's dwelling, to find you and guide you back to the warmth and safety of His father's dwelling once you realize you are lost.

Like one who walks on land then puts to sea, once you have experienced the feeling of God being with you, the assertion that God does not exist will seem as absurd as the assertion that land does not exist, even when you cannot see it.

Or at least that has been my experience.

--Nathan Carman

Holy cow.

In my humble opinion God was not planning on saving Nathan Carman. So I figured an Inquisition was in order. Based on his media and other statements I knew he would feign ignorance on one inquiry and deny everything else. Did you murder your mother? Shoot her? Strangle her? Bludgeon her? Stab her? No, no, no, no, no. But the key question followed from Nathan's *20/20* comment to Linzie Janis: "I did not cause my mother's death" and when I asked could you have saved her by giving her a hand or a life jacket, predictably, Nathan couldn't say. With all that chopped bait from the cooler and an hour-long slick as Linda went missing, I also wanted to ask again, as I had in the EUO, what else he might have observed from his life raft. One thing he did not see was any sharks. Also entirely predictable. *Hmm.*

About six hours into the deposition, with 317 pages of testimony and thinly veiled attorney crankiness back-and-forth, there was still one subject we had not addressed and for which I had saved adequate time.

Real fun, even though I got nowhere fast, began when I abruptly asked a long series of questions regarding the missing Sig Sauer. Nathan had nothing to say, didn't open his mouth. Not validly objecting, claiming the grandfather's murder was not relevant, Attorney Anderson simply instructed Nathan not to answer. So I laid the groundwork for another motion to compel Nathan's testimony on questions which Judge Sullivan had already authorized on "the specific firearm that has been associated with the death of his grandfather," and we adjourned the deposition's first session so we could go back to court.

16
MORE CHUM

Liam and I turned to and prepared our next motion to compel further testimony from Nathan on the Sig Sauer. Here are the topics we told the court we needed answers on to questions we had asked in the deposition, without response:

> a. Where and when did Defendant purchase the Sig Sauer 716 Patrol .308 caliber rifle?
>
> b. Are there any Sig Sauer purchase and sale documents?
>
> c. Is the Sig Sauer now in Defendant's possession, custody, or control, and if not, where is it and what happened to it? When did he last have possession of it?
>
> d. As referenced in Coast Guard records, who went with Defendant for a boat ride the night his grandfather was murdered?
>
> e. As with his mother, was Defendant the last person to see his grandfather alive? How much did he inherit so far and how much more did he expect?

Attorney Anderson filed his brief objecting to any more deposition time and the lawyers appeared for a hearing on March 26, 2018 before Judge Sullivan. A few days later she issued her written order and we won on all points.[80]

Judge Sullivan first summarized that during Nathan's deposition, he "was instructed not to answer any questions" regarding his grandfather's murder, with Attorney Anderson arguing it was "beyond the scope of permissible discovery." She pointed out, however, that he "did not reference any privilege or limitation imposed by the Court" and "each instruction was accompanied by inappropriate and time-consuming colloquy."

Concerning Anderson's relevancy objection to my questions, Judge Sullivan echoed our argument that the Court had already ruled:

> [A]s Plaintiffs correctly point out, this ship has already sailed—the Court has already ruled that discovery in this case may focus on facts bearing directly on an alleged scheme to procure a substantial inheritance by murdering, first, his grandfather and then, his mother through the intentional sinking of the vessel, because such facts bear directly on his intent in making the changes and repairs to the vessel that Plaintiffs allege resulted in its loss.

More specifically, Judge Sullivan reasoned:

> In light of the centrality to this case of Defendant's intent in taking the actions that led to the insurance claim for the loss of the vessel, and in light of the law enforcement records suggesting that family members and neighbors suspected that Defendant's intent was to sink the vessel deliberately as the culmination of a unified scheme that began with the murder of his grandfather, Plaintiffs asked these questions. Viewed through

[80] ECF No. 59.

> the lens of Defendant's intent, this inquiry is plainly focused on seeking evidence that "has a tendency to make a fact more or less probable than it would be without the evidence." Fed. R. Evid. 401(a); *see also* Fed. R. Evid. 404(b)(2) (evidence of crimes, wrongs, or other acts may be admissible to prove motive or intent).

Judge Sullivan went on to dismiss "Defendant's suggestion that he has been sandbagged by the introduction of the issue of his intent at this late stage of the case" as "disingenuous." She noted, "Defendant ultimately conceded...that he himself produced" a set of Coast Guard documents which themselves raised the issue of intent by connecting the possible common motive for the two deaths. Furthermore:

> [A]s Plaintiffs highlight, their theory that Defendant's intent traces back to the murder of his grandfather is reflected in material produced in Plaintiffs' initial disclosures (including their reference to an ABC *20/20* television broadcast).
>
> Moreover, whether or not discovery focused on Defendant's intent may begin with the murder of the grandfather was openly litigated during Plaintiffs' prior motions to compel.... Defendant's newly-made argument that he is now surprised by the Court's ruling on the scope of discovery is belied by this record.
>
> After carefully considering all of Defendant's arguments, the Court finds that the inquiry into Defendant's intent that Plaintiffs propose to pursue by focusing on the topics blocked by Defendant's improper instructions at the deposition is not sand-bagging, but an appropriate examination regarding relevant matters that may proceed forthwith.

Judge Sullivan's always professional, thorough, and thoughtful approach, with little tolerance for attorney antics, is a shining example of how the grinding wheels of justice should be administered, typical of federal court litigation but less common in state court. Her order granted us two more hours to depose Nathan and specifically authorized us to ask him about the Sig Sauer. But that got delayed when Defendant filed an objection to the order for review by Chief Judge William E. Smith, who would be presiding at our trial. That objection was summarily dismissed on June 29, 2018.

So finally, after five months, we were going to get two more hours of deposition time with Nathan.

We had not, like we might in state court, sat on our hands awaiting a final ruling from Chief Judge Smith because there was a firm fact discovery deadline on the horizon. During those five months we diligently did more grunt work while waiting for the judicial go-ahead to resume Nathan's deposition and we came up with some stunning and critical new evidence, in the logical order of our case development, on the following issues:

Nathan's poor repair of the trim tab holes.

Which way did he go?

His life raft drift.

His Sig Sauer.

Sr. and Jr.

The apple falling not far from the tree, the only witnesses Attorney Anderson identified as supportive of Nathan were a sad father-and-son act, Roth Sr. and Roth Jr. They both had worked for Brian Woods a short while during the years he was refurbishing the *Chicken Pox*.

My Boston longtime go-to DiNatale Detective Agency ran some background investigation. I had used the DiNatale brothers in 1994 for airplane surveillance to show no wheelchair ramps at the very secluded Neponset River marsh home of two slip-and-fall liars, one of whom was a Jones Act seafarer. He had been Coast Guard-helicoptered to Savannah off the 688-foot oil tanker *Cherry Valley* en route from Venezuela to New York, but there was nothing wrong with him in the hospital or afterward.[81] His longshoreman gunrunning brother and demonstrably not wheelchair-bound nurse wife both had almost identical unwitnessed on-the-job accidents, and all three dopes went to the same doctors and specialists.

That case, too, could probably be a book. Plaintiffs' lawyer, Tom Hunt, showed up in court with a bodyguard and dismissed the case the morning that jury selection was to begin.[82] At the pretrial conference ten days before, Boston Federal Judge Mark L. Wolf had promised, "I will walk the trial transcript myself to the US Attorney's Office" if Plaintiffs' lawyers Hunt and Ed White did not immediately drop the case, and that next weekend White jumped—or maybe he was pushed—off the old Carlton Bridge over the Kennebec River in Bath, Maine, never to be seen again.

This time the DiNatales determined that both Roths had serious substance abuse problems and a string of financial failures. Apparently, Roth Sr.'s girlfriend had a child on the spectrum. To please her and get some notoriety, likely hoping for expert witness pay, he contacted Dave Anderson and claimed to have information that would help Nathan.

Liam and I needed to discover what these two guys were going to say at trial, and we were all set to take their depositions in Chatham, but Attorney Anderson reported one of them had just had a DUI and the other one's truck had broken down, so they had to cancel. I hunted around for a place in their South Shore town and contacted our law firm bank's branch office there, which was right down the street from where the two lived, so there could be no more excuses.

I met Liam the morning of the depositions in the bank parking lot on a raw spring day, having borrowed my niece's car since I couldn't

---

[81] John DiNatale, *The Family Business: Memoirs of a Boston Private Eye* (PFP Inc., 2013), 249–50.

[82] The *Cherry Valley* master disembarked the ship in Mobile and flew to Boston as the corporate representative at trial and as an eyewitness. I was very happy to take him to lunch after our quick win, but as it turns out, he would have preferred staying aboard. His relief obtained the largest marine salvage award ever, $4.125 million, for rescuing the barge carrying a NASA space shuttle fuel tank in a tropical storm. *Margate Shipping Co. v. J.A. Orgeron*, 143 F.3d 976, 1998 AMC 2383 (5th Cir. 1998).

climb into my truck. I didn't know it at the time, but I had torn the meniscus in my left knee two days before doing speed work on the hated treadmill and could barely walk. Liam tried to grab my crutches out of the car, but I insisted "No crutches," accepting instead his kind assistance with my best FDR accent, "The only thing we have to fear is fear itself," adamant that Anderson witness no infirmity.

After the three of them arrived I started with the son, because you always work your way to the top. The reasoning is, by starting with the crew you get revelations that constrain the officers' retelling of events to their advantage.

Roth Jr. was a broken young man. He spoke glowingly of his father's boatbuilding abilities but had virtually nothing relevant to say besides some garbled testimony about stripping the boat's interior and finding the hull so thin he could push through it with a screwdriver. Why would you do that? No good reason in reply, some more garbled nonsense, and finally I asked, knowing the answer from DiNatale's work that very morning:

> Q: Did you take Methadone today?
>
> A: Yeah, at six this morning.
>
> Q: When were you sentenced six months in the Plymouth House of Correction?
>
> A: I mean, if you need to know my criminal past, you know, and like, you want to pay me to talk about it, I'm more than willing to talk about it.
>
> Q: I don't want to pay you. I want you to—
>
> A: All right. Well, I'm not saying anything about it then.

We were pretty sure we would not be hearing from Roth Jr. at trial.

Next up, Roth Sr. started out with some bravado about his small-boatbuilding skills, which may even have been accurate, but his recollection was definitely not, and his testimony only helped us.

He claimed he himself had installed the trim tabs and drilled seven-eighths-inch holes in the transom. That must be what Anderson liked about his story—almost the size of half-dollars, or certainly quarters. But it all quickly fell apart, since Roth Sr. testified he only drilled two holes, for the "cable" that operates the trim tabs. So I asked him to diagram it.

> Q: And what about the trim tabs? Tell me more about that. Where did you drill the holes?
>
> A: In the stern.
>
> Q: How many?
>
> A: I believe two.
>
> Q: Okay. And where?
>
> A: Above the waterline, for the cable that operates the trim tab to come out.
>
> Q: Where on the transom, from the centerline, port and starboard?
>
> A: About a foot and a half in from either side, so about eighteen inches in from either side from the exterior of the outside of—
>
> Q: I think we might need a piece of paper.
>
> A: Well, I can draw what I think. It's always just a thought. My guess is here's your waterline, so your boat—I would say these were your scuppers on the top.
>
> Q: That's above the waterline?
>
> A: Yep.

Q: So my question was, Where is the location of the holes that you drilled?

A: It would be right on the photograph, which shows it coming out. My guess is right around here.

I exploded at opposing counsel's blatant attempt to coach the witness by flashing photos of the trim tabs on the transom with the four actuators in an effort to have Roth Sr. change his testimony from drilling two holes to four holes.

MR. FARRELL: Mr. Anderson, keep your papers to yourself. I don't want you coaching the witness, I don't want you doing it again, I don't want him seeing any photographs now. You do what you want on cross-examination. Keep your papers to yourself now.

MR. ANDERSON: I have not shown him a photograph at all.

MR. FARRELL: You've got them in your hand.

MR. ANDERSON: I have—I do have photos in my hand. They are not within his vision.

MR. FARRELL: They damn well are. Move them away.

MR. ANDERSON: No, they are not.

MR. FARRELL: Hide them. Hide them, Mr. Anderson.

MR. ANDERSON: They are not within his vision.

MR. FARRELL: Keep them away.

MR. ANDERSON: They are not within his vision and they never have been. I don't know what's wrong with you today.

MR. FARRELL: They are directly in his vision if you put them down like that—

MR. ANDERSON: Let's ask the Witness. Can you see the photographs in my hand? Can you see the photographs in—

MR. FARRELL: You can ask your questions at the end.

MR. ANDERSON: I will, but you just stop to cause these problems. He couldn't see the photographs. I wasn't showing them to him. You're just making stuff up.

A: I don't—I honestly don't need photographs to determine where trim tabs go on a boat. I mean, this is what I do for a living.

Q: Okay. Let me ask you then the question that I was trying to get at. Can you draw on this diagram where the holes are that you drilled?

A: I can't accurately, so I won't even try to do it because I don't want to, you know, impose any false information if I'm wrong.

That was a close call.

Then I asked him to assume Nathan had removed the trim tabs and that left exposed holes in the transom.

Q: Based on the record, the assumption that I'd like you to make is that Nathan Carman took the trim tabs off and there were these exposed holes in the transom one evening or afternoon, and that he went fishing just six hours later.

A: Uh-huh.

Q: Okay. With these holes that were in the transom, what should he have done to fill them?

A: I mean, you could have taken a two-by-two square of plywood and four screws and went right over it. You could have filled it with some sort of a putty, epoxy, or something. You know, I mean, to do it right?

Q: Yes.

A: Yeah, I mean, there's several ways. I mean, the old days, they would use a wooden plug.

Q: Tapered down?

A: A tiny bit, yeah.

Q: And then pounded in there?

A: Yep.

Q: And then what would you do?

A: Leave it if you want or you could sand it down flush.

Q: You could cut it off and sand it down flush?

A: Yeah, you could do a lot of things.

Q: You might then fiberglass over that?

A: Yeah.

Q: Would that be the preferred way to do it?

A: Yeah, I mean, if I was going to do it, yeah, I would have glassed over it. I mean, I just would have glassed over it, thrown a patch over it, in an hour it would have been dry and been fine.

Depositions don't go much better than this. Nathan's only witness just testified that the right way to seal the transom holes was with fiberglass. Nathan didn't do it that way. As I hobbled out with Liam, we both figured we'd just won it on the faulty repair policy exclusion.

Ping

An intriguing reference in the Coast Guard records attracted our great interest, and Liam and I expended lots of energy on it, but in the end it yielded no tangible fruit, at least on the technical information we were able to muster.

We had gotten our hands on "float plan" text messages between Linda and her friend Sharon Hartstein,[83] which is a good idea for any boater, to let someone ashore know the trip itinerary, in case something goes wrong. Particularly if heading out with Nathan Carman.

> *From Linda to Sharon, Friday 9/16/2016 at 11:11 am:*
>
> leaving Rams Point Marina around 1am heading out to Striper Rock, Southeast of windmills.
>
> Back by 9 am. call me 12 noon if you don't hear from me. thanks for being there.

Linda attached a photo of the boat with its Rhode Island registration numbers—just in case that was needed.

> *From Linda to Sharon, Friday 9/16/2016 at 9:15 pm:*
>
> We are NOT going out tonight
>
> maybe tomorrow night…
>
> *From Linda to Sharon, Saturday 9/17/2016 at 10:54 pm:*
>
> leaving the dock shortly. be in contact by 9am.

---

83 Tr. Ex. 18.2.

From Sharon to Linda, Sunday 9/18/2016 at 5:18 pm:

Should I worry?

Yes, but by then it was too late. Sharon spoke with the Coast Guard reporting the overdue boat. Linda never texted Sharon that they were heading further offshore.

From Sharon to Linda, Wednesday 9/21/2016 at 4:56 pm:

Missing you. Hurry Home

Based on the float plan Linda had texted to Sharon, the Coast Guard first focused on the nonspecific Striper Rock in the vicinity of the wind farm southeast of Block Island. That was consistent with a ping from Linda's cell phone there (and also roughly consistent with what Nathan testified to in his examination under oath and his deposition and chart drawings).

But not long after there is another entry in the Coast Guard records that Linda's cell last pinged ten miles southwest of Block Island at 12:45 a.m. Sunday morning, with the Coast Guard therefore shifting search assets to that side of the island. And that would have been consistent with what Nathan wrote to Martha about first stopping to fish southwest of the island.

Could he have gotten there by 12:45 a.m.? Yes, if he went straight from Point Judith; no, if he first went to his Striper Rock.

The Coast Guard file confirmed that Nathan's truck and Linda's car were in the Ram Point Marina parking lot and its surveillance video showed the boat departing at 11:13 p.m. on Saturday night September 17, 2016. If Nathan had scooted right along through Point Judith Pond on the clear night with a nearly full moon and a pretty high tide, once outside in the Harbor of Refuge he could have hooked it up to twenty knots and gotten to the ping spot ten miles southwest of Block Island in an hour, by 12:45 a.m. Sunday morning.

Liam and I pursued this hard, continuing to wonder, which way did he go? To the east or west of Block Island? Which of the two pings from Linda's phone was accurate? We subpoenaed Verizon, Block Island and

Long Island cell towers, and retained a cell phone/cell tower expert. He ended up concluding that since there was only one nearby cell tower registering the pings, which was on Block Island, and Long Island towers were too far west, there was no usable second axis to pinpoint either ping along the first axis. So we were left with an arc of about twelve miles, centered on the Block Island cell tower, east to south to west, or over 180°, and the 12:45 a.m. ping theoretically could have happened anywhere on that arc. And it seems like that's just what happened—the other ping from Linda's phone, just two minutes earlier, was southeast toward the wind farm, pretty much on the same arc. So much for using one cell phone tower to pinpoint a phone at sea.

Adding to the which way did he go question, in his deposition Nathan would not rule out the possibility that the ping ten miles southwest of Block Island was accurate and they had actually been there.

This was all very murky. Liam and I always had that in our hip pocket to use against Nathan to impeach his sworn voyage story about going to the east but our gut was to leave it alone. It seemed like a vestige of Nathan the Desperado trying to confuse us. Our better course was to just hold Nathan to his twice-sworn eastside story culminating with his Block Canyon 140-fathom sinking, the starting point to discredit his life raft drift fiction. And we would go to the ends of the earth to do it.

Jazz

Which Liam did, the man for the job, on the ride of his life, for the evidence capstone of the wet case against Nathan.

Growing up on Massachusetts's other Cape, Cape Ann, to the north and rocky, Liam went to St. John's Prep and Massachusetts Maritime Academy, becoming a platoon leader and standout Ferris Bueller student rebel. The maritime industry education available there for the really smart or very hardworking is terrific, and even better for people like Liam who possess both attributes. He's a fast learner and quick on his feet, gifted at concocting outrageous conspiracy theories out of one or two alleged factoids.

Starting out after graduating and serving as a mate on Mass Maritime's training ship *Patriot State*, the Coast Guard grabbed him to serve in Texas as a Marine Safety Officer for the bustling Houston Ship Channel. Ships from all over the world call there, huge tankers and container ships, all subject to routine Coast Guard safety inspection and, should that lead to the discovery of something illegal under US and/or international law, the Coast Guard and Department of Justice, Admiralty Division, will go hard to convict. Liam was involved in hundreds of investigations on foreign-flag ships involving every conceivable vessel system, from navigation electronics to engine room mechanics, tanks and ballast systems, cargo operations, spills and casualties, and electronic data storage. He testified as a litigation expert witness for the US government and, post convictions, served as a parole officer, monitoring sanctioned foreign-flag vessels and fleets.

Commanding Coast Guard armed escorts for Navy nuclear subs in Groton, Connecticut, was another plus for reliability on his resume. I met him after he finished law school and had been admitted to practice. I knew he had good offers from top US admiralty law firms.

But Liam wasn't interested in doing that initially and wanted to develop a criminal defense practice in state court. *Say what?*

Liam knew what he wanted and was sure he'd get a lot of courtroom and trial experience along the way, becoming a better maritime lawyer as a result. I was impressed with his approach but wondered how he was going to get the writing experience he would need in federal court.

Dave Smith and I figured we'd let Liam go both routes. He soon started working on our maritime cases along with his criminal practice and picked up fast on federal court strict writing requirements, erudite briefing style, and exacting citation rules—which in turn helped his state court briefing. And he got all sorts of day-in day-out courtroom experience from his evidentiary suppression motions, witness examinations, and bail hearings. He defended his clients from DUI and drug possession and A&B and gun charges before six-person juries and judges.

That's normally not the kind of courtroom credentials a corporate lawyer can collect. To have the foundation of his maritime law practice grounded on the shipping industry with fully developed courtroom skills put Liam on a fast track to surpass his peers and elders.

And it just so happened that Liam was going to Singapore on business to meet fleet operators with our friend David Smith, a former British Merchant Navy Master Mariner, who was our big-ship marine surveyor. Liam nicknamed him "Union Jack" to contrast with law partner David U.S. Smith.

The Asian client visit with Union Jack was great timing. We had been tracking *Orient Lucky* for some months, monitoring its ports of call with Chet Hooper. At one point we were thinking about trying to have someone board it in South Africa, but the ship sailed before we could make arrangements there, and headed to Dumai, Indonesia, on the island of Sumatra, across the strait from Singapore.

Liam has himself to thank for what happened next. He had earlier pointed out that the email from *Orient Lucky* to Coast Guard Station Boston reporting the latitude/longitude of Nathan's rescue location could be inadmissible hearsay even if the Coast Guard receipt of the email would be admissible as a business record. We couldn't risk failing to get that location 106 miles south of Martha's Vineyard into evidence for use in Richard Limeburner's reverse drift analysis. And the only way to eliminate doubt would be to get the *Orient Lucky's* official chart with its course plot and deck log entries documenting where Nathan was "rescued."

We knew that *Orient Lucky* was owned by a one-ship Chinese entity but had no luck contacting it. But we also knew *Orient Lucky* was entered in the West of England Protection & Indemnity (P&I) Club, one of thirteen international mutual insurers, which together insure 90 percent of the world's shipping. I had done work for West over the years and Union Jack was very close with its higher ups. Thanks to his entrée, Liam got terrific help from West's Paul Barnes and authorization to board the ship and get the ship's documents certified. That grant of permission alone was a major accomplishment.

But it was only half the battle, the rest of which was right out of James Bond. Liam flew twenty-five hours from Boston to Singapore, the cushy part of his mission. Checking in to his hotel to shower and drop off his bags, our International Man of Intrigue then flew out of

Singapore with detailed instructions from the *Orient Lucky*'s local vessel agent on how to get through customs at the Pekanbaru airport in the middle of Sumatra.

Heavily armed guards, presumably official Indonesian military and not some coup, flanked the queue, Liam towering head and shoulders above all. When it was his turn at the customs booth for questioning on the purpose of his visit, Liam dutifully answered as instructed, "Tourism." And where precisely? "Dumai." Eyes very askance, Dumai being a pit, and for how long? "Twenty-four hours."

Liam's passport was inexplicably stamped, and he was on his way, deeply relieved he did not end up in an Indonesian jail.

To his next connection—the man in the terminal holding a sign, LAIM. Then into a rundown car with no air conditioning for a five-hour drive. The driver lit up a khat cigarette, which Liam knew can produce hallucinations, paranoia, and hyperactivity, so he breathed out the window in hopes of avoiding secondhand delusions, ready to grab the wheel if needed.

The two-lane road (well, mostly), frequently unpaved and muddy, cut through villages and thick jungle, drilled by Chevron to access the picturesque Port of Dumai. That doesn't mean it lacked traffic. Whole families on one motorcycle, multi-vehicle accidents, and overturned tractor trailers littered the way. After more than enough time for Liam to become acclimated to this exponential bumper car ride, the driver turned to introduce himself: "I Jazz. I Muslim."

Normally this would not matter one iota to Liam. But, under the overseas circumstances, should it? What if the Wild Men of Borneo paddled over to attack?

Unhealthy fears continuing to dance through his head, Liam upgraded his readiness posture (another Coastie phrase) when it was time to pull over for gas and a bathroom break. Yuck. Outside he took a selfie, texting it to me to establish his last whereabouts in case he ended up in a wooden cage deep in the jungle.

At the fly-infested café of sorts, Jazz purchased the fried ears of a large mammal, probably (Komodo dragons lack ears, right?), and coffee from locally grown beans, served in a nice cup and saucer, into which he flicked the ashes from yet another khat ciggy. Time to get back on the road, he swilled some coffee with the ashes and slurped it all down from the saucer. Concerned that psycho Jazz might now take off, Liam downed his own jet fuel java but otherwise fasted, his rising blood pressure exacerbating his worries.

The harrowing ride continued in searing heat and humidity through more impoverished humanity and squalor than a US citizen can imagine.

Upon arrival at the Port of Dumai, Indonesia Jones was relieved, as we always are, to see that in fact thar she blows, steam fumes even in equator weather billowing from the stack, with cargo operations in full swing, the words *Orient Lucky* high above the quay, knowing now with certainty that after all his efforts, the ship was actually there and had not sailed away after some last-minute change in itinerary. Finally within reach by the same steep gangway that Nathan was videoed negotiating without a misstep, Liam climbed up, on the exact opposite side of the world during his own mission to weld the evidence sinking Nathan's drift story into a known known—a flat-out lie.

Admitted aboard at the top by the gangway watch as one of the vessel's few authorized visitors, Liam was escorted to the captain, who was not the same as the one who took Nathan to Boston. But no matter, Federal Rule of Evidence 902(12) provides self-authentication of foreign-flag vessels' official logs and nautical charts, for automatic admission at trial. Liam had, in advance, prepared paper certifications to accomplish that, and with photos memorializing the captain's signatures, Nathan's fate was sealed.

The log established that on September 25, 2016 at 1320 local time, *Orient Lucky* picked up "survival Nathan Carman" at 39°-38.05'N,

070°-34.40'W,[84] 106 miles south of Martha's Vineyard, as plotted on British Admiralty Chart 2860, "Outer Approaches to New York."[85]

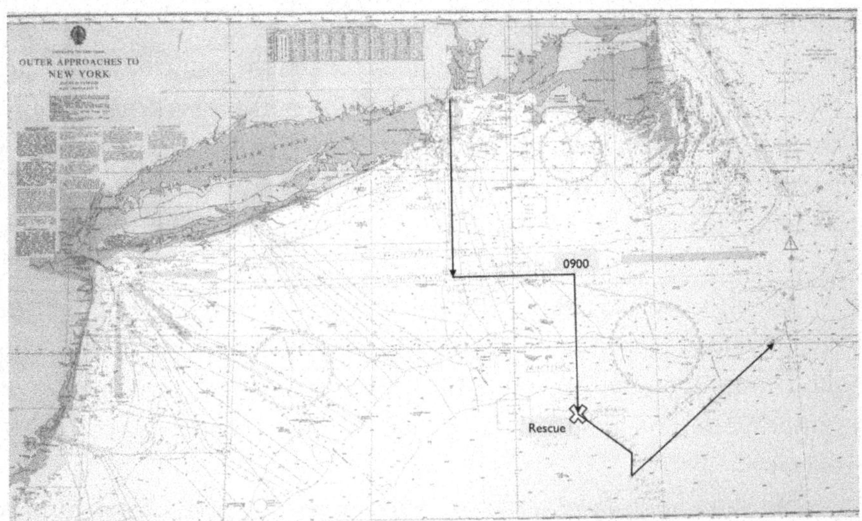

Fait accompli, Liam texted me with photos, which I received while in Göteborg for a half-marathon with the Swedish Club, another P&I Club. It gave me an endorphin high before I even got to the starting line. Sumatra was my running mantra that day, intriguingly my first navigation lesson on our West family friends' *Sumatra* melding with this navigation prize from Sumatra helped by our firm's West friends.

But Liam still had an Ironman competition ahead of him much more challenging than my 21K *Varvet*. First, Jazz let Liam know that it was too late to venture through the jungle back to Pekanbaru before dark, so they would have to stay overnight at the seedy Dumai hotel, something Liam dreaded. And second, Liam wore a coating of red odoriferous dust from the cargo all over his boots and clothes and hair.

---

84 Tr. Ex. 32.02.

85 Tr. Ex. 5.4.1. https://www.rid.uscourts.gov/sites/rid/files/documents/17cv38/082319/P5.4.1.pdf. With *Orient Lucky's* course line enhanced, note that the ship when south of Martha's Vineyard turns south from the outbound shipping lane at 0900. At the end of that leg Nathan was "rescued," and the ship then turned southeast and then northeast towards Boston.

Asking the chief mate what it was yielded this grim response—fertilizer. Liam might be able to depart on the plane from Pekanbaru, but arriving at Singapore with bomb ingredients detected could get him caned. At the hotel, he scrubbed and scrubbed.

The next morning, tour guide Jazz reversed their suicide alley route back to the airport for Liam's two-hour flight and another tense customs entry. But in a shipping hub like Singapore, it greatly helps to have a US passport and a maritime law business card. Terrorist residue notwithstanding. Liam somehow slid into the city-state and had a unique story with which to regale Union Jack and the clients.

He also had something else, which could have been any number of contagions picked up at the truck stop, aboard *Orient Lucky*, or in the Dumai Ritz. Feeling lousy, Liam went to a Singapore clinic before venturing west on his circumnavigation, with chart and log as carry-ons, of course.

With a raging fever and rash when he got back to Logan Airport in Boston, our hero was unable to enjoy the welcome awaiting him at home. Really sick, internet searches yielding a dengue fever self-diagnosis, Liam dragged himself to his family doctor's front porch that Sunday morning.

Emerging in his tighty-whities and a wife beater to examine six feet, four inches and 235 pounds of red pustules that made chickenpox look tame—a nice visual for which fortunately no photo is available—the roundish five-foot-four MD declared, "No Liam, it is not dengue fever. *Dengue* means 'crazy' in French. You are crazy, but not *that* crazy. Just stop taking the sulphur drug they gave you."

Sig

Windsor, Connecticut Police Detective Renee LeGeyt wanted to help us.

She'd read in the papers that we were all over Nathan and were hoping to get more on the John Chakalos murder. Her department had taken the lead on that investigation, but she would not talk substance to us without a subpoena.

One problem was, if we served the Windsor Police Department with a subpoena for its whole file, we would also have to serve Attorney Anderson a copy of the subpoena, and he would no doubt move to quash it as beyond Judge Sullivan's scope of discovery order. She, in turn, would grant that motion as a fishing expedition into all sorts of things beyond Nathan's intent.

So Liam and I toyed with narrowing a Windsor police subpoena to just seeking information about the Sig Sauer. But that presented strategic problems. Then Attorney Anderson and Nathan would know what we knew, and any surprise factor in the deposition resumption would evaporate. So I figured it was worthwhile to see if we could, on the off chance, first hunt down the Sig Sauer gun shop on our own. If we failed, we could always fall back on a Windsor police subpoena for whatever they knew about Nathan's purchase of "a Sig Sauer 716 Patrol .308 caliber rifle from a gun store in New Hampshire," as stated in the 2014 search warrant affidavit.

I directed my staff to go online and put together a list of all gun dealers in New Hampshire on a map and get prepared to canvass them all. While that was in process, two things jumped out at me. First, there was a Sig Sauer Academy in Epping ("Sunday, Sunday, New England Dragway"), New Hampshire. And second, while hundreds of gun shops were sprinkled all over the Granite State, there were some just off major highways which Nathan could have more easily accessed from his Connecticut apartment.

I made my first telephone call. A woman at the Sig Sauer Academy told me that a Nathan Carman had not purchased anything there, although he had signed up to take a course which he did not attend. Pretty good for a first call. She also gave me the names of several major Sig Sauer retailers, and I figured that's where cost-conscious Nathan would have been able to find the best price. Plus, he wouldn't so much stick out to some mom-and-pop gun dealers as the only customer that day.

After more calls—this all came together in about twenty-four hours—I scored with Shooters Outpost in Hookset, right off Interstate 93.

Unlike southern Maine's Kittery Trading Post, with fly rods and camping gear mixed in with hunting rifles and giant stuffed moose and bears, Shooters Outpost is more a big-box store for machine-gun and assault rifle enthusiasts, displaying only a couple of stuffed varmints. Hell, if you machine-gun a coyote there'd be nothing left to stuff.

A store like this was a new experience for me. I shuddered on reading a handwritten display card, "Ghetto Blaster," on a shelf, probably left by a customer because it contrasted with other printed display cards. It shocked me into realizing that a subgroup of assault rifle enthusiasts, which I had never given much thought to, actually felt that way.

Of more pertinence, the Shooters Outpost employees and owner Jim McLoud were very helpful and professional, aware of Nathan from the news. They gave me the name of the salesman, Jed Warner, who no longer worked there. I telephoned him at home. He clearly remembered the transaction with Nathan five years before. Nathan had done his homework and wanted to make sure the Sig Sauer he had his eye on could interchangeably fire Winchester .308 and NATO 7.62 ammunition. I arranged to get an affidavit from him, but unsurprisingly, Shooters Outpost would not give me the Sig Sauer purchase and sale records without a subpoena.

As much as we were getting warmer and warmer on the Sig, we were also getting pretty far afield from maritime law. I started wondering, what if some higher up at our marine insurance clients started squawking about our legal fees on the dry murder and decided to dump that on Holland & Knight to pursue on their own? But when I told Vince I'd found the New Hampshire gun store, any concerns lifted and he congratulated me in a way I'd never heard before, or since, in my career—"That's why you get the big bucks." Debatable.

Better yet, I had Vince's full support that he'd deal with any internal naysayers, and I knew his convincing feistiness would always prevail. We were onto Nathan like no one else, no one else knew it, and Vince would not let cost-conscious executives' knee-jerk reactions end our just pursuit of insurance fraud involving murder.

Vince was also 100 percent with me that we deal with the Sig Sauer ourselves and not hand it off to Holland & Knight for the Sisters' Slayer Suit. That might have been the cheaper way out for the Insurer, but we were just about to resume Nathan's deposition and could make better use of a Sig Sauer surprise in the Rhode Island federal case than Holland & Knight could in the New Hampshire state case where depositions had not started. Plus which (as they used to say on *LA Law*), Magistrate Judge Sullivan was receptive to our pursuit. New Hampshire Judge King, not so much. I informed Holland & Knight in strict confidence that they were going to have to wait, and they understood. Dan Small even told me on the phone, "You're my hero." Hold on, not yet.

After confirming with Vince and Martha, Liam and I refined our plan to resume Nathan's deposition and try to trap him on Sig Sauer testimony without his knowing we knew where he'd bought it. Only afterward would we let the cat out of the bag, an all-important legal concept not taught in law school.

We had a knowledgeable team. Liam knew all about firearms from his Coast Guard patrol boat days. Vince was a gun collector—I always found him to be a jack-of-all-trades—and he sent me an article, "The Truth About 7.62x51 mm NATO and .308 Winchester."[86] Highly technical, I gleaned that 7.62x51mm NATO military cartridges and .308

86 Lapua product catalog (2020). https://docslib.org/doc/13582199/the-truth-about-7-62x51mm-nato-and-308-winchester.

Winchester big-game cartridges are indeed interchangeable. The difference in their "chamber pressures," or power, is statistically insignificant, and while they share very similar exterior dimensions for the cartridge casings, there are minor yet certainly detectible differences.

Was that part of Nathan's plan? The Windsor police search warrant affidavit referenced "a Sig Sauer 716 Patrol .308 caliber rifle" but the Sig Sauer website showed the 716 as 7.62 NATO caliber. That seemed to confirm it could use both ammunition calibers interchangeably but did that double reasonable doubt that Nathan wanted to exploit? Was there a simple approach to avoid getting bogged down on technical ballistic details? We retained Richard Ernest from the Lone Star State, of course, as a firearms expert to explain all this.

17

HOOKED

Upon resuming Nathan's deposition on July 17, 2018, we still had to be efficient due to the two-hour time limit Judge Sullivan imposed. I started by knocking out some follow-up questions from the last deposition session.

Nathan's rationale for removing the plywood bulkheads during the summer of 2016, it became clear, was further specious. Using a RIDGID brand reciprocating saw, like a small Sawzall, Nathan testified that he cut the plywood at the bottom, where it was fiberglassed to the curve of the hull, but the cut wasn't flush and clean. Sharp splinters and shards of resin-hardened plywood still remained and there was no way to secure the rods or strap them down in those spaces.

So as the bow bounced up and down in the waves, not only would his expensive striper and more expensive tuna rods and reels get thrown around, sweating from the tropical humidity of bilge moisture, grease, and diesel heat, but the monofilament lines, too, would suffer abrasions. One little nick in the mono with a fish on—*snap*—it would be suddenly gone, as any heartbroken ten-year-old angler knows.

Someone as fishy as Nathan would never store rods that way. Seems Ed Niejadlik was right when he told Liam he never saw Nathan's fishing rods. Plus which, Nathan never produced any receipts for the rods despite our discovery requests. Nathan was a cheapskate, as we knew from his $600 stunt with Woods, so maybe buying tuna rods and reels costing hundreds of dollars was an unneeded expense. Save that money, cut out the bulkheads at no cost, use that as cover for no rods, and sink the boat faster. Brilliant. But only to Nathan the Genius.

We spent a little time on the life raft story. Besides deploying the life raft's drogue anchor six out of seven days adrift to slow it down, Nathan did not do anything else to maneuver the speed or direction of the life raft. No way he could have, but I wanted to rule out any later Nathan waffling in an effort to detract from oceanographer Richard Limeburner's still-secret opinion. And in collecting hypothermia evidence for the physician we were consulting, Nathan testified he was "uncomfortably cold at periods of time" and constantly needed to use "sponges to soak up the water and then ring them out overboard" and got wet "lying on the floor with water on it."

With that out of the way, I changed topics and bore in on specifics related to the grandfather's murder. Not long after his grandfather's death, Nathan testified he received unrestricted access to $560,000, comprised of inheritance, a related gift from his mother, and cash from a college savings plan. This was all due to changes his grandfather made to two accounts eight months before his death, with Nathan's knowledge. And with that money, he later bought his JC 31 from Brian Woods.

Getting into the Sig Sauer, I referenced where it was mentioned in the 2014 search warrant and asked Nathan, "Did you buy a .308

caliber firearm from anywhere prior to your grandfather's death?" He answered, "No." When I asked him about the Sig Sauer 716 .308 Patrol Rifle mentioned in the 2014 search warrant he testified, "I've never owned a Sig Sauer 716 .308 caliber gun." And while he admitted that on the morning of the murder, he and his mother had gone fishing on a Frances Fleet head boat out of Point Judith which lasted most of the day, he denied throwing any firearms off the boat then.

It struck me that Nathan was either flat-out lying or extremely precise about the highly technical differences between .308 Winchester and 7.62 NATO interchangeable ammunition. He even testified, "I believe that there is no such thing" as a "Sig Sauer 716 Patrol .308 caliber rifle." We might only find out by looking at the Shooters Outpost purchase and sale records' description of what he bought after we subpoenaed them. So I simply dropped the .308 inquiry, asking more broadly, "Did you ever buy a Sig Sauer rifle of any caliber?" Nathan's answer was just what we were looking for.

> A: On the advice of Counsel, I invoke my Fifth Amendment privilege against self-incrimination on the basis of the Fifth and Fourteenth Amendments.
>
> Q: Did you ever buy a Sig Sauer 716 Patrol rifle?
>
> A: I invoke my Fifth Amendment privilege.
>
> Q: Did you ever own a Sig Sauer 716 Patrol Rifle?
>
> A: I invoke my Fifth Amendment privilege.
>
> Q: Did you ever purchase a Sig Sauer rifle from a gun store in New Hampshire?
>
> A: I invoke my Fifth Amendment privilege.
>
> Q: Did you buy a Sig Sauer anywhere prior to your grandfather's death?

A: I invoke my Fifth Amendment privilege.

Hooked!

While the US Constitution protects citizens from criminal self-incrimination, it is very different in civil cases. Nathan's taking the Fifth not only made him look bad, under civil case law it generally supports an inference that his withheld answers were detrimental to him.

A couple of quick, related questions on the grandfather's murder set the hook. The Windsor search warrant affidavit alleged Nathan discarded his computer hard drive and his truck's GPS after his grandfather's murder, and Nathan admitted doing that—but he took the Fifth on why.

Maybe we couldn't hide our glee at the same time that Attorney Anderson couldn't hide his torment. But he wasn't quite sure why. Which made him stress even more. He finally couldn't stand it and started barking, and I passive-aggressively suspended the deposition for a second time, for another motion to compel. I then looked at Liam, and we nodded to each other, not trying too hard to conceal that from Attorney Anderson. Liam pressed Send on his laptop, and an email with a copy of a subpoena to Shooters Outpost landed in Anderson's inbox.

We then had the subpoena immediately served on Shooters Outpost and shortly in return received certified paper records of the Sig sale to Nathan on November 11, 2013. He had falsely claimed New Hampshire residence on the federal Bureau of Alcohol, Tobacco, Firearms and Explosives (ATF) form required of all firearm purchases, using his grandfather's West Chesterfield address. Dan Small then checked Nathan's credit card records, of course paid for by John Chakalos, evidencing Nathan's gas purchases and Massachusetts Turnpike toll charges on his trip from Connecticut to Shooters Outpost and back to Connecticut that day. The younger Desperado had left tracks, for the last time.

18

NATHAN'S RUN

As a nursing home magnate, John Chakalos was more familiar with hospice than most. That was his wife Rita's plight on November 11, 2013, the day Nathan bought his Sig Sauer. She succumbed to cancer ten days later. For Nathan, that meant one domino down, two to go. And for John? He was already a step ahead. The whole thing triggered Nathan back then. Five years later, now firmly on the hook, he did whatever he could to shake free.

But Nathan's 2018 run in our case bore no resemblance to the powerful yet graceful flight of a hooked sailfish, which he was never going to catch. It started with Nathan entirely out of sight when it first went public.

It was just the lawyers in front of Judge Sullivan on September 18, 2018 (two years after the claimed sinking) with another of our Insurer's motions to compel testimony from Nathan. The real parties to a lawsuit (the Insurer and Nathan in this case) don't attend motion hearings like this; typically lawyers tell their clients, interested though they might be, to stay home and thereby avoid getting called to the witness stand by the other side, unprepared. This time Liam and I were primarily seeking answers on the current whereabouts of the now very-well-documented Sig Sauer and Attorney Anderson was fighting his utmost to prevent that.

There was a lot of back-and-forth between Judge Sullivan and me, and between Judge Sullivan and Attorney Anderson, and between Attorney Anderson and me. Judge Sullivan kept it from becoming a free-for-all, repeatedly pulling the lawyers back to the issues before the court. I was arguing that the Insurers needed a discovery cutoff date extension, which had expired, so we could complete Nathan's deposition. I made the point that we did not have the Shooters Outpost records at the time of Nathan's second deposition and deserved another opportunity to question him about them. After more back-and-forth, Judge Sullivan announced:

> The noncompleted discovery is not the product of inactivity and doing nothing by the Plaintiff. Clearly, you've been pursuing it. You've met with barrier after barrier. You had a breakthrough through your own investigative efforts. Now you need to complete the deposition. Discovery needs to be recalibrated, the deadlines, so all that can happen.[87]

Whew, very good.

That opened up the next logical dispute on whether Nathan had waived his Fifth Amendment right against self-incrimination on questions we wanted to ask in the deposition about the Sig Sauer as described in the Shooter's Outpost records. Liam briefed that Nathan had waived it, by already answering some of my deposition questions about the Sig Sauer without asserting the Fifth.

But Attorney Anderson was now arguing that the only reason Nathan took the Fifth in the first place had nothing to do with his grandfather's murder but everything to do with the post-Sandy Hook, Connecticut assault rifle ban. If Nathan's testimony showed he ever simply had possession of the Sig Sauer in Connecticut, he'd be slapped with

---

87 ECF No. 91 at 20.

an automatic prison sentence under the Sandy Hook statute. He had to clam up for that reason and that reason alone. A very nice argument. But it too had holes.

Judge Sullivan from the bench weighed the opposing arguments, concluding it a close call, but she was not going to handcuff Nathan from taking the Fifth in our third deposition session. She gave us ninety more minutes and limited my questions to those arising from the Shooters Outpost records. And she agreed with Liam's briefing that in this civil case (as opposed to a criminal case), any question Nathan refused to answer by taking the Fifth could give rise to an "adverse inference" against him.

This was all received by Attorney Anderson, hemming and hawing, as very grim news indeed. He had no need to consult with the absent Nathan. If things went south for them at the hearing, Attorney Anderson already had his marching orders.

Nathan, with a hook firmly set in his own mouth, through his mouthpiece peeled off line, starting his frantic run for innocence and freedom, initially with a down and dirty deep dive. Announced Attorney Anderson, abruptly and with fanfare, in open court:

> There is evidence that the night of the murder, that the decedent, Mr. Chakalos, had a fairly lengthy telephone conversation with a woman with whom he was having a relationship which involved an exchange of money for sexual favors.
>
> There is evidence that on the morning of his death, that he went to a store, that he purchased an item which one could reasonably conclude was to be used with this woman.
>
> There is evidence that this individual had ties with organized crime, specifically running drugs, including marijuana—excuse me, heroin and cocaine.[88]

---

[88] ECF No. 91 at 34-35.

So much for Nathan's abiding love for his grandfather.

Attorney Anderson's argument continued, if the Insurers get to depose Nathan for a third time, Defendant should be able to defend himself by taking three new depositions on the grandfather's murder, citing "what's good for the goose is good for the gander" as precedent.

We'll go through the three deponents in order, all women, who supposedly exculpate Nathan. They do not.

Mistress Y

First, there was the newly revealed mystery woman in John Chakalos's life. Because there was later a court order protecting her name from public identification, it will not be mentioned here. It certainly added intrigue to Nathan's criminal reasonable doubt for Attorney Anderson to only identify her salaciously as Mistress Y.

Liam and I knew something like this was coming. We had enough intel from our own investigation and a tip from Holland & Knight to have seen Facebook photos (deleted long ago) which can accurately be described as depicting an alluring young woman, including one photo of her in a cheap Halloween getup. Not only old men would be tantalized.

Particularly in person…which grandfather and grandson both got to experience when (still just) Ms. Y began working for one of the Chakalos companies. The three met in the spring of 2013—John Chakalos the boss, Nathan Carman his unpaid interlocutor, and Ms. Y, immediately aware of longing stares from both.

Alas, poor Nathan was destined to lose out to the rich old buck. Lunch dates soon ensued, but only on one leg of the triangle. According to Attorney Anderson's October 22, 2018 brief,[89] John gave "'Mistress Y' increasingly large gifts of cash ranging from $100 to $800…in exchange for sexual favors." Nathan, the odd man out, would be left behind, fuming, jealous, salivating, instead heading alone to Keene State to look at college girls, creeping them out.

---

[89] ECF No. 88 at 4-10.

When wife Rita died on November 21, 2013, any guilt felt by the John evaporated. The weekend preceding his murder, the two like birds headed to the opulence of Connecticut's Mohegan Sun casino for an overnight. The standout couple strolled the adult playground as yokel jet-setters. After some celebrity chef's foodie creation, no doubt, piled atop a tender bed of arugula, crowned with a plop of locally sourced pureed turnip, an exciting night of fun and games lay ahead.

To warm up, John sponsored Mistress Y's gambling to the tune of $3,500 in cash, as a kind gesture toward her newly minted "boob job."

Then back to the multiroom hotel suite, the swanky likes of which Mistress Y had never seen, where the sex games were set to kick off. But she elected not to receive. Although "she showed him her boobs," due to the recent surgery she wasn't quite ready for the red rubber thing John had packed, the same color as his Jaguar. Of course it was! In any event, she thought it "way too big." So all they did was sleep together. She kept it to "kissing and heavy petting" and "never had sexual intercourse with him."[90]

Not one to give up, the aged machine-gunner battled on. With Christmas without Rita around the corner, Chakalos family celebrations would be subdued this season of grief, so John made it known he planned to lie low, and who could blame him? Better to sneak off to New York City with Mistress Y.

Rockefeller Center Christmas Tree and Rainbow Room plans took shape. Titillating teasing by telephone in the wee hours. Presents to purchase. On John's last day—Thursday December 19, 2013—he shopped for more "sexual paraphernalia" at Luv Boutique in Hartford, as Attorney Anderson wrote in his brief fingering suspects not named Nathan Carman.

That brief constituted Nathan's best shot to dispel allegations that he murdered his grandfather. "Evidence from 'Mistress Y' dramatically alters our preconceived notions of what 87 year old grandfathers do with their spare time,"[91] wrote Attorney Anderson, adopting the trendy

---

[90] ECF No. 88 at 5-6; ECF No. 88-2.

[91] ECF No. 88 at 9.

legal strategy of throwing someone, anyone, under the bus. *The Boston Globe* headlined, "In twist, Nathan Carman's lawyers point at 'Mistress Y' in grandfather's murder."[92] A *Boston Herald* article, "Nathan Carman lawyer airs dirty laundry," reported that the Sisters were incensed, quoting Dan Small, "Nathan's shameful attack on his Grandfather today shows there is no depth to which he will not sink to avoid producing his gun, which is the probable murder weapon."[93]

Interviewed in 2014 several times by the Windsor Police Department, Mistress Y was deposed absent her own counsel in 2018 by pro se Nathan in the New Hampshire probate case. Judge Sullivan also granted Attorney Anderson's motion to subsequently have at her, but strictly limited his deposition to nothing repetitive or harassing. The only notable exchange during that second deposition was Mistress Y's newly retained Attorney Andrea Kramer's passionate dressing down of Attorney Anderson. It was reassuring to see that he irritated non-maritime lawyers too. Regrettably for the reading public, these two depositions are subject to confidentiality court orders that protect the innocent, although it is unclear who that is.

Assuredly, though, Mistress Y was innocent of murdering her geriatric suitor, despite Attorney Anderson's briefing that robbery was the motive.

> [S]he was directly involved either individually or through an accomplice. "Mistress Y" had knowledge that John Chakalos was worth millions, that he was 87 years old, hard of hearing, that he always had large amounts of cash… Simply stated "Mistress Y" had knowledge that John Chakalos was a very easy &

---

92 Travis Andersen, *Boston Globe*, "In twist, Nathan Carman's lawyers point at 'Mistress Y' in grandfather's murder," October 22, 2018. https://www.bostonglobe.com/metro/2018/10/22/new-twist-nathan-carman-lawyers-point-finger-mistress-wealthy-grandfather-murder/P3Akk0GBh93tOMghKyMB0J/story.html.

93 Laurel J. Sweet, *Boston Herald*, "Nathan Carman Lawyer Airs Dirty Laundry," October 26, 2018 (updated November 14, 2018). https://www.bostonherald.com/2018/10/26/nathan-carman-lawyer-airs-dirty-laundry/.

> lucrative target… It is also plausible that "Mistress Y's" boyfriend, motivated by jealously or greed, committed the murder.[94]

The huge problem with that defense theory, though, was police photos documenting the remaining presence of hundreds of dollars of cash out in the open all over John Chakalos's home/office after the murder, on his desk, in his bedroom—left behind by Mistress Y and/or the greedy boyfriend "who had a history of drug abuse"[95] and has since died.

In sum, Mistress Y and her young ex-boyfriend did not do it. The murder, that is.

Aunt Valerie

A deposition of Nathan's Aunt Valerie Santilli (the lead Plaintiff in the Sisters' Slayer Suit) was also approved by Judge Sullivan, notwithstanding Attorney Anderson's attempt to throw mud against the wall, hoping some would stick. Claimed Attorney Anderson in his October 22, 2018 brief:

> [Valerie Santilli] had a far stronger motive to murder John Chakalos and in fact the evidence of her involvement with the murder is stronger than the evidence of Nathan Carman's involvement. It should be noted that Defendant is not suggesting that the evidence of Mrs. Santilli's involvement is particularly strong, it is not, but it is stronger than the evidence against Mr. Carman.[96]

One problem with that assertion was that Valerie, and also Linda and the other two sisters, had passed lie detector tests. And when Attorney Anderson deposed Valerie, he turned up nothing remotely suggesting her involvement in her father's murder. To the contrary,

---

94 ECF No. 88 at 9.

95 ECF No. 88 at 7.

96 ECF No. 88 at 11.

Valerie's deposition backfired on Nathan, with his long-term financial motive solidly put into evidence.

Aunt Valerie was the executrix of John Chakalos's estate. While she did not know the intricacies of his very complex estate planning documents, and deferred on those particulars to Attorney Caroline Demirs Calio, her father's trust and estate attorney, and Bill Rabbitt, her father's financial advisor, Valerie's testimony was very clear on the big picture. She testified, as both Attorney Calio and Mr. Rabbitt had confirmed to me, that Nathan was unusually involved in his grandfather's finances, frequently attending estate planning meetings with them. Extraordinarily, the grandfather would often give in to his oldest grandson's demands.

Aunt Valerie provided fascinating financial testimony in her deposition, stating that in 2012 Nathan, then seventeen years old, had created an intent road map consisting of written inquiries he posed to Attorney Calio. Nathan had requested in writing that she provide him "a copy of the organizing documents for the trust of which I am a beneficiary" and wanted to know "what the trust(s) mean(s) to me now."[97]

Perhaps nothing terribly alarming there, a pretty basic question from a would-be heir, I suppose. And it was all fine by the grandfather.

But from a seventeen-year-old? As Aunt Valerie questioned during her deposition:

> When most children are out there educating themselves or working or trying to make for their own, his obsession was this money trail, and I mean, I don't know how many teenagers would call up an estate attorney and have a meeting with an estate attorney to understand, you know, their benefits in the future when their mother is dead. I mean, who thinks of their 40-year-old mother as being dead? I mean, she's not even sick. We're not talking a cancer patient here.[98]

---

97 Deposition of Valerie C. Santilli (hereafter Santilli Dep.), Ex. 2.

98 Santilli Dep. at 290.

Check out Nathan's specific written questions: What happens "if or when certain scenarios present themselves in the future?" To wit, what happens "[u]pon my grandfather's passing?"

Having "already learned that upon the death of my mother I will take her place as the primary beneficiary of the dynasty trust," and "I will begin to receive the regular payments that she currently receives from the trust," Nathan then asked, "When this happens," (like he expected it would, sooner rather than later), "Is there a stipulation stating that I am not to receive such payments until a certain age even if my mother passes prior to my achieving that age?"[99] Nathan's roadmap to his Dynasty Trust dollars eliminated Attorney Anderson's contention in his brief that "Nathan Carman did not have a financial incentive to murder his grandfather." And mother.

Furthermore, despite Nathan's testifying that his immediate post-grandfather haul was $560,000, Valerie testified that Nathan had unrestricted and immediate access to as much as $850,000 upon his grandfather's death. This consisted of a "second-to-die account" which Nathan jointly held with his grandfather (pretty good odds for Nathan, age seventeen, *v.* John, age eighty-seven) and which Nathan had earlier demanded during a "heated argument" in Bill Rabbitt's office; a tuition account (which the flunked-out genius would not need now); and also $300,000 Linda had earlier signed over to Nathan, upon the death of her father.[100]

These are strong reasons for steeper estate taxation.

Aunt Valerie also testified that Linda had disinherited Nathan in her own will, its major asset being her house. This was also conveyed in a video Linda filmed for Nathan in case she wasn't around. She probably had a fatalistic inkling that might be the case, and/or if she cut him out face-to-face, that might be it, then and there.

"Hey, Big Guy. I guess if you're watching this, you're watching this," Linda's video started out, with a tautology even someone who thinks "differently than many people" could understand. As a genius, he could

---

99 Santilli Dep., Ex. 2.

100 Santilli Dep. at 288-89.

also comprehend that Linda's disinheritance of him from her house did not affect his big-ticket item—the Chakalos Family Dynasty Trust—as she made clear.

The nursing home millions in the Dynasty Trust were split four ways among the four sisters, and with Linda's irrevocable signature there was no way she or anyone else could prevent her quarter share upon her death from going to Nathan—her only issue—as the law used to call offspring. As Aunt Valerie testified in her deposition, Linda had "signed a piece of paper that said her trust must flow directly to Nathan. She couldn't alter the flow of her trust.... So once she signed that paper, it was set in stone that her trust—the benefits of her trust—would go directly down to Nathan," her only offspring. While he would not be getting it as a lump sum, because all the Sisters were currently receiving amounts "distributed every month," it meant that Linda's quarter portion of the Dynasty Trust's millions and millions of dollars would end up going straight to Nathan as soon as Grandmother Rita, Grandfather John, and Mother Linda were out of the way.[101]

But her Big Boy needed all three dominos to fall first. Which is what this story is all about. The last domino was stickier than Nathan had envisioned.

It surprised me that with the Sisters' Slayer Suit stating that Linda "has been missing at sea since September 2016,"[102] when I asked Valerie whether she believed Linda "died on the boat trip," she answered:

> A: I'm just thinking, you hear crazy stories about whatever. What I can affirmatively say, that what I believe, is that Nathan took Linda out that day with the intent of not bringing her back and her not coming back. I can only imagine what

---

[101] Santilli Dep. at 299.

[102] Petition for Declaratory Judgment, Replevin, Restitution & Other Equitable Relief, & to Impose a Constructive Trust, *Santilli v. Carman*, No. 313-2017-EQ-00396 (N.H. 6th Cir. Prob. Div. July 17, 2017).

> happened to her out there, but I can say that his intent was for her not to come back to dry land.[103]

Why was Valerie so disingenuously hesitating?

> A: It's difficult for me to believe that Linda is dead.
>
> Q: Why is that?
>
> A: She's my sister, and to think of what she went through on that boat—I mean, who knows what she went through, didn't go through. A million scenarios go through your mind. I can say I believe she's not coming home, or to any home; that Linda is out at sea.[104]

What?

> A: My sister is not deceased.
>
> Q: Meaning Linda?
>
> A: Correct.
>
> Q: In the eyes of some court or state, is that the point?
>
> A: Correct.[105]

It would take seven years after Linda first went missing—not until September 17, 2023—for her to be deemed dead under the law of Connecticut, her state of residence. Valerie did not want to accelerate that date so that Nathan could accelerate receipt of his blood money.

---

[103] Santilli Dep. at 294.
[104] Santilli Dep. at 317.
[105] Santilli Dep. at 293.

Neighbor X

The third witness Attorney Anderson wanted to depose, and Judge Sullivan approved, on paper seemed like a possible exculpatory witness. Attorney Anderson called her "Neighbor X," again adding intrigue, even though he provided her name in public docket filings.

Neighbor X lived with her mother next door to the Chakalos residence. At 2:00 a.m. on Saturday December 21, 2013—about twenty-four hours after the murder—Neighbor X reported to Windsor police that the morning before, "at about 0200 hours" she heard "a loud bang" coming from the Chakalos house and her dog "began barking." Then "[a]t about 0300 hours," she woke up to "squealing" tires and "was annoyed and then went back to sleep."[106]

According to Attorney Anderson's brief:

> Deposition testimony from "Neighbor X" is highly relevant because this testimony tends to establish that John Chakalos was **not** murdered during the one hour time period (0257–0400) which the Warrant Affidavit claims Mr. Carman is "unaccounted for." Simply stated, if John Chakalos was shot at 2:00 am, then Nathan Carman clearly was not the murderer.[107]

Tellingly, however, Attorney Anderson never took Neighbor X's deposition. If she was truly Nathan's salvation, so "highly relevant" as claimed, the rule is, depose her now and compile a transcript that can be submitted in lieu of her testimony at trial—in case she dies or for whatever reason becomes unavailable—the same sort of thinking that compelled us to depose hole saw Mike Iozzi ASAP.

Attorney Anderson scheduled her deposition but then cancelled it—perhaps an indication that she was not going to be a very good witness for Nathan. Why was she up at 2:00 a.m. both days? Was she just off by an hour? Maybe the clock she'd been looking at was simply

[106] ECF No. 88-1 (Windsor Police Department Supplement Report).

[107] ECF No. 88 at 4 (emphasis in original).

incorrect? Did she need an unrelated alibi? Maybe she was worried someone would point to her as the culprit? Do two or three Sig Sauer rounds "a loud bang" make? Then followed by squealing tires, but no 911 call? Maybe those squealing tires were indeed Nathan's?

Neighbor X's simple written statement raised lots of questions. And it was just paper. Nathan on his desperate run and his mouthpiece chose not to turn her supposed observations into admissible evidence.

***

There were other speculative suspects not named Nathan Carman. A Chakalos bookkeeper was convicted of absconding with several hundred thousand dollars. And there were the other two sisters, and their husbands, who might have wanted the patriarch out of the way to pave quickened paths to heightened luxury. But if Attorney Anderson didn't finger them or anyone else, we didn't see any reason to spend much time chasing them down either.

None of them, to our knowledge, ever owned a .308 Winchester/7.62 NATO caliber assault rifle.

19

WHAT WE HAD LEARNED ABOUT THE LAST SUPPER

(DECEMBER 19, 2013)

John Chakalos's final evening, Thursday, December 19, 2013 was right after Nathan's fall semester grades came out. Admitting his community college four F's at a Greek restaurant to the Emperor of Education could not have gone well at all. Despite his genius and business acumen, the Heir Apparent (if only in his mind) to the Chakalos business empire was about to be cut off from everything he had worked so hard in his nineteen years to achieve—his own truck, his own apartment, and his own credit card—all expenses paid.

Nathan had contingencies for this personal disaster, however.

With Grandmother Rita already out of the way, the second of his financial road map's "certain scenarios" presented itself, triggered by a phone call Nathan overheard between Mistress Y and his quite deaf grandfather a few hours after the four-F dinner. As briefed by Attorney

Anderson, after answering Mistress Y's December 19, 2013, telephone call at 8:36 p.m.:

> John Chakalos told her that Nathan was just leaving and asked "Mistress Y" to give him a minute "to say goodbye to my grandson." Thereafter John Chakalos and "Mistress Y" spoke on the phone for approximately 20 minutes. This 20 minute conversation was sexual in nature. During this 20 minute conversation on the evening of his murder, John Chakalos told "Mistress Y" that he was not happy with what happened at Mohegan Sun.[108]

And neither was lingering big ears Nathan, whose unhappiness far exceeded his unhappiness regarding the apparently unused red thing. It came down to his bottom line, about to bottom out along with his grades. So he came back a little later. From a safe distance outside the splatter zone, the Sig blew a hole in his sleeping grandfather's head, with a second shot to the right lower back. According to an unclassified FBI report dated July 18, 2014:

> Based upon the confusing layout of the multi-level home, it appears the offender was familiar with the residence and the location of the victim's bedroom....
>
> The use of a high power rifle to kill an 87 year old man reflects the offender's need to use a weapon that would ensure the victim's death. The number of shots fired into the victim highlights the motivation which was to kill the victim. The final round was a coup de grâce shot fired to ensure the death of the victim.

Nathan immediately picked up the shells and made his escape, breaking a backdoor window to make it look like forced entry by an outsider. But he got it backwards, busting the glass from the inside so

---

[108] ECF No. 88 at 7.

it fell outwards. He perhaps got a big break. He left behind a black hair with the broken glass, but the police apparently lost it. But knowing Nathan, maybe it was someone else's he'd planted there.

Recall that other important things got lost too—the GPS from Nathan's truck and his computer hard drive, both of which the Desperado destroyed, to cover his tracks. Nathan was supposed to meet his mother at 3:00 a.m. in Glastonbury, and he, too, went missing, as Attorney Anderson admitted. On December 20, 2013, actually between 2:50 a.m. (video showing him leaving his apartment) and 4:11 a.m. (Glastonbury gas station video), Nathan is "unaccounted for."[109] His cell phone was off during that time too, his mother's four "where are you?" calls during that hour unanswered, eliminating a very good shoreside tracking tool. He weakly explained to police he had gotten lost driving around—within a few miles of where he had lived all his life.

A most significant event in the murder evolution, a word that works well here too, is Nathan's and Linda's departure a little later that morning, before sunrise Friday, December 20, 2013, for the fishing trip aboard the *Gail Frances* out of Point Judith. This was no Boston Whaler but a ninety-foot vessel headed offshore in winter.

While there are some people who like to catch a nice December codfish, this is hardly a widespread Yuletide festivity, but it fit perfectly with Nathan's plans. He bought tickets a few days before, knowing his grades would be coming out. They'd be fishing fifteen miles or more southeast of Block Island in over one hundred feet of water. And there is Frances Fleet video of him boarding that morning with a duffle bag which surely could contain a broken-down Sig Sauer.

Nathan testified during our second deposition session that he was seasick much of the trip. (He never mentioned that affliction in the life raft.) More likely throwing up in guilt, if he felt any. While outside to get some air, and out of passenger and crew view, he discreetly tossed the Sig Sauer barrel here—miles later, the stock there, and miles later, the remaining components everywhere, never to be reconstructed or ballistically tested.

---

[109] ECF No. 37-4; ECF No. 80 at 3.

When they got back late that afternoon, the Windsor police already wanted to talk with Nathan, interviewing him on video.

> DETECTIVE DeJESUS: Do you own any firearms?
>
> MR. CARMAN: I do have an air gun. I'm not sure if that counts as a firearm, but—
>
> DETECTIVE DeJESUS: Is that the only—
>
> MR. CARMAN: Yes, it is.

Certainly it's hard to say Nathan wasn't telling the whole truth and nothing but the truth on those questions, having just relinquished Sig ownership to the sea.

Then, after the weekend, on Monday December 23, 2013, perhaps the most bizzarro scenes in this case took place at the Hartford Greek Orthodox Cathedral. This would have been before the John Chakalos funeral. Attorney Dan Small and Nathan, pro se, later deposed the Reverand Dr. Gheorghita Zugravu in the New Hampshire case, during which the priest set the cathedral stage.

Father Zugravu testified that John Chakalos was one of the cathedral's "great benefactors," annually contributing thousands and thousands of dollars, including a good chunk for the cathedral dome's "twenty-three-carat gold" leaf. He was "gruff on the outside, but inside always a very good soul." Even if John once "smashed the door" in the good Father's office and there is still a "hole in the sheetrock." After Rita died, "John Chakalos was saying he would like to do something for my angel." (Particularly since he had done something for the less than angelic Mistress Y?)

Sometimes John brought Nathan along on these tithing meetings, beseeching and negotiating with God's rep.

> I want, Father, for him to be standing on his legs, and just to be self-sufficient. I want him to do well with school and everything else, please, can you pray harder

> for that? I'm paying all this money for the church, but can you pray harder, can you do that for me?

Anyway, the transactional prayers didn't work, even if Father Zugravu did not so testify. But what he did say was that he observed Nathan on December 23 in the front of the church, kneeling at the steps to the altar, in the orans position—fervently praying with his hands out, palms up—for five hours while Linda waited in the back.

Several times Father Zugravu approached Nathan, intending to offer condolences and compassion, when at one point he heard Nathan say, "'God, please forgive me,'" repeated a "couple of times."

There was no other conversation until just before 4:00 p.m. in the back of the church. "I said that I'm so sorry about your loss, of course. I embraced them, and obviously Nathan and Linda, they were pretty traumatized." And "[w]e were discussing about how much we are going to miss John, and Nathan was saying that, you know, 'I loved him' and all that, but then it came out of nowhere," and Nathan said that "'whoever did this should be forgiven.' And I think that Linda turned to him and said, 'Well, I'm not ready for that.'... She was really—I don't want to call her mad, but she was quite 'I'm not ready for that'— very articulate, and very stern in speak."

Father Zugravu then made the point that none of this was "given to me in a confessional setting," meaning that it was not protected by the priest-penitent privilege and was all out in the open.

What did it mean legally? Was it admissible evidence? As Nathan quite properly asked Father Zugravu on cross-exam during the deposition, "Do you know if I was recounting specific occasions when I had been less than a perfect grandson before each time I said, 'Please forgive me?'" Nathan neither got an answer to that nor very far when he tried to engage his witness on the Lord's Prayer—"'Forgive us our trespasses, as we forgive those who trespass against us'"—but Nathan strongly made his point. Anything he said during, and maybe everything about the cathedral scene, would probably be excluded as an arguable admission of his guilt because the "probative value is substantially outweighed" by the danger of undue prejudice against him under Federal Rule of Evidence 403.

Then again, combining the unconventional post-deaths cathedral scene and Nathan's letter to Captain Zhao might with some creativity come in.

Nathan faced a bigger evidentiary problem, however, with what he said a few weeks later on January 14, 2014, in another police interview following up on his air gun and a shotgun he purchased after his grandfather's murder. Note that Nathan not only administered himself the oath of truthfulness, he also did not invoke the Fifth Amendment.

> MR. CARMAN: You can assume it's the truth when I say something to you here....
>
> DETECTIVE MacGREGOR: So you have one air gun and one Remington shotgun?
>
> MR. CARMAN: That's correct.
>
> DETECTIVE MacGREGOR: I just want to make sure. So one air gun and one shotgun. No other?
>
> MR. CARMAN: That's correct.
>
> DETECTIVE MacGREGOR: Any other purchases of a firearm at any time?
>
> MR. CARMAN: No.

Certainly, it's easy to say Nathan wasn't telling the truth on that question.

***

It wasn't just the police who were interested in Nathan's firearms. After Linda disappeared, the Sisters insisted on getting to the bottom of the missing Sig Sauer as key evidence that would tie together the two deaths and Nathan's attempt to fast-track his inheritance.

A meeting was held in a Connecticut coffee shop, with Nathan proposing a *laissez-faire rapprochement,* translated by Aunt Valerie as "things are where they are, why can't we just move forward and all get along?" Sipping with a similarly suspicious Sharon Hartstein, Aunt Valerie responded that before exploring any possible *entente*, "Nathan, you have to answer this question for me, for us to move forward. Where is the gun Nathan? Where is the gun?… If you're innocent, clear your name. Do the right thing…. If you're truly innocent, we will work together to help you through this. Where's the gun?"

But Nathan told them nothing. Because he knew that Valerie knew "that was the gun that was used to murder John."[110]

[110] Santilli Dep. at 303–06.

20

HARPOONED

We decided to resume Nathan's deposition, Act III, in a Brattleboro, Vermont law office on October 29, 2018.

I contacted Brattleboro Attorney Jonathan D. Secrest, who cordially let us rent his firm's conference room for the morning. Knowing full well that Nathan's Sig Sauer would never again see the light of day, we nevertheless demanded that Attorney Anderson produce it, as identified in the Shooters Outpost invoice, at the Brattleboro law office concurrent with the deposition resumption. This would foreclose any refusal to produce the Sig in Massachusetts, which also bans assault rifles, or in Rhode Island, which has no ban, since Nathan would have to travel through the Massachusetts and Connecticut bans in order to get there from Vermont.

The afternoon before I drove up to get a lay of the land. I still use road maps and was surprised, I suppose, to see a village named Satan's Kingdom, Massachusetts, just over the border from Nathan's town of Vernon, Vermont.

I first conducted a half dozen drive-bys of Nathan's house, on cruise control at thirty-five mph, spread out over the course of an hour. This southeast corner of the Green Mountain State near the Connecticut

River is flat, sprinkled with small farmhouses, none affluent. Nathan's ugly structure stood out, with a lot of clutter outside and a collapsing barn. It was hardly unique for New England, or anywhere. Objectively looking at it, and similar properties, say, a long unpainted Maine antique with old washing machines in the door yard, or a California desert stucco fortress plausibly with a meth lab underneath, you always imagine there's some sort of economic/psychologic/sociologic issue going on with the inhabitants, with violent crimes something you wouldn't be at all shocked to learn about on the evening news. In sum, nothing about Nathan's home at 3043 Fort Bridgman Road dissuaded me that he murdered both his grandfather and mother.

He didn't seem to be there. So I headed to the Chakalos estate on the New Hampshire side of the river in West Chesterfield, fifteen miles away. Playing nosy tourist, I just drove up the hill and turned around and slowly went back down. Again, no one around. A nice spread, but the whole place was way too ornate for my New England tastes; sculptures in rural settings are like oil and water.

I followed Route 9 back to the West Brattleboro rotary for supper and the Hampton Inn for free breakfast near a Dunkin' Donuts for more fuel, and the next morning got to the law office early. I had arranged for coverage by the Windham County Sheriff and the Deputy's car was already parked outside. I advised him there was no way Nathan was going to show up with the Sig Sauer but I didn't know whether he might otherwise be packing, and of course the Deputy got it. Nathan had been a local person of interest for a couple of years now.

Then Liam arrived, liveried by his mother in his big black GMC pickup so he could get work done on the three-hour drive. I thought that was great, and thanked them both, as it was the kind of thing my parents would do for me when they were alive. They parked next to my big white Silverado pickup.

It was raining hard as we two cowboys strode inside. We don't know if the Desperado got frisked when he arrived, but we were much obliged that Deputy Dawg was there. Plus which, his presence must have piled on for Nathan the seriousness of this videoed deposition, and he had to be (or any reasonable, normal thinking person, and counsel, should have been) regretting the misguided decision to make his $85,000 hull insurance claim.

Court reporter Lauren and the videographer were all set up. Pretty promptly in came Attorney Anderson and Nathan to the conference room. With the barest minimum of exchanged pleasantries, we got rolling. Wearing the same outfit as his last deposition, Nathan, wet to begin with, was about to get dunked.

Attorney Anderson had responded in writing overnight that Carman did not have the Sig Sauer in his "possession, custody, and/or control." When I asked on the record in the deposition whether he had possession, custody, or control of it, Nathan asserted the Fifth Amendment.

We were here to find out how Nathan lost possession, custody, and control of the Sig Sauer. Judge Sullivan had limited the ninety-minute deposition to questions that "relate to the newly procured information derived from the New Hampshire firearm store where it is claimed Defendant purchased a weapon."[111] Opposing our efforts to do just that, counsel escalated his attempted distractions and disturbances, while his client whimpered at times, not just in response to my targeted questions, but also due to his counsel's eruptions.

I handed Nathan a copy of the subpoenaed Shooters Outpost invoice.

[111] Text Order, September 19, 2018.

Shooters Outpost
1158 Hooksett Rd
Hooksett, NH 03106
Phone: (603) 232-6125
shootersoutpost@gmail.com

INVOICE

INVOICE NUMBER	INVOICE DATE	FORM 4473	PAGE
R 73929	11/11/2013	8885	1 of 1

COMPANY:

Shooters Outpost
1158 Hooksett Rd
Hooksett, NH 03106
Phone: (603) 232-6125

VENDOR:

BILL TO:

CARMAN, NATHAN
140 POND BROOK ROAD
WEST CHESTERFIELD , NH 03443
Phone: (860) 759-0649

SHIP TO:
12243
CARMAN, NATHAN
140 POND BROOK ROAD
WEST CHESTERFIELD , NH 03443

CUSTOMER #	ORDER #	ORDER DATE	P.O. #	EMP	SHIP VIA	SHIP DATE	TERMS	REG	DRW	USR
12243	73929	11/11/2013						1	1	

Item #	...	Description	Serial #	NICS	Shipped	Ext Price
24015	P	HOPPE'S BORE SNAKE RIFLE CLEAN .308, 30-30, 300 CALIBER			1	19.99
K207	P	KLEEN BORE 30/7.62 RIFLE CLEANING KIT			1	22.99
R716-16B-P	P	SIG SAUER 716 PATROL 308 QUADRAIL, MAGPUL FURNITURE	22C012970		1	2,099.99
XM80C	P	FEDERAL 7.62X51MM 149GR FMJ 20			3	50.97

Sub Total: 2,193.94
Total This Invoice : 2,193.94

Change Due: 6.06

Payments

Type	Date	Amount
Cash:	11/11/2013	$2,193.94
VOID:	11/11/2013	$0.00

SO000001

We Strive to Exceed our Customers Expectations.All ammunition, firearm, & reloading sales are final.

The invoice shows Nathan Carman indeed did buy a Sig Sauer .308, specifically contradicting his .308 caliber denial during his second deposition. Which he had lied about to the Connecticut detectives too. Listed on the invoice as a SIG SAUER 716 PATROL 308 QUADRAIL, MAGPUL FURNITURE, Serial # 22C012970, it cost $2,099.99, which Nathan paid in cash. He also bought interchangeable NATO 7.62 ammunition, a rifle cleaning kit, and a bore snake to clean it. Five weeks before his grandfather's shooting.

Then I handed Nathan a copy of his subpoenaed federal ATF Form 4473, which needs to be filled out accurately and honestly in any legal firearms purchase in the USA. It showed that nineteen-year-old Nathan had gotten his New Hampshire driver's license and registered his truck in New Hampshire on November 6, 2013, to support his untrue claim of New Hampshire residency, just before he bought the Sig Sauer on November 11, 2013. If he had presented Connecticut identification at Shooters Outpost, salesman Jed Warner would not have sold Nathan an assault rifle, knowing them to be illegal in Connecticut. Furthermore, Nathan checked "NO" on "Have you ever been adjudicated mentally defective OR have you ever been committed to a mental institution?" Although not a well-phrased question, no holdup or background check resulted, with this another likely reason Nathan wanted to keep his medical records out of our case.

Cocking my prehistoric weapon while referring to the invoice, I asked:

> Q: Where is this item listed, Sig Sauer 716 Patrol 308 Quadrail Magpul Furniture with a Serial Number of 22C012970 now?
>
> A: In response to that question, I'm going to invoke the Fifth Amendment and decline to answer on that basis.
>
> Q: Is it at the bottom of the sea?
>
> A: In response to that question, I'm going to invoke the Fifth Amendment and decline to answer on that basis.
>
> Q: Was it jettisoned when you went fishing with the Frances Fleet on December 20th, 2013?

A: In response to that question—

> MR. ANDERSON: Wait. Wait...[soliloquy]...I'll have Mr. Carman invoke the Fifth.

A: In response to your last question, I invoke the Fifth Amendment privilege and decline to answer.

Stuck!

We could use all of Nathan's EUO, his videoed deposition testimony, and his Fifth Amendment pleas as adverse inferences against him in our civil insurance trial. Simply put, like the "Lost at Sea" *20/20* episode, Nathan was again cooking his goose.

To recap, here's the chronology of Nathan's conflicting Sig Sauer statements:

1. Owns no firearms besides an air gun, per December 20, 2013 police interview.
2. Besides the air gun and a recently purchased shotgun, never purchased any other firearm ever, per January 14, 2014 police interview.
3. Never purchased a Sig Sauer .308 and did not throw any firearm overboard from Frances Fleet boat, per July 17, 2018 deposition.
4. Takes Fifth Amendment on whether he jettisoned Sig Sauer Serial Number 22C012970 while fishing with the Frances Fleet on December 20, 2013, per October 29, 2018 deposition.

Another half dozen or so other questions on the Sig Sauer also ended with Nathan taking the Fifth. As noted earlier, Attorney Anderson claimed the only reason Nathan did that was because of the Connecticut assault rifle ban, and it had nothing to do with the Chakalos murder. But there wasn't a complete overlap between the two. The deposition testimony and video at the end had some nice drama on his lawyer's purported distinction and regrettably remains under a protective order. But I don't see a breach of it in revealing a question I asked that Attorney Anderson would not let his client answer.

Referencing the other three items on the Shooter's Outpost invoice—the Hoppe's Bore Snake Rifle Clean, the Kleen Bore Cleaning Kit, and the 7.62 NATO ammunition—all legal in Connecticut, I wanted to know how its assault rifle ban could be the basis for asserting the Fifth on those three purchases.

With that, Nathan Carman, at one end of their monkey-rope, was yanked away as his attorney stormed out of the conference room, falsely haranguing that my question was beyond Judge Sullivan's scope of interrogation to matters that "relate to the newly procured information" from Shooters Outpost. The deposition was over. "We're done," and they were gone.

So Liam and I picked up our papers, making sure Lauren's exhibit numbers matched our list, and tail-wrapped our catch for the ride home. On top of the Shooters Outpost rifle cleaners and 7.62 ammo, Nathan's destroyed hard drive and GPS from December 2013 had zero to do with the Connecticut assault rifle ban, so those Fifth Amendment invocations could only relate to John's murder. Plus, jettisoning the Sig Sauer from the Frances Fleet boat the morning of the shooting was offshore of Rhode Island and had nothing to do with Connecticut. Nathan's taking the Fifth on that, too, could only relate to John's murder.

Then less than three to five minutes later—the time elapsed from Nathan's hearing a funny engine sound to the boat's falling out from beneath him—back they came, hoping to continue, in over their heads, desperately searching for a life raft.

Bemused by our opponents' indecision, Liam and I huddled, pumped fists, and promptly and authoritatively decreed, "Negative."

We would leave the deposition record just as it was, with Nathan Carman walking out on his attorney's direction. A dramatic ending to an hour of lively video, there was no reason to give them a chance to muddy the blood in the water.

As Liam and I were leaving the law office, Attorney Secrest met me in the hallway. I thanked him and apologized for how noisy it had been, but he still seemed miffed at me. It only dawned on me much later that he must have mistakenly thought I had been repeatedly roaring, "That's a big fat lie" to the deponent, when in fact it was the deponent's lawyer yelling it, falsely, at me.

2019

21
SPANKING

After the defense duo's performance in Brattleboro there were several motions we had to file, including our fifth motion to compel, seeking production of Nathan's deposition transcript and paper discovery in the Sisters' Slayer Suit, and our second motion to amend our affirmative defense that Nathan's insurance claim was a fraud, along with a request for a new expert witness disclosure date, since we still had not finished up our fact discovery needs. We e-filed the Brattleboro deposition transcript in support of our motion papers without reference to the difficulties encountered in conducting that deposition.

Judge Sullivan opened the January 29, 2019 hearing on our motions with comments that would have mortified me had I been on the receiving end.

> THE COURT: What the Court has observed, and it was pertinent to our two motions which are on for hearing today, is a pattern of behavior by the Defendant only, not by the Plaintiff, of engaging in misconduct during depositions which has had the effect of stringing

> out the case. I do not see that conduct by counsel for the Plaintiff at all....
>
> I'll use a word I do not often use when I sit in this chair, shocking.... [A]nd this is really material—the witness repeatedly indicated that the conduct of his own attorney was preventing him from testifying truthfully. And that is very disturbing to the Court....
>
> Disparaging personal remarks or acrimony towards other counsel, parties, or witnesses is prohibited...by the Rhode Island Rules of Professional Conduct. That rule was repeatedly breached....
>
> I'm simply looking at a raw transcript, and "big fat lie" are three words that are strung together multiple times in that transcript. That had no place in obstructing the attempt to procure testimony.[112]

Our motions were granted. The best result of the hearing was Judge Sullivan's allowing us to file our updated fraud affirmative defense to Nathan's counterclaims. It summed up the Insurer's case, detailed solidly on the evidence we had developed through our investigation and fact discovery as of January 22, 2019. Below, the legal pleading we then e-filed with the Court is reproduced,[113] omitting a couple of citations. It was written with every attempt to make it clear to anyone reading it.

> 88. Defendant Nathan Carman's amended counterclaim, including his insurance claim, are denied and barred by fraud because his boat's sinking was not accidental or fortuitous, and/or was caused intentionally by, with the knowledge of, or resulting from criminal wrongdoing by Nathan Carman. His Policy states:

[112] ECF No. 130.

[113] ECF No. 122 at 9–13.

Fraud and Concealment

> There is no coverage from the beginning of this policy if you or your agent has omitted, concealed, misrepresented, sworn falsely, or attempted fraud in reference to any matter relating to this insurance before or after any loss.

Similarly, under general maritime law, Vermont state law, and any other law of fraud applicable here, insurance coverage for the sinking of Nathan Carman's boat and any other claims related to it are denied and barred. In accordance with Fed. R. Civ. P. 9(b)'s requirement to plead fraud with particularity, the Insurer alleges Nathan Carman not only fraudulently attempted to obtain $85,000 hull insurance proceeds from the sinking but he also criminally attempted to accelerate receipt of his inheritance from his maternal grandfather and mother as the evidence assembled in discovery will show, chronologically:

(a) While his maternal grandmother was in hospice, on November 11, 2013 Nathan Carman purchased a Sig Sauer 716 Patrol Rifle, Serial No. 22C012970, from Shooters Outpost in Hooksett, NH for $2,099.99. Based on Nathan Carman's own deposition testimony in this case and adverse inferences against him in civil litigation due to his invoking the Fifth Amendment of the U.S. Constitution, plus other evidence, he and the Sig Sauer were criminally involved in his grandfather's murder on the night of December 19/20, 2013. The Sig Sauer rifle was capable of firing the same caliber rounds which killed his grandfather and Nathan Carman was the last known person to see him alive. In the morning Nathan Carman went fishing on a head boat out of

Point Judith, RI, jettisoning his Sig Sauer rifle which now lies at the bottom of the sea. Because he no longer has possession, custody, or control of the Sig Sauer rifle, he could not produce it in his home state of Vermont during his October 29, 2018 deposition re-resumption and it is unavailable for ballistics testing. After the murder Nathan Carman also destroyed his lap top's hard drive and his truck's GPS. Following the murder, he obtained unrestricted access to roughly $587,000.

(b) Lacking gainful employment or educational pursuit, Nathan Carman then engaged in a similar scheme with chilling parallels. Using part of those monies, in December 2015 at the age of 21 he purchased a 31-foot diesel boat for $48,000. He insured it with the Insurer under the terms of the Policy, first registering it in New Hampshire. Upgrading the boat, he increased its insured value to $85,000 on March 25, 2016.

(c) On April 26, 2016 Nathan Carman failed to open a cooling water valve and overheated the boat's diesel engine while inside the Point Judith Harbor of Refuge. He called 911, with emergency assistance provided by the U.S. Coast Guard, and made an insurance claim, getting his engine replaced under the terms of his Policy.

(d) During the summer of 2016 Nathan Carman removed two forward structural bulkheads from the boat, thereby also diminishing its buoyancy. During September 2016 the boat experienced electrical problems with its forward/port bilge pump, which Nathan Carman replaced on September 17, 2016 without ever testing the boat's aft/starboard bilge pump. That afternoon and evening he also removed two trim tabs from the transom, thereby opening four ½ inch diameter thru-hull holes for the trim tabs' hydraulic actuators, just above the waterline and below the scuppers (which had outboard baffles). Using an electric hole saw, he then increased the size of those four holes to half dollars or larger and he failed to properly seal them. All this made the boat unseaworthy.

(e) In this unseaworthy condition the boat departed Ram Point Marina several hours later, around 11:12 p.m., with Nathan Carman and his mother aboard. He testified they first fished for stripers southeast of Block Island but that is contradicted by other evidence including Verizon records of his mother's cell phone putting them off the course line he swore to by about 10 miles southwest of Block Island at 12:45 a.m. on September 18, 2016.

(f) Testifying they then went about 75 miles south of Block Island to fish for tuna and billfish in Block Canyon off the Continental Shelf—for the first time ever—Nathan Carman claims that while trolling north at 4-6 knots around midday he discovered the boat's bilge suddenly full of water. He instructed his mother to reel in the lines but he neither gave her a life vest nor told her the bilge was flooded. Despite the boat's open deck design, he never saw, spoke with, or heard from her again and as with his grandfather, Nathan Carman was the last person to see her alive.

(g) Nathan Carman immediately prepared to abandon ship and then had three opportunities in the pilothouse to summon help by using the VHF radio or setting off the EPIRB, both of which he installed, but he did not. This contrasts with his previous April distress call while inside the Point Judith Harbor of Refuge. He disingenuously testified the reason he did not place a distress signal in offshore ocean waters 140 fathoms deep was that he would only do so when in jeopardy of losing life or limb. Then, he claims, the boat quickly sank bow first, but if true, that would only be possible given his prior removal of the forward bulkheads.

(h) Along with the sunken boat, its electronic navigational equipment went missing, just like Nathan Carman's Sig Sauer rifle and his truck's GPS after his grandfather's murder. Also, he says he kept the forward/port bilge pump he took out the day he departed onboard as a spare, so it, too, has gone missing as evidence.

(i) Nathan Carman testified his life raft automatically deployed and he was able to swim and get inside with his survival gear, including 30 days of food and a water maker. The life raft then drifted in the winds and seas for seven days, he claims, until he was rescued by a passing Chinese ship, the ORIENT LUCKY, on September 25, 2016 about 40 miles southeast of where he testified the boat sank in Block Canyon. Cold and wet during that claimed ordeal, video nevertheless shows him swimming toward ORIENT LUCKY and climbing its steep gangway without apparent difficulty or need for medical attention. His seven day life raft story is further deflated by Woods Hole Oceanographic Institution analysis showing that if deployed at the Block Canyon location where he says the boat sank, the life raft could not have drifted 40 miles southeast but rather would have drifted in the opposite direction, about 40 miles northwest, and if it had it would have been seen by Coast Guard search and rescue aircraft on September 19, 2016.

(j) In Nathan Carman's initial October 19, 2016 written description of his boat's sinking to Martha

Charlesworth in support of his hull insurance claim he failed to mention anything about his removal of the forward bulkheads, anything about electrical problems and his replacement of the forward/port bilge pump, or anything about his removal of the trim tabs exposing transom holes which he enlarged and inadequately sealed. These actions materially increased the risk of the boat's sinking and Nathan Carman breached his Policy by not reporting them to the Insurer before departing and/or in his October 19, 2016 written description.

(k) Nathan Carman's false testimony precluded the Insurer's and others' efforts to recover the sunken boat and their ability to inspect it and the unseaworthy alterations he made to it in furtherance of his fraudulent marine insurance claim so that he might obtain $85,000 in hull insurance proceeds. Similarly, Nathan Carman attempts to mislead Plaintiffs and others into concluding he did not criminally cause his mother's death and is entitled to her ¼ share of a multi-million dollar family trust owning several nursing homes.

(l) In sum, Defendant Nathan Carman executed a common scheme with striking, chilling, parallel losses of evidence, omissions, concealments, misrepresentations, false testimony, and fraud to procure a substantial inheritance by causing first his grandfather's murder and second his mother's death at sea through the sinking of his boat which Nathan Carman intentionally, knowingly, and/or criminally rendered unseaworthy before leaving port in an effort to claim its $85,000 hull insurance proceeds. Nathan Carman has thereby caused injury to the Insurer who continues to incur attorneys' fees and costs in denying his fraudulent insurance claim. Therefore, this Court should declare Defendant Nathan Carman's Policy cancelled and void

> as of September 17, 2016 and that all coverages under it were properly denied by the Insurer.

Let me explain why I included this whole thing verbatim. This book is about how we put our case together, chronologically, based on the factual evidence we assembled, with Nathan's testimony the most critical evidence. The foregoing serves as a status report summarizing where we were in early 2019, approaching a likely District of Rhode Island trial date later that calendar year.

And there's another reason to include it now. We hoped it would prompt criminal prosecution.

22

"I HATE THESE THINGS"

There were several depositions in early 2019 that Attorney Anderson conducted. They may have given him an inside look at marine insurance but nothing came out that damaged the Insurer's case. Attorney Anderson also deposed two of our expert witnesses.

Depositions of the Insurer's Representatives

First he deposed three Insurer witnesses—claims handler Martha Charlesworth, the Insurer's vice president for underwriting, and the Insurer's financial representative. Anderson got two seven-hour shots at Martha, one as Nathan's claim handler, and one as the Insurer's corporate representative on claims handling.

There were two shots also at the VP who oversees another important part of an insurer's business. Called "underwriting," it means signing up insureds and taking in their premium payments—an insurance company's revenue source. The underwriting VP testified both about overseeing Nathan become an insured and also as a corporate representative about underwriting in general.

The third part of an insurance company financially manages all those revenues minus claims payouts with all sorts of investments, about which I am clueless, but I'd wager the three operations are roughly one-third, one-third, and one-third important for any insurance company.

Altogether these five deposition sessions took over twenty-five hours, with Attorney Anderson compiling as exhibits not only Nathan's full underwriting and claims files, but also the Insurer's website pages, training manuals, and confidential business and financial documents.

Attorney Anderson knows what he is doing in this realm, and he diligently and thoroughly explored everything, but all was on the up-and-up in the Insurer's business practices, generally, and in the particular case of how the Insurer treated Nathan Carman. This is tedious stuff, not just for the patient reader but also for everyone in the deposition room and you won't get dragged through it.

The Insurer's witnesses were smooth but not slick, and nothing of any detrimental consequence was unearthed. There was no reason to think Nathan would be able to prevail on the allegations of his bad faith insurance suit.

Depositions of the Insurer's Experts

Attorney Anderson's two depositions of our expert witnesses, oceanographer Richard Limeburner and longtime recreational boat marine surveyor Jonathan K. Klopman, were more entertaining. Still, no one would want more than a quick summary of the two seven-hour ordeals.

We also had five other experts Anderson decided not to depose.

Two, marine surveyor Bernie Feeney (whom we adopted thanks to Nathan), and naval architect Eric Greene, both just amplified their earlier written reports.

A third, Patrick J. Modic, is a professional mariner who sailed with Exxon and was one of Liam's professors at Massachusetts Maritime Academy. Modic would testify on Nathan's navigation, various possible routes, and marine electronics in case we needed expert testimony on that.

Fourth, N. Stuart Harris Jr., MD, is a Harvard Medical School faculty wilderness emergency physician with Massachusetts General Hospital who evaluated Nathan's apparently excellent physical condition after being plucked from his seven days in a life raft. I couldn't believe I found someone with those credentials. They enable him to charge a hefty fee for expert testimony.

And fifth, we had firearms ballistic expert Richard Ernest to address the Connecticut State Police lab report[114] and other technical issues, and the impossibility of further testing on the missing Sig Sauer. Ernest opined in his report that, "Two (2) .30 caliber class jacketed bullets with boat tailed bases, each with a rifling structure of 6 lands and grooves with a right hand twist" were recovered from decedent John Chakalos. Ernest made clear that ".30 caliber class" bullets include both "the 7.62 NATO cartridge and the .308 WIN cartridge," which "are interchangeably used in firearms chambered for either cartridge," such as the Sig Sauer model Nathan purchased at Shooters Outpost.

All seven of our experts had submitted very detailed written reports laying out everything they would be testifying about at trial, and more—their education and training, specific expertise, data relied upon, prior testimony and publications, how much we paid them, and their opinions—which, if it's not disclosed in the report, won't be admissible at trial.

It's my guess Attorney Anderson has cross-examined enough marine surveyors, naval architects, mariners, physicians, and engineers at trial based only on their written expert reports that he decided to not bother deposing Feeney, Greene, Modic, Harris, and Ernest. That is not uncommon practice, because if you depose an expert, you might hear a changed or even a brand-new opinion that becomes admissible after you've beaten up the written opinion. Better to do that at trial if you think you can and then jump up and down to keep the expert from coming up with a new opinion.

But Jonathan Klopman is in a league of his own on recreational boating forensics, and he had thoroughly discredited Nathan's bow-first

114 ECF No. 86-1.

sinking claim. And with Nathan repeatedly testifying that he sank, even after Attorney Anderson came aboard, at 140 fathoms, they now realized that oceanographer Limeburner was the linchpin of our case that Nathan was a "big fat liar." So Anderson figured he had to take both of their depositions to see if he could undo their opinions.

There are a couple of reasons the Insurer didn't take any depositions of Nathan's expert witnesses. One, Attorney Anderson did not disclose any. Two, and related to that, he probably could not find anyone willing to testify. All they could muster was fact witness Roth Sr., who hurt their case.

Limeburner, at least prior to the Carman case, was best known for figuring out where Paris-bound Air France Flight 447 crashed in the mid-Atlantic killing all 228 aboard after taking off from Rio de Janeiro in 2009. Employing his "reverse drift" analysis, he backtracked from where floating debris and bodies were found five days after the crash to where the floaters would have been when first surfacing. And not far away, side-scan sonar found the debris field and fuselage more than two miles below.

Limeburner came across as professorial yet practical, and his life raft drift report was precise and compelling. He had lots of photos and charts showing currents overlaid on and contradicting Nathan's claimed drift from 140 fathoms at the Block Canyon Fishtails to the *Orient Lucky* pickup spot. Both of those locations were now solidly in evidence with Nathan's charting and his reiterated, confirming deposition testimony and with Liam's retrieved *Orient Lucky* deck log and actual paper chart with its dead reckoning. And right there, in the middle of Nathan's claimed drift, were Woods Hole Oceanographic Institution and US government super-duper oceanography buoys measuring on-scene currents and surface winds in real time, all publicly available on the web. Limeburner called those buoys the "frontal array," placed right over the Shelf Break south of Martha's Vineyard. He also attached to his report graphics showing AIS vessel traffic during the week Nathan was supposedly adrift.

Admirably fighting for his client, Attorney Anderson doggedly went at Limeburner and his data and plugged and plugged away, but the net result was Nathan's claimed seven-day life raft drift from 140 fathoms in Block Canyon to the *Orient Lucky* did not happen. Had he really sunk where and when he said he did at the Fishtails, his life raft would have drifted northwest toward Long Island and not to the south of Martha's Vineyard.

Nathan was "Dead in the Water," figuratively if not literally, unlike his mother, who was definitely both. He had concocted a colossal, multifaceted, science fiction tale, not just on where and when he repeatedly testified the JC 31 sank, but consequently over the next week, too, as USCG SAR assets crisscrossed sixty-two thousand square miles searching for him in vain—a week that he did not drift in his life raft into the wind and upstream into the current to an *Orient Lucky* rescue. A week that he was not wet and cold, constantly sponging out water. A week not rationing his food and cranking his water maker to survive the confines of his bobbing cocoon in up to twelve-foot seas. It was, in short, all a big fat murderous lie.

But it was highly respected yacht surveyor Jonathan Klopman who during his deposition brought out the worst.

I wanted Klopman, rather than Mike McCook, who had initially been involved for us and is a solid pro, because McCook regularly worked closely with the Insurer and his opinion might get impeached as biased.

Klopman is meticulous and able to translate engineering principles into simple concepts, which he demonstrates with convincing models he creates. A Tufts magna cum laude history major, he's refreshingly insolent when dealing with pushy or wrongheaded people. He's been all over the world (once with me to the Mediterranean) re-creating and assessing the cause of boat sinkings and collisions.

Among Klopman's demonstrative exhibits, he built several "exemplars," which has become marine surveyors' preferred term for models. Both are decent word choices actually, as they are key physical re-creations for easy comprehension by the judge or jury. For example, Klopman took a simple short plank of lumber and drilled three half-dollar-sized holes, leaving one empty, filling a second with epoxy putty, and fiberglassing over the third puttied hole, to show how easy that would have been for Nathan.

Klopman also built a full-size model, with precise measurements, of a JC 31 transom cross section using a JC 31 he located in a boatyard—a nice exemplar to have in court. On it he installed two actuators and an adjustable trim tab.[115]

Klopman had figured out what Nathan was talking about in his post-lunch deposition testimony when he said the transom holes were the size of silver dollars that are slightly larger than a quarter. Klopman realized Nathan meant Susan B. Anthony or Sacagawea dollar coins which the US Mint removed from circulation because they were so easy to confuse with quarters. It was another way Nathan was overly cute in his attempt to downsize the half-dollar holes.

Klopman's written report contained construction photos of the boat from Brian Woods and also photos produced by Nathan and compelling graphs depicting bilge water levels as observed by Nathan when he first looked forward of the engine compartment[116] and a scant minute later when he took off the aft port deck hatch.[117] Knowing the components, Klopman tracked down the same items in marine stores for measurement references. Contrasting Nathan's two observations, the water levels were ten to twelve inches higher aft, as shown by the large double-ended arrows on the two graphs.

---

[115] Tr. Ex. 32.27.

[116] Tr. Ex. 32.43; Tr. Ex. 32.45.

[117] Tr. Ex. 62; Tr. Ex. 32.50.

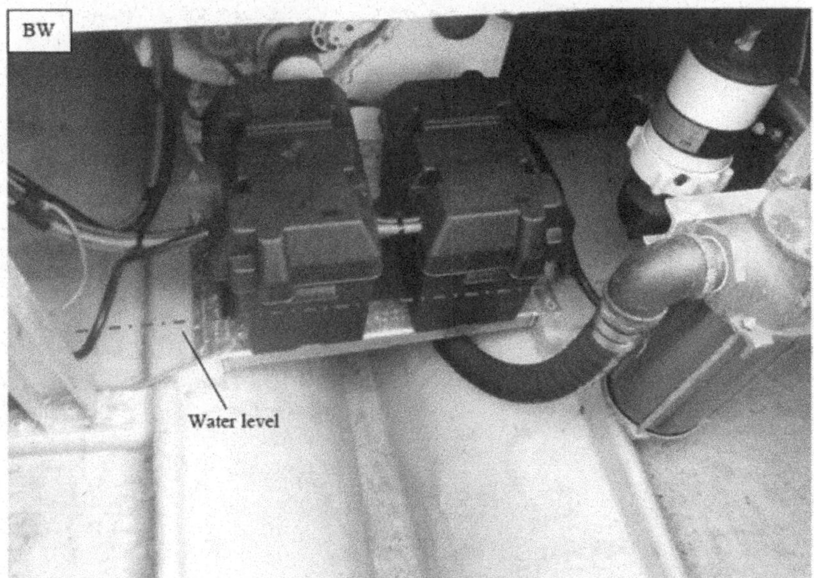

Photo 34 View inside the forward hatch looking aft. The statement says that the water level was halfway up the batteries. Note the relationship of the engine behind the batteries to the battery platform. This platform is approximately the same height as the motor mounts.

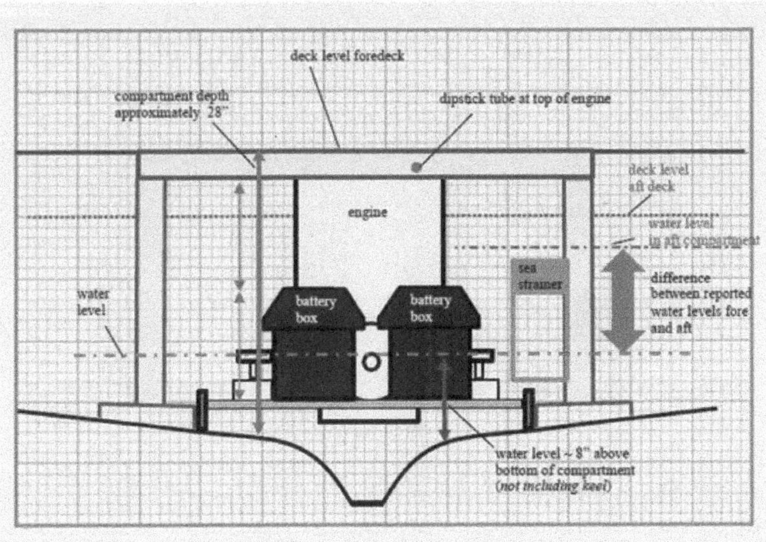

Figure 7 Forward compartment looking aft. Note water level as referenced to half way up the batteries. Compare with water level in aft compartment. The water level is well below the level of the dipstick near the top of the engine. Refer to Photos 32, 33.

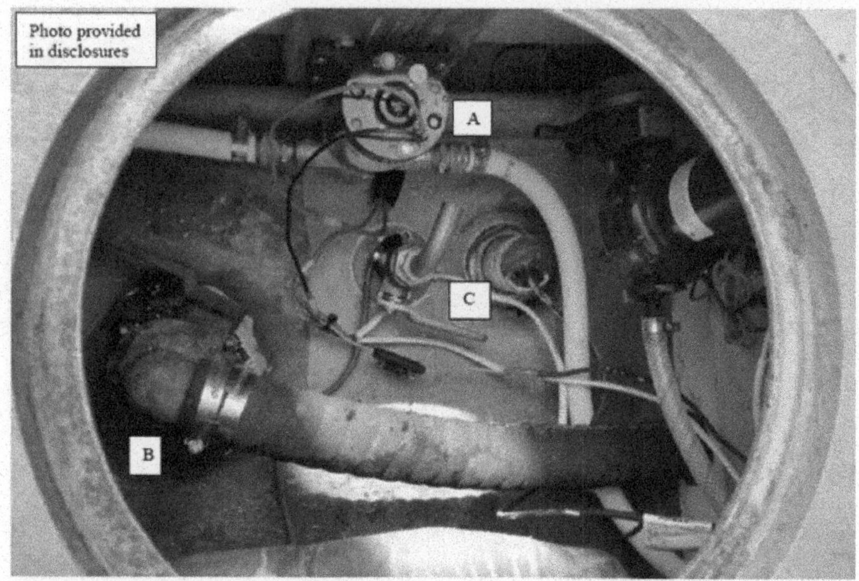

Photo 38 View looking in port aft hatch. Note the water puppy pump (A), engine sea water intake seacock (B), and washdown pump seacock (C). Photo taken on April 8, 2016 when the washdown pump was installed by Point Judith Marine. Note the depth of the compartment relative to the height of the water puppy pump (6.75" length)

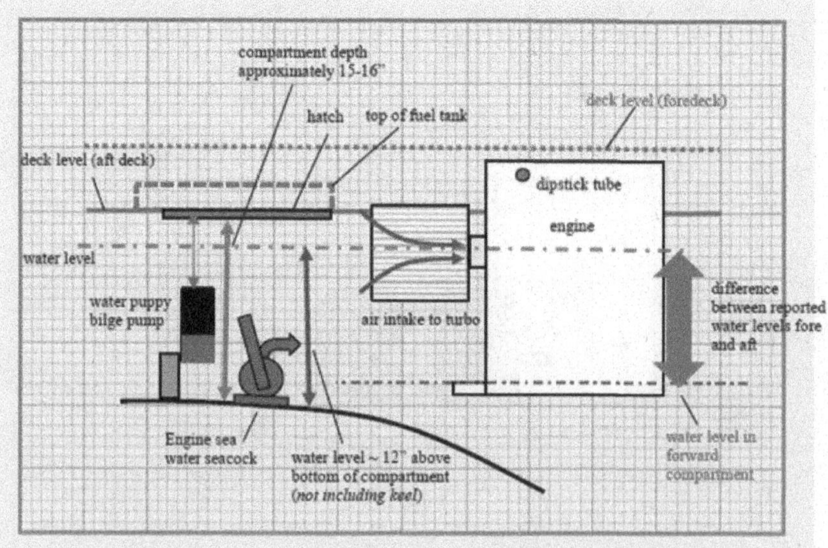

Thus, on Nathan's observation, the boat had to go down by the stern, weighed down by much more water, and his sudden bow-first sinking was impossible, graphically summarized, another lie.

Klopman had a terse, well-supported answer for every deposition question from Attorney Anderson, backed up by photographic evidence of the boat. This eventually got under Anderson's skin, who had perhaps too much skin in the game, perhaps too much empathy for his client to step back objectively.

> Q: Do you think Nathan Carman actually took a hole saw on Saturday afternoon and, in front of a bunch of people on the dock, drilled four holes into the transom of his vessel?
>
> A: Yes.
>
> Q: Okay. You really believe that?
>
> A: Yes, I do....
>
> Q: You would agree with me that if you, if it was your intent to sink your vessel, that it would be a lot easier to remove the hose clamp on the pressurized side of the pump...and turn on the pump as compared to drilling, leaning over the stern of your vessel with an electric drill and a two-inch hole saw or an inch-and-a-quarter hole saw, and drilling four holes in the transom. Do you agree with that?
>
> A: Now we're discussing the process of fraudulently sinking your boat. It depends on what your goals are. There's the ease of the initial cutting of the hose or removing the hose, or there's the thoroughness of using many different holes to sink the boat quickly. Depends on what the person is after. I can't speak to the motive of someone who would be doing that.

After more of these losing skirmishes, Attorney Anderson kicked off his never-appropriate Crocs, started running around the conference room table in his stocking feet, repeatedly thrusting photos in front of Klopman's face—only for Klopman to parry with more unassailable opinions, which sent Anderson retreating to his chair, muttering, amplifying his distress. Then his antiquated flip phone started ringing—"God dammit. I hate these things"—whereupon a small black boomerang from across the table whistled at eye level right between Jonathan and me, ricocheting off the conference room door and onto the floor, in pieces, its ringer terminally defunct.

Why didn't I go ballistic and rat out my adversary to the court? That's why. But I decided then and there that if I ever did write a book, I wouldn't sugarcoat his incivility. Recognizing that there are no saints in my business, and that everyone can have a bad day or bad patch, as a profession we need to commit to showing respect and collegiality to our adversaries even as we zealously scrap for our clients. It is particularly important during these divisive times. Boorish behavior distracts from the real issues, drives up attorneys' fees, and sullies the Rule of Law. Federal judges across the country commonly compliment Maritime Law Association members on their ability to get along and cooperate with each other while fiercely litigating. Guess who is not a member?

23

OUR PRETRIAL WHIRLWIND

After fact and expert discovery are completed, most federal civil cases, regardless of whether a bench trial to a judge or to a jury, are closely scrutinized by the lawyers for the chances of getting an early dispositive ruling from the judge, and not proceeding to trial.

Commonly, the defendant will argue there is a defect in the plaintiff's case requiring dismissal of the complaint. Less frequently, the plaintiff will argue nothing more needs to be proven, based on documents or what the defendant has already admitted, and that judgment can be granted now without further wasting everyone's time.

Judge Smith made it clear at a pretrial telephone conference that he was not interested in disposing of this case short of trial. When there are central factual disputes, like whether puttied transom holes and removed bulkheads result in a bow-first sinking, it means a full trial is necessary, so the judge or jury can watch witness testimony and assess credibility, and so the judge can protect the record in case of appeal.

What does that mean, when a judge protects the record? It means the judge issues rulings during the case which cannot be easily second-guessed on review by an appellate court. In a bench trial, when the trial judge makes a factual finding regarding the truthfulness or credibility of witness testimony, the appeals court is virtually always going to affirm that finding. After all, the trial judge watched the direct testimony and the cross-examination and is in a firsthand position to assess witness credibility, demeanor, and substance.

This starkly contrasts with appellate judges, who review the trial's written record and do not hear witnesses. Talk about an ivory tower. Federal appeals court judges are typically brilliant, scholarly and detailed, even nerdy, but they are insulated from the trial lawyers' trench warfare and have to defer on witness observations made by the presiding trial judge. So when a judge in a bench trial finds that one witness is credible and another witness is not credible, that is virtually locked in and should be taken by the losing party as a real discouragement to pursuing an appeal. Thus, the trial judge protects the record and avoids getting overturned by the higher-ups.

Another way the record can be protected is when the trial judge seems to be signaling who is going to win but then starts issuing evidentiary rulings that go against the projected winner. That forecloses the loser's argument on appeal that the trial judge was biased in favor of the winner.

That Nathan's insurance claim was going to trial is not the typical situation in federal court civil litigation. Of all civil cases filed, only 1 percent go to trial. Settlement or a pretrial dispositive ruling is almost always how lawsuits terminate.

So when Judge Smith gave us an August 11, 2019 trial date and set out the filing deadlines for each party's witness and exhibit lists, evidentiary motions *in limine* advocating for or against the admission of certain evidence, and proposed findings of fact and conclusions of law, those dates were pretty much cast in stone. For the lawyers, our calendars were now jammed with time-consuming tasks, requiring methodical preparation that not only covers the bases but also anticipates future in court battles.

Done the right way, preparing findings of fact and conclusions of law for a bench trial is extreme deskwork drudgery for the lawyer drafting them. A judge is required to issue a written decision after a bench trial, so it makes it easier for the judge if the two parties prepare drafts.

The opposing versions will necessarily be slanted—that's the way our adversary system works—and many judges ask for the drafts after trial has been completed, covering the evidence as presented at trial.

Increasingly, and especially in a fully litigated case with multiple depositions, because trial testimony will generally conform, judges want the proposed findings of fact and conclusions of law drafts before trial, to force the lawyers to sift through in advance what is really essential. This makes for a more efficient trial. The lawyers' best practice is to spend the time crafting a winner with extensive citations and quotes from deposition testimony and exhibits, using a chronological storyline, making compelling arguments, and providing case law to fully educate and persuade the judge to rule for your client even before the clerk convenes the first day of trial with "All rise."

Liam and I split up sections to handle, and our partner Olaf Aprans threw in some good insurance case precedents to supplement our maritime cases. I ran it confidentially by my longtime consigliere Eric Biss, a professional skeptic, who gave it his thumbs-up, and the fifty-eight-page Plaintiffs' Pre-Trial Proposed Findings of Fact and Conclusions of Law[118] we filed were outstanding, if I do say so myself. Fully citing and quoting Nathan's pretrial testimony, our filing taught the trial judge about all the issues in dispute, addressing the evidence that would be presented at trial and applying the governing law, showing why the Insurer absolutely should win. As an example, we wrote:

> 102. The similarities between the deaths of Carman's grandfather and mother can be summarized in the below table:

Grandfather's Murder	**Mother's Death at Sea**
Bought Sig Sauer, Serial # 22C012790, November 11, 2013 in NH	Bought boat December 2015; first registered in NH

[118] ECF No. 139.

Last known person to see him alive, December 19, 2013	Last person to see her alive, September 18, 2016
Grandfather murdered with .30 class ammo December 19/20, 2013	Mother dies on boat September 18, 2016
Hard drive and truck GPS destroyed; unaccounted inconsistencies in Carman's truck route	Navigation electronics sunk; unaccounted inconsistencies in Carman's course
Fishing with mother immediately after murder	Fishing as mother goes silent
Lies, takes 5th Amendment, Sig now "at bottom of the sea" per adverse inference, not produced at deposition	Lies about Block Canyon, boat never will be found
$560,000 unrestricted funds	$85,000 hull insurance claim

With the ultimate goal his $10 million inheritance from the Dynasty Trust.

You might ask why we bothered to lay out a double murder case when we were so confident we would win on Nathan's unseaworthy repairs causing the sinking and voiding insurance coverage. The easy answer is, impartial Judge Smith refused to consider granting us summary judgment on our unseaworthy repair issue, so maybe we were overconfident. Another reason is the whole enchilada, as stated in our fraud Affirmative Defense 88, rebutted Nathan's counterclaims. But it really came down to this: When at war, you want all your weapons available.

***

While deep in the throes of trial preparation, preparing exhibits and witness testimony, it is also critical that the lawyers step back and take a last-chance, big-picture overview of all the evidence, reexamining assumptions, ensuring exhibit admissibility, identifying gaps and weaknesses, and refining strongest arguments.

We were finally able to review Nathan's deposition transcript from the Sisters' Slayer Suit after Judge Sullivan ordered its production to us. Generally consistent with what Nathan testified in our case, there were a couple of significant tidbits. For one, he reconfirmed his boat's normal speed was 16 knots and added that their southernmost point in Block Canyon was 80 miles from his Block Island Striper Rock X, which perfectly fit 5 hours of travel, D = S x T. Once again, he had to.

Also, pro se and without a lawyer representing him in his New Hampshire deposition, Nathan took the Fifth dozens of times in response to Dan Small's questions related to the John Chakalos murder.

However, an alarm went off when I read that Nathan volunteered without any prompting a navigational twist in his New Hampshire deposition when describing the fishing leg as they trolled north in Block Canyon. After our examination under oath, our first deposition, and now his New Hampshire deposition, with Nathan confirming the sinking at the 140-fathom mark, later in his New Hampshire deposition he added that, as they trolled, their course northward was not a straight line but instead "an S, like a semicircle to the left and then a semicircle to the right of centerline course" by autopilot option selection.[119]

Why did the Genius in his last deposition meander his course, trolling north in smooth, continuous semicircles, conceptually even simpler than his sine waves? I had to figure this out.

True to form, the Genius also demonstrated how he thinks "differently than many people." Nathan actually testified in his New Hampshire deposition that every day adrift he would wake up at 8:00 a.m. to eat breakfast. Then brunch, lunch, and dinner. C'mon, the

[119] Tr. Ex. 6.2.

quotidian routine of a cruise ship, including *brunch*? And it was Nathan who yelled out to the *Orient Lucky* crew from thirty yards away to attract their attention.

There was also a loose end we had not yet tied down—the West Marine store in Middletown, Rhode Island. So I did, and then drove the same forty-five miles Nathan would have taken back to Ram Point Marina, where I wanted another pretrial look. On the drive, I then knew that on the day of the last voyage Nathan had bought not only a new bilge pump in Middletown but also two very different safety harnesses.

While poring over Limeburner's report, it also occurred to us on studying the AIS data he had included in an appendix, that there was a vessel that had been in the Block Canyon area at the time of Nathan's alleged sinking, Sunday September 18, 2016. How we had missed that is hard to explain, but better late than never. Plus, that same vessel's AIS signature showed up further east the week that *Orient Lucky* came upon Nathan's life raft. Could it be that this F/V *Prudence* was his ride east against the wind and current, his partner in crime?

We didn't want this cat getting out of the bag until we knew more. We did some quick but intensive background checking on the *Prudence*, an offshore lobster boat, helped by our partner Kirby Aarsheim's fishing industry connections, and could only conclude that the company and the captain were both finest kind. With even more confidence, because Liam and I had spent around fifteen hours studying Nathan face-to-face at that point, we deemed it humanly impossible for him to conspire with anyone else. Not only does he think differently from others, he acts differently too. No one would ever be able to have an oral meeting of the minds with him on anything, as demonstrated by Brian Woods's experience with the title transfer. We decided it was safe to get in touch with the *Prudence* owners, which Kirby helped arrange, to see if we could talk with the crew.

After some serious cajoling to overcome the common instinct to not get involved, Liam established a good rapport with *Prudence* Captain Alex Aucoin, who finally agreed to testify at trial about what he did not see while lobstering that week.

In the New Hampshire case, however, things were going nicely for Nathan. Shedding his pro se status, he found a law firm (or maybe it found him) to represent him in filing a motion to dismiss the Sisters' Slayer Suit. The simple argument was that the State of New Hampshire lacked jurisdiction for the probate suit since John Chakalos was not a New Hampshire resident and actually lived day-to-day in Connecticut at his Windsor home/office.

Around this time, our good friends at a large New England firm, Hinckley Allen, and also a Chicago "Big Law" firm, got involved on behalf of the Sisters. Michael Connolly of Hinckley Allen and Bill Michael from Chicago drove down to the Cape to visit me. Our Rhode Island federal court case was on a rocket ship to trial while the Sisters' Slayer Suit in New Hampshire was indeed dismissed and appealing it looked like a loser. So when Bill announced, "I'll be quarterbacking this from now on," somewhat taken aback, I harrumphed in my best Big Law dialect but gratefully accepted their offers to help in whatever way they could with the trial.

They provided an excellent sounding board and support, and it was a pleasure dealing with them. However, we had different end goals. The Insurer just wanted the judge to void Nathan's policy and deny insurance coverage. With the Sisters' Slayer Suit dead in the water, their focus was on getting Nathan convicted, and they wanted to use our trial as a springboard to convince prosecutors to file criminal charges. It didn't seem our goals were mutually exclusive, but as it turned out, they almost were.

***

With less than a month to go before the start of trial, Liam and I were ANAT (All Nathan, All the Time). Liam decided to rent a vacation home in Chatham, bringing his family along, so he and I could feverishly work together.

We were getting lots done, and even enjoying evening cookouts with our families, when Chatham experienced its first ever tornado. We know a lot about storms here, but this was surreal, coming on so suddenly, dissipating so quickly, so different from a multiday omega block northeaster.

In a minute I had seven scrub pines in the woods shorn halfway up their trunks, falling 360° around the compass, proving cyclonic surface winds, even if only EF1. Cleanup briefly disrupted our trial prep, but I couldn't stop cogitating Nathan's S curves, just like the twister bearing down on the Gales's farm, and started thinking I might be able to make sense of his semicircle course northward.

Our whirlwind morphed five days before the start of trial into a litigation maelstrom, as big as any I'd ever seen of the invariable hurdles that pop up as the first day approaches. Out of nowhere again, there was a change in District of Rhode Island chief judges, with Judge John J. McConnell, Jr. taking over from the prior Chief Judge William E. Smith.[120] A pretrial conference, the second one for this case, was set for August 8. This brought out wild cackling like seagulls in the morn from some of our team, while others prognosticated with the certainty of the Larry's PX breakfast counter at half past six. No one got it right.

During the August 8 teleconference, after counsels' introductions, Judge McConnell started right off commenting he had been learning all about trim tabs over the previous twenty-four hours and concluded that the case could be most efficiently handled by bifurcating it.

Shiver me timbers, where and what was he going to chop in two?

The judge announced it was going to be intentional sinking. We would be trying what he called Phase I of our case limited to whether Nathan's repairs and alterations made the JC 31 unseaworthy and caused it to sink, thereby excluding coverage under his insurance policy, but with the proviso that if we lost Phase I, we could then try our criminal intent counts for sinking, murder, and fraud in a second trial, Phase II.

Gut punch or gift?

Liam was convinced it was the former, sapping us of some of our best evidence—Nathan's inheritance road map, his jettisoned Sig Sauer, and Fifth Amendment pleas. Liam and Vince were freaking that Judge

[120] There is a routine rotation of the chief judge's administrative job among a district's judges. There is nothing to my knowledge suggesting that the Carman case had anything to do with the switch from Judge Smith to Judge McConnell.

McConnell, an Obama appointee, must have an axe to grind against insurers in general.

Although this bifurcation was another twister we didn't see coming, I tried to remain cautiously optimistic. We would have to clean up our witness and exhibit lists, but that made our case simpler. I could only interpret the bifurcation to mean Judge McConnell already got it from reading our proposed findings of fact and conclusions of law and felt he could comfortably deny insurance coverage based on faulty-repair policy language in Phase I and did not need to open up a Phase II can of worms of unwitnessed deaths motivated by millions of dollars. He could dispose of the civil insurance case and properly punt the sinking fraud and murders for due process handling by prosecutors and criminal defense lawyers. This made complete sense since judges like to efficiently clear their dockets and not bite off more than they need to close a case. Reassuringly, Michael Connolly checked with his Providence office and got solid reports that Judge McConnell was fair and not some radical jurist whose default was to rule in favor of the underdog.

But Liam and I were unwilling to give up on at least trying to get certain evidence admitted in Phase I which related to Nathan's nefarious intent—specifically, Limeburner's drift analysis—because it so disemboweled Nathan's overall credibility. I was sure Nathan and Attorney Anderson would try to distance themselves from the 140-fathom sinking spot to pull the rug out from underneath the starting premise of Limeburner's drift opinions. I was guessing they wanted to move the sinking as far south as possible to argue the Gulf Stream as a natural and very appealing explanation for Nathan's eastward life raft drift.

To do that, they would have to disavow three different pretrial occasions when Nathan swore to sinking at 140 fathoms in Block Canyon. I had to make sure I held their feet to the fire—and blister them.

24

THE FEDERAL COURT TRIAL

Our team's headquarters was the Homewood Suites by Hilton, two blocks from the federal courthouse in downtown Providence. Liam and I checked in the weekend before trial with all our exhibits, computers, printers, and scanners. I worked hard on the S-course navigation and got it all down on paper late Saturday night using basic geometry. I presented my thoughts to Liam, who called me "Rain Man," an autistic savant.

Our staff had made overnight reservations for our witnesses, who checked in and out as their trial appearances dictated. With easy travel and parking, there was a small gym, and a breakfast buffet and heavy happy-hour snacks were included in the accommodations package. It was a convenient setup for going over testimony with our witnesses before they took the stand and for conferring in private with Martha and tying in Vince by phone to discuss developments. Our group got a kick out of watching the local evening news lead stories about the trial on the big screen, as well as the uninvolved guests' show of support that Nathan looked as guilty as sin going in and out of the courthouse. The Hilton even allowed us to use luggage carts to roll our stuff over to the courthouse. Altogether, it was a very efficient setup, without distractions. Logistics matter.

Jury trials with citizens deciding the case and a federal judge-tried admiralty case are different animals. After forty years, I am convinced the latter are won or lost on the opposing parties' proposed findings of fact and conclusions of law. As ours had summarized for the judge, you the reader already have the bulk of the evidence before you by now—and this may be disappointing to the true crime aficionado—but 90 percent of your work evaluating Nathan Carman is already completed. Few unexpected bombshells went off—at least for the courtroom's public consumption—but watch for behind-the-scene surprises.

This case would largely turn, as is typical of admiralty cases, on technical nautical evidence, and specifically here on circles—holes and courses—with Nathan's demeanor, of course, playing a tremendous role. And don't forget, as bifurcated, Phase I was going to be a trial concentrating on one clause in an insurance policy.

Besides his counsel, a mysterious young gray-haired goth woman showed up around halfway through trial; she was Nathan's only fan in attendance. During breaks, there would be occasional public displays of muskrat love between the famous Defendant and his groupie. This even elicited the one and only smile I ever saw flash on Nathan's face, and while anthropologically fascinating, our team didn't have time to study their flirtations, unlike many courtroom observers.

The news reporters, though, more often gathered around the Sisters' PR consultant, a nonlawyer, who held seminars during breaks on what had just gone on or was coming up. Occasionally Liam would send someone to listen in and report back, and it was clear that Mr. PR was trying to stoke media interest to pressure some prosecutor somewhere to indict Nathan.

The way we saw it, the media was primarily present just to watch Nathan in person, well aware he wasn't going to be pronounced criminally guilty, but salivating for anything and everything they could learn about him and hopeful for a big headline. It's a real temptation for lawyers to play into that, which is why cameras are still not allowed in federal courtrooms. And in a bench trial there is no question that the better approach is disciplined focus on supplying only what the judge wants.

Opening Statements

On the morning of the first day, August 13, 2019, both trial teams arrived early to set up in the grand wood-paneled courtroom. Defendant Nathan Carman and Attorney Anderson sat at the table to the judge's left. At the table to the judge's right were Plaintiff Insurer represented by Martha Charlesworth, with Liam and me plus Vanessa DiDomenico, our summer associate, a sharp Tulane Law student by way of Mass Maritime, a quick legal researcher, and a tech-savvy wiz.

Shortly before the 9:30 a.m. start, a tall, sixtyish gentleman in a dark suit entered from a side door and introduced himself to us. "I'm Jack McConnell." Neither party's counsel had met him in person before and we all appreciated his collegial gesture. But I for one would never ever call a federal judge by his or her first name, even at a cocktail reception. They have my deepest respect, confirmed by the Senate, appointed for life, responsible for a vast array of federal legal topics, civil and criminal, and constitutional. My limited capability is but a drop in the bucket of their jurisprudential scope, and it has always been a privilege to educate a federal jurist on maritime intricacies, with some more knowledgeable in the areas of my peculiar proficiency.

Judge McConnell, in his robes, quickly took his place on the bench and crisply framed the case.

> THE COURT: Good morning, everyone. So we're going to get started. Let me just recap. We're here to try the Plaintiff insurance companies' claims that require this Court as the factfinder to determine three matters. As to Count II, whether Mr. Carman breached his continuing duty of utmost good faith by failing to disclose material information about any increased risk associated with the work that he did on his boat; as

> to Count IV, whether Mr. Carman made incomplete, improper, or faulty repairs that caused the loss of his boat; and, Count VI, whether Mr. Carman knew his boat was unseaworthy when it left from Ram Point Marina and whether any unseaworthiness caused Mr. Carman's loss.

Judge McConnell then set out time limits that constrained the lawyers.

> THE COURT: The Court has previously allotted each side fifteen total hours to put on their case. I have this nifty little clock that I'm going to use, and I encourage counsel to check with me during the course of the trial to see where they are so that we're not surprised at any point.
>
> And with that, we'll have opening statements from the Plaintiff.

Liam and Vanessa were ready with slides of evidence we would be admitting, and which they would display on the courtroom monitors, and I referred to those slides and other demonstrative exhibits as I spoke.

> MR. FARRELL: Thank you, Your Honor.
>
> This is a case about a boat that left Point Judith with holes in it and it sank twelve hours later. As bifurcated it becomes a rather routine marine insurance case, but there are still some nonroutine facts that need to be considered.
>
> The evidence will show that Mr. Carman's boat was in great shape when he bought it. Our first witness will be Brian Woods, who over the course of several winters refurbished an old lobster boat turning it into a highly functional, walk-around deck, fishing vessel with an aluminum pilothouse.

He added bulkheads in the forward compartment. These provided some structural support for the bow so that it wouldn't twist and torque and send vibrations throughout the hull, and it further enclosed two floatation voids forward that help keep the boat afloat.

Mr. Woods also added two trim tabs on the stern of the boat. And here's an exemplar model, Your Honor, of what the trim tabs looked like, a courtroom version.

Mr. Woods, when he installed them, drilled a half-inch hole, as the directions require, through the transom to put in a bronze pipe that connects to the actuator with a threaded screw, and then there's a rubber hydraulic hose, and this is how the hydraulics work.

Mr. Feeney will testify next. He's a marine surveyor who Mr. Carman hired to conduct a prepurchase survey of the boat, and Feeney found the boat to be in good shape, and based on his documented condition and his written survey report with photographs that was sent to the Insurer, the boat was insured for sixty-six thousand two hundred dollars.

But Mr. Carman tends to lose things. He lost the boat, electronics, other things, and he says he never received his insurance policy. But he admits that he has problems with the US mail, which sometimes gets misplaced in his house which was under construction.

He nevertheless contacted the Insurer when he made additions to the boat. He purchased marine electronics and a life raft worth a lot of money, and so he increased the value of his hull insurance up to eighty-five thousand dollars.

But Mr. Carman failed to contact the Insurer when he subtracted assets from the boat, when he made it less safe, when he made it unseaworthy, and when he increased its risk of loss. I'm talking about his removal of the bulkheads in the forward compartment with a Sawzall that chopped the plywood out of the bilge, thereby structurally weakening the boat, letting it vibrate, and removing those two large floatation voids.

He also on the day of the fateful voyage removed the trim tabs, and he took off the actuators from the transom and he says that he thereby found half-dollar holes in the hull, which are a lot bigger than the half inch holes Mr. Woods drilled. And the evidence will show that Michael Iozzi observed Mr. Carman using an electric power drill with a hole saw attached to it while he was bent over the transom at the waterline.

Mr. Carman then filled these four half-dollar holes with epoxy putty that he purchased at West Marine that day, but he only used about three-quarters of this stick to fill the four half-dollar holes. The holes didn't have any backing on them; they were just holes into the hull.

Mr. Carman claims to be a genius, but this is what the directions say: "For use on fiberglass, wood, metal, and plastic surfaces."

Not gaping holes.

What he didn't do is every bit as important because he also bought that day a fiberglass boat repair kit that has matted fiberglass that he could have easily placed on the outside of the hull to seal those holes so that seawater wouldn't get into the bilge.

He also replaced the port cockpit bilge pump that day.

It's the second time he replaced the bilge pump in six months. He had continuing electrical problems blowing fuses to the bilge pump which Bud Smedberg, a marine mechanic from Point Judith Marina, will testify needed to be addressed.

If Mr. Feeney had seen the boat in that condition when he did his survey, he would not have authorized even launching it into the water, and he will testify it is perfectly predictable it sank the following day.

Another marine surveyor, Jonathan Klopman, will try to explain Mr. Carman's removal of the trim tabs in the water while Mr. Carman remained on deck and didn't even get onto the dock, tried to work with power tools at the waterline, reaching over, and what a difficult job it would be. He will also talk about the sinking sequence, if we can get into that at all. I don't know if Your Honor will consider that intentionality, but there are a lot of questions about what happened in the sinking.

Klopman will also testify that had he come across the boat in the course of being a marine surveyor and observed the putty in the transom holes, he would have immediately called the insurance company and said this boat shouldn't even be in the water.

Finally, a naval architect, Eric Greene, will show you why those puttied holes likely failed and seawater entered the bilge and filled it up just twelve hours later.

On those facts alone, Your Honor, this case can end.

The non-routine part of this case, though, is Mr. Carman's testimony about where the boat sank. This chart is where he marked his voyage, and right here is Block Canyon.

He marked two spots here and he said he sank right in between at 140 fathoms at the northern edge, within the walls of Block Canyon. He'll probably try to wiggle away from that, but it's very clear that's where it was.

He then drifted in a life raft for seven days and ended up over here, 106 miles south of Martha's Vineyard, where he was picked up by the *Orient Lucky*. That could well be the only fact that we have independent confirmation of in this entire case—because Mr. O'Connell was on business in Singapore and the *Orient Lucky* was in Indonesia and he trekked over to the ship and came home with this chart from the *Orient Lucky* showing where they picked Mr. Carman up at 1320 on September 25th, with the latitude and longitude reflected also in the ship's log that Mr. O'Connell also obtained.

We'll have Richard Limeburner from Woods Hole Oceanographic Institution, who will testify that he conducted an analysis of the life raft drift. And fortuitously there is a buoy right in the middle of where Mr. Carman was picked up and says he sank, a Woods Hole buoy, that measures wind speed and direction and current speed and direction. And based on that information, Limeburner did what's called a reverse drift analysis, calculating where Carman's life raft would have had to start, seven days before, to get to the *Orient Lucky*; and that is all the way to the southeast.

Limeburner also did a forward drift analysis, starting at Block Canyon at the 140-fathom mark. Where would Carman end up seven days later? Northwest; an eighty-mile difference. So Limeburner will say that the oceanographic evidence does not support a sinking in Block Canyon on September 18th. He's backed up by Fishing

Vessel *Prudence* Captain Alex Aucoin who will testify he was fishing in Block Canyon that day and he didn't see anything.

And we'll also hear from Dr. Stuart Harris from Harvard Medical School and the Massachusetts General Hospital Emergency Room Department, who has a specialty in wilderness medicine and hypothermia. Based on very good photographs and video from the *Orient Lucky*, Dr. Harris will testify that after seven days adrift, Mr. Carman's physiological condition and his fine and gross motor skills would have suffered, he would in no way be able to stand up in the life raft and wave a flag.

He would in no way be able to swim to the life ring that was tossed to him and hold on, as he is with his right hand.

He would in no way be able to fend off the ship with his fingertips.

And he would in no way be able to walk up the steep gangway without missing a step while firmly holding onto the handrails with his fingers.

So, Dr. Harris will testify that Mr. Carman must have been in the life raft significantly shorter than seven days.

Despite all of this, Mr. Carman submitted a marine insurance claim for eighty-five thousand dollars, and on October 19th he submitted this one-page written description of the accident and the sinking. But Mr. Carman in this report, despite talking about how much water was present in the bilge, makes no mention of the bilge pump problems and his replacement of the bilge pump the prior day. He mentioned nothing about the

> removal of the bulkheads, and he mentioned nothing about the holes in his hull that he filled with putty.
>
> After receiving that report, Ms. Charlesworth, with us at counsel table, asked that Mr. Carman submit to an examination under oath, as required under his insurance policy and on December 16th Mr. Carman did come in, and I took a five-hour examination of him under oath.
>
> We then denied his insurance claim in January 2017 and filed suit seeking the Court's judgment that the denial was proper.
>
> Your Honor, Plaintiffs appreciate the opportunity to present evidence in this truncated version of a tragic case which still reverberates three years afterwards. Thank you.
>
> THE COURT: Great. Thank you.
>
> Mr. Anderson, do you want to open now?
>
> MR. ANDERSON: Yes, Your Honor.

Anderson didn't have to. He could have waited until we finished with our case and he started putting on his. But that almost never happens.

Attorney Anderson also referred to coming exhibits during his opening statement.

> So first of all, I guess there's two issues in this case, at least in this first bifurcated part of the case. The first revolves around this boat, the *Chicken Pox*, and the second revolves around the policy, about the practices of the Insurer in terms of dealing with consumers purchasing recreational boat insurance, and also what are the terms of the policy and then the application of maritime law to those terms of that policy.

Let me start with the boat, the *Chicken Pox*. It was never built as a boat. It started life as what's called a plug. The plug was built in '74, so we're talking about a plug which got turned into a boat which apparently worked some unknown place for twenty years until eventually, in around 2007, Mr. Woods bought it.

It was configured as a lobster boat when he bought it. It sat in the yard just out in the rain, with leaves and water sitting in the bilge, for a couple of years. He finally stripped it down to the bare hull, and then rebuilt the boat first as a speedboat, but the thing couldn't even get up on a plane because it was so darn heavy. And that's when he put in the trim tabs.

It still wouldn't get up on a plane. So then he reconfigured it as a center-console boat where he had a single center console which was enclosed, fully enclosed and with a door, sitting directly on top of a new engine. Then he, with his experience as an aluminum fabricator, he then basically made it look pretty nice by putting aluminum, basically aluminum frame and decking on top of what was about a thirty-five-year-old waterlogged hull, which was never built as a hull but rather was built just in order to make a mold. So that's the boat.

You're going to hear evidence that a gentleman named Mr. Roth, way back in 2008, and his son was working with him doing some work for Mr. Woods and they asked him, "Do you want us to cut this hull up and just throw it in the dumpster?" Mr. Woods was told at that time that that thing is not structurally sound, you're wasting your time and money trying to turn it into something. And it turned out that was correct. Mr. Woods had what he thought would be a quick flip, you know, fare it out, paint it up, you know, make it look nice and sell for big money. It didn't turn out that way.

In fact, no one made offers on the boat until Mr. Carman came along. And at the time Mr. Carman, you know, he's a young twenty-two-year-old kid with more money than experience.

But the reality is that the boat, that this *Chicken Pox*, the boat that sank, was really—it was like a thirty-five-year-old boat which was never designed to be a boat in the first place, which had seen way too many years, and structurally really had deteriorated.

And we found out during the course of this case why the boat was named *Chicken Pox*, and you're going to hear from Mr. Roth the reason they called it *Chicken Pox* is there was water weeping out of these little chicken-pox-looking things, little blisters that come out with water or some liquid dripping down from them. And these are photographs taken when Mr. Woods was trying to rehab the boat.

So there were real problems with the *Chicken Pox*. It looked pretty good on the surface, but underneath it really wasn't a great boat, okay, in terms of structural. That's not something Mr. Carman knew. It's not something the insurance company knew. But it's a fact.

And let me address the insurance policy. And you're going to hear that Mr. Carman was looking to buy the *Chicken Pox*. He had a quote from the Insurer that described the type of policy it was, which was an All Risk policy, and he called them up and said, "Okay, I want to buy the insurance you quoted me."

And you'll hear evidence from Mr. Carman that he never got the policy. He acknowledges maybe it came in the mail and I threw it away or lost it or whatever, but I never got it.

So an important distinction in this case, as opposed to perhaps cases under state law—the general maritime law, in connection with insurance, imposes upon all parties a duty of utmost good faith and fair dealings. That means you cannot keep your cards to your chest; you've got to lay them on the table. You've got to give your counterpart all the information that a reasonable counterparty would want to know and that you know they want to know, and so you've got to be fair with them. It's not buyer beware under the general maritime law. You've got to treat them fairly. And that's true of both sides.

Even with respect to Mr. Carman, he has exactly the same duty. He has an obligation to treat the insurance company fairly, when asked for information, to provide them the information that he knows. A twenty-two-year-old kid, you know, very little practical experience, a lot less knowledge than he should have or that he thought he had, but he treated them fairly. Never lied to them, always treated them fairly, never withheld anything. He fulfilled his obligation under the duty of utmost good faith and fair dealing, and from the inception the Plaintiffs in this case didn't, because what they really did was a bait and switch.

So, about the way the boat sank. There's a lot of things that could have caused this vessel to sink, okay, and we're not going to be able to prove what it is.

What Mr. Farrell is trying to prove—and I don't know where he's going as to this trial with respect to the location of the sinking—but Block Canyon does not have a clearly defined boundary. You know, it's not like the city limits of Providence. Block Canyon, I mean it's a place, and you'll see it on the charts, but you're going to see that all of these different charts label Block Canyon at different places and that the shape, that classical canyon shape on the chart, varies with the scale of the chart.

And so the evening before the boat sank, Mr. Carman didn't pull out a chart, you know, decide which longitude and latitude he wanted to go to, plot a course with a pencil and ruler and all that sort of stuff. What he did was he took this plotter, this electronic device, it runs off electricity, and he looked at where Block Canyon was, and he decided he wanted to go to one end of Block Canyon and then troll through the length of it. So he went to the far south end of Block Canyon, as depicted on the chart on the plotter as zoomed out, tapped the plotter, it gives you a waypoint, and then hit some buttons on the side that told the autopilot controlling the wheel to go there, and he went there. And it's like he—it's just like he's working off the electronics and having the electronics take him there.

But in terms of actual real knowledge of where am I, he had none. It's like these kids who, like, you know, grow up with iPhones and they want to visit a friend in upstate New York and they just whip out their iPhone and they just put it in the car and they drive. They don't really know where they are; they just listen to the iPhone tell them to take a left, go straight, etc. And that's what occurred here.

And so I think the evidence in this case is going to be that Mr. Carman was significantly farther south than where Mr. Farrell has him.

So I don't know what Mr. Farrell is talking about, about the drift and so forth. Nonetheless, you're obviously going to hear evidence of it, and the reality is when you're out there and you're looking around and all you see is water, your only point of reference is your ability, how you navigated there. But if how you navigated there is sort of the modern way, if you will, which is you just go to electronics and you tap it and say go there, it's not really—you don't really have a strong sense of direction of where you are.

So I think when you hear the evidence, I think you've got to ask yourself, Is this how I would want to be treated if I was a consumer, not super knowledgeable about this stuff, you know? I work as an accountant and I have a boat I take out, on the bay on the weekends, is that how I would want to be treated both in terms of the marketing, the sale of the product, and then afterwards when they're trying to get out of paying and they're bringing up all sorts of clauses which clearly don't apply? And so, with that, I'm done.

THE COURT: Thanks, Mr. Anderson.

Mr. Farrell, your first witness.

MR. FARRELL: Thank you, Your Honor. We call Brian Woods.

Unseaworthy Alterations

Brian Woods's testimony on my direct exam demonstrated his lifelong professional boatbuilding expertise. He narrated photo exhibits showing his work on the JC 31 as it progressed. Essentially, he took the old lobster boat apart down to its skin and bones, sanding the solid hull comprised of the mahogany plug sandwiched between fiberglass on the inboard and outboard sides.

Woods testified there was no waterlogging problem but at some point someone used sheetrock screws on portions of the hull which had bled drops of now-hardened greenish resin. About that *Chicken Pox* name—Woods said it was a follow-up to his parents' boat named *Goose Bumps*, which might not have completely convinced anyone. More convincingly, he used sturdy two-by-ten-inch pressure-treated lumber to replace athwartship ribs, which, along with the longitudinal stringers, he fiberglassed to the bilge. As well, he added layers of fiberglass on both inboard and outboard sides of the hull with nice, finished gel coating outboard. The boat was "solid as a rock."

A little levity entered the courtroom when I asked about his employees.

> Q: And what did the Roths do to the boat?
>
> A: Make a mess.
>
> THE COURT: Why don't we stop on that high note and take our mid-morning break. We'll be back in fifteen minutes.

Woods went on describing his first refurbished rendition of the JC 31 plug as a sleek-looking aluminum speedboat, which did not live up to its visuals. It was then, in 2009, that he added the extra-long trim tabs to help it get up on plane. He followed the Bennett instructions, personally drilling four ½ inch diameter holes through the transom hull for the four actuators, connecting each to a bronze tube fitting through the transom hole which attached to a bronze elbow inside the bilge, then to a flexible hose from the hydraulic pump.

As Attorney Anderson had described in his opening, the trim tabs didn't help at that point. So Woods revised the design with the walk-around wheelhouse amidships and replaced the gas engine with a used, lighter yet stronger diesel. He added the forward bulkheads, fiberglassing them to the bilge, and tightly adhering them to the aluminum fish box with 3M 5200 sealant.

A "Mr. Carmine" contacted Woods about buying the boat. The prospective buyer said he was a "homebuilder" and looked like he was in his "mid-forties" due to his "full beard and long hair," not anything like his appearance today in court, Woods testified. Woods offered him an option for secure storage of ten fishing rods under both port and starboard gunwales, but he decided against that.

Wrapping up with Woods, we showed the video of the boat, which looked "gorgeous" planing through the Cape Cod Canal after Nathan took delivery in December 2015—without final payment—all of which Woods recounted for the court. He was incredulous that Carman planned to take the boat to Rhode Island in winter without any life preservers and Woods insisted he take some along.

It was then Attorney Anderson's time to cross-examine Woods. They started waltzing aimlessly with no apparent goal in sight until, quite suddenly, Attorney Anderson showed his smarts and courtroom skill, focusing for no discernible reason on Woods's installation of the ribs and the perpendicular stringers at the stern, and his subsequent securing of the deck on top of them. Soon Anderson's point became clear. Since Woods installed the trim tabs after the deck was down, he would have been unable to fit the brass tube screwed into the larger brass elbow through the ½ inch diameter holes from the outside.

> Q: Okay. How did you get it inside the hull?
>
> A: I believe before the deck was painted over there were holes cut into the deck to reach in to fit this in.
>
> Q: Whoa. Do you remember reaching your hand through holes in the deck for that purpose?
>
> A: I vaguely remember doing that.

Q: When did you first vaguely remember doing that? You've testified in this case in a deposition. You testified this morning. You never mentioned a vague memory of reaching your hand through holes in the deck which had been left there in order to install trim tabs. You agree with that?

A: I do agree with that.

Q: So when did you first have this vague memory of doing this?

A: Actually, it's happening as we sit here.

It was ten years ago, after all. Woods remained unflustered.

Q: Okay. Do you have a single photograph that shows how big these holes were?

A: I don't recall, but I'm thinking it was a four-inch hole, just enough to get your hand in.

Q: So today it occurred to you, you must have drilled a hole in the deck, correct?

A: Your questions allowed me to think more about this, actually. The way you walked through it, I realized that, yes, there was another alternative.

Attorney Anderson then charged ahead, offering more alternatives. One was that Woods could have used an electrician's snake to grab and pull the flexible hose from the hydraulic pump around or through stringers and ribs, and Woods agreed that, too, was theoretically feasible. And there was another way.

Q: And so you might have to drill a little bit bigger transom hole or widen the hole out in some manner. True?

A: If that was the way it was done, yes.

This was a terrific (and terrifying) point. Attorney Anderson was suggesting that the four ½ inch diameter thru-transom holes Woods says he drilled for the actuators must have been bigger in order to push the wider bronze elbow into the bilge from the outside since it couldn't otherwise get inside the bilge if no access holes were cut into the deck.

Would Anderson then press Woods to admit that the transom holes were as big as a half-dollar? Surprisingly, no. Instead, his questioning went back to confirming that Woods's holes were only ½ inch in diameter:

Q: So, thinking about it, do you think that's probably what you did?

A: Since your description, I've been thinking about it quite a bit, and honestly, I can't remember how it was done.

Q: And sitting here today, you just don't remember exactly what fitting you used or exactly how you installed the trim tabs. Is that a fair statement?

A: I remember installing the trim tabs. The exact fittings I used for the hydraulics and how exactly they were connected, I can't say that I remember exactly.

Q: Bennett's got fittings for everything. Wouldn't you think you could just look in the catalog and they'd have a ninety-degree fitting, they would have a straight fitting, they would have a bunch of different things?

A: They very well may, but I don't remember. I can't remember using a ninety-degree elbow, I can't remember using a straight.

Q: And if you'd only used a straight fitting, and Mr. Carman were to have removed the trim tabs, he could pull the three screws out of the actuator, and then he could grab the actuator and then the hydraulic line would come straight out. And then he'd take a utility knife, cut the hydraulic line, push it back in, and now he's got a hole; but that would be—if, in fact, the way I described it is how it was done—it would have been very easy for Mr. Carman to do what I just described. Is that true?

A: That would be true if it was done the way you described.

Q: And sitting here today, you can't say one way or the other whether it was or whether it wasn't done the way I described; but you do agree the way I described is the easiest and simplest way to do it?

A: Yes, which is different than my deposition.

Q: And your testimony earlier this morning.

A: Yeah.

This sounded very damaging—but was it? No doubt Attorney Anderson had done an excellent, tenacious job bringing out that Woods now could not recall precisely ten years ago how he connected the hydraulic lines to the actuators. I didn't see it coming.

But Attorney Anderson asked one too many questions, leaving the final impression that the thru-transom holes Woods drilled were indeed only ½ inch in diameter, with the flexible hose running straight from the hydraulic pump in the bilge to a bronze tube in the transom hole screwed into the actuator without employing any elbow inside the bilge. If the hose was reachable as Nathan bent over the transom, and easily cut, that would obviate his need to use a hole saw to drill a bigger hole in order to access any bronze elbow that may or may not have been inside the bilge.

All told, however, Anderson's points were at most a field goal. Because in the grand scheme of things, whatever way Woods attached the hydraulics did not critically matter. Nathan was forever stuck with observing four half-dollar-size holes at the actuators ever since Attorney Santos's October 12, 2016 letter. And in any event, however they got there, the Genius chose not to seal his sloppy putty job with the fiberglass repair kit he bought the very day he removed the trim tabs.

My re-direct exam questions ignored the precise hydraulic hookup and planted the seed for the cause of sinking. Confident that it was Nathan who increased the ½ inch holes to half-dollar size, which of course were below the scuppers and opened straight into the bilge, I asked:

> Q: Mr. Anderson asked you about those baffles on the outboard side of the scuppers on the transom.
>
> A: Yes.
>
> Q: And you remember he asked you about backing down for tuna fishing and not letting the water come back into the deck because of those baffles?
>
> A: Yes.
>
> Q: Would those baffles be effective were the boat moving forward in a following sea?
>
> A: Yes.
>
> Q: And what would their effect be?
>
> A: They would prevent water from washing onto the deck.
>
> Q: And when I talk about a following sea, I'm talking about waves from the stern.
>
> A: Yes.

Oh, and that field goal? They were the very last points Nathan and Attorney Anderson would score.

***

Next up, Liam called marine surveyor Bernie Feeney, hired by Nathan for a prepurchase survey, chronologically the next logical witness.

We hired Feeney too, as an expert witness, but he had never before testified. He was completely down-to-earth likable and charmed the judge. Feeney had been an aircraft mechanic in Vietnam and president of the Massachusetts Lobstermen's Association for fifteen years. He was also personally familiar with the JC 31 plug during its life as a lobster boat and knew its owner then.

Feeney initially used an ultrasound moisture meter and percussion testing with a nylon hammer, finding the "hull was in very good shape," with moisture readings within acceptable ranges. Any elevated moisture readings were attributable to the mahogany core, which has an inherent moisture content, and not excess water. He went on a sea trial with Nathan and Woods and all systems worked well.

Feeney was critical of Nathan's transom hole repairs with putty without inboard backing, his bulkhead removal, and his failure to remedy chronic bilge pump problems. Very familiar with Down East-style boats, Feeney had seen several sink. "They sink stern first; the bow would be upward, where the air pocket would be," he said.

During all this Attorney Anderson was objecting so often, almost always getting overruled, that Judge McConnell told him, "You can have a standing objection Mr. Anderson." But Anderson kept objecting, with the professionally patient but personally exasperated judge at one point even imploring, "David, David, David...."

After more Anderson objections, Judge McConnell eventually ruled, "The Court finds Mr. Feeney eminently qualified to be able to give expert opinion in this case based on his qualifications, his training, and his experience in this area, and particularly on the issue of causation." This meant that Feeney could testify not only that Nathan's work on the boat was poor quality but also that it caused the sinking, and he did.

THE WITNESS: Just putting epoxy into these holes without backing meant that the epoxy had the ability to get pushed through the hole by water pressure outside the boat.

Having four holes in the back of a boat is just lending itself to taking water on, and he had bilge pump issues, you've got water coming in. He was using the boat for approximately—I think twelve hours was about the trip length. He could have been taking water in all the time while he was fishing.

So we had four 1½ inch holes versus the original holes that were there, which were ½ inch or so for the fittings.

THE COURT: So your opinion is dependent on it being a 1½ inch hole?

THE WITNESS: No, the fact that it has holes. Boats aren't supposed to have holes.

THE COURT: So, if the hole were the same as when the trim tabs were originally put in, if they followed the instructions, at ½ inch, you'd have the same opinion?

THE WITNESS: Yes, I'd have the same opinion.

Feeney then addressed the removed bulkheads.

THE WITNESS: Had the bulkheads been sawn out at the time of my survey, the boat should not have been launched. The bulkheads are there for a very specific reason, actually two reasons, one being for the structural integrity of that portion of the boat, and two, although they weren't watertight, they were pretty well tight to the deck. That would have been an air pocket that would have been a reserve if, in fact, the boat flooded. So it would have had some more buoyancy at that portion of the boat.

THE COURT: So in your opinion, Mr. Feeney, to a reasonable degree of scientific certainty, did the removal of the bulkheads increase the risk that the boat would come into safety troubles?

THE WITNESS: It increased the risk, if the boat flooded, of that area of the boat no longer having that air pocket. So it would flood the entire bilge area.

Tie that with an intermittent bilge pump issue and holes in the back, there's a certainty that boat's going to be in peril at some point in time.

MR. O'CONNELL: Nothing further, Your Honor.

THE COURT: Great. Thanks, Mr. O'Connell.

After Attorney Anderson's cross-exam went absolutely nowhere on hull moisture levels, specifically as to Nathan's JC 31 and as to mahogany boats in general, Liam on re-direct asked:

Q: Last question, Mr. Feeney, and I probably should have asked before. Do you specifically have experience with mahogany-core boats?

MR. ANDERSON: Objection, Your Honor. It's not in his report.

THE COURT: Overruled.

A: Absolutely. I've owned three mahogany boats in my life. Two were mahogany, not fiberglassed, a regular old-fashioned boat. I had one built brand new in 1982, 1¼ inch mahogany over oak. It was built up in South Bristol, Maine, by Bruce Farrins, a great boat builder. The last boat that I used, that I retired out of, was made in Plymouth, Massachusetts by the Jesse's yard in 1959. It was 1½ inch mahogany on oak. It was fiberglassed on the outside, with a ½ inch of fiberglass material, and that boat is still working today, sixty years old.

I know mahogany boats, and I know mahogany wood, and I know fiberglass over mahogany.

MR. O'CONNELL: Thank you, Your Honor.

Liam was done with his re-direct and Attorney Anderson had done his cross, so the lawyers' questioning of Feeney was finished, yet there was more to come.

THE COURT: Mr. Feeney, I have a few questions for you.

THE WITNESS: Sure.

As you have already seen, it is common in a bench trial for a judge to jump right in and ask questions of the witnesses. Often top-notch trial lawyers themselves, federal judges know what facts they think are critical in the case they are hearing, and usually they just can't help themselves. But now we were ringside to an uncommon way for a lawyer to jab a judge.

THE COURT: So removal of the bulkhead in your expert opinion would have made the boat unseaworthy?

MR. ANDERSON: Objection, Your Honor. I'm going to object to your question, which I think I can do. I recognize I'll probably get overruled on it, but this is beyond the scope of his expertise, beyond the scope of his disclosure.

And insofar as the question probably can only tend to hurt my client, I am going to object even if you're asking the question.

For Attorney Liam O'Connell, opportunity knocked.

THE COURT: Do you want to defend me, Mr. O'Connell?

MR. O'CONNELL: Yes, Your Honor. I'll represent you here. Mr. Carman used Mr. Feeney's survey report in order to purchase the vessel and obtain insurance. Clearly it's within the realm of Mr. Feeney's testimony to say the boat was seaworthy or not.

THE COURT: "Seaworthy" is a word that's not used in the insurance policy. It affects the insurance policy because it's used in maritime law.

I ask you, Mr. Feeney, whether the boat was seaworthy when Mr. Carman bought it and your opinion whether it was seaworthy after he made certain repairs on it.

THE WITNESS: Seaworthy when I did my initial report and not seaworthy, using that same definition, after knowing what he had done to the boat.

THE COURT: Great. Mr. Feeney, thank you. You can step down.

Feeney not only scored a touchdown for us—Anderson gave up a safety.

***

Our next witness was the Insurer's VP of underwriting, to address Nathan's marine insurance policy. Incessant objections from Attorney Anderson to my questions and the judge's occasional questions unduly dragged out the testimony with nothing much of great importance to further bore you. The VP's key testimony was that after receiving the Feeney prepurchase survey report describing the boat's good condition and insuring it on that basis, had the Insurer been made aware of Nathan's bulkhead removal, bilge pump problems, and transom hole repairs, the Insurer would have put the boat on "port risk ashore"—continuing to insure it only if the boat was taken out of the water.

Liam then called Point Judith Marine mechanic Bud Smedberg, who had worked on Nathan's boat during the summer of 2016.

The original diesel had developed several problems, and after Nathan overheated it in the Harbor of Refuge, Smedberg installed a newer model. It was sturdily supported by and securely lag-bolted to longitudinal stringers. Smedberg sea trialed the new Cummins diesel, reaching a wide-open-throttle maximum speed of 20 knots.

But Nathan had recurring problems with his port cockpit bilge pump. Four times Smedberg had to go to Ram Point Marina to deal with its blown fuses and pump out accumulated rainwater, but Nathan would not authorize Point Judith Marine to otherwise troubleshoot that obvious electrical problem. The opposite of genius.

Next, eyewitness to the trim tabs removal, Mike Iozzi was a handful. With Nathan alive and well, Iozzi continued fearful and reluctant to testify against him. Liam had Iozzi come to the Hilton to prep the morning before testifying, but the tough old coot brought his policeman son along and was pleading, almost crying, and refusing to testify despite his trial subpoena. But he did, telling the court he had cut concrete for "forty years" and "I would say probably in the course of a year, we probably drill a couple, five hundred holes" with hole saws. Plus, Iozzi said he owned an eighteen-foot Boston Whaler, a thirty-two-foot Chris-Craft, and a thirty-six-foot cabin cruiser.

Iozzi clearly had knowledgeable background but he was so nervous, chomping on his dentures throughout, that he looked like he might expire midsentence. There's a reason these proceedings at the center of our legal system are called trials. Nothing is easy.

Iozzi was sitting on the Ram Point Marina dock around 5:00 p.m. on the Saturday before "all the media" excitement, visiting his friends the Ferreiras, whose boat was docked near Nathan's.

> Q: And did you talk to Mr. Carman?
>
> A: He said he was fixing the—what do you call the flappers?—trim tabs. Looks like he was drilling holes in the transom. Two holes I saw him drill, maybe eight inches apart.
>
> Q: And what's the diameter of that hole saw?
>
> A: It's about approximately two-inch.
>
> Q: Could you see what Mr. Carman was doing with the drill?
>
> A: Well, the dock is higher than the waterline on the boat, so I wasn't able to see the actual hole.
>
> I saw him bending over, doing that—you can get electrocuted—and he wasn't polishing the water, that's for sure.
>
> And then he applied some adhesive over the holes. It was all stuck on his hands.

***

Marine surveyor and yacht accident reconstructionist Jonathan Klopman was next. He displayed a RIDGID reciprocating saw, the exact kind Nathan said he used to cut out the forward bulkheads.

On my questioning, Klopman showed the illogic of Nathan's trim tabs removal. Klopman explained how he had built his exemplar of the transom based on measurements he took from another JC 31 and added an exemplar trim tab, pointing out that the actual trim tabs on the boat were forty-two inches wide. Referring to his exemplar, Klopman testified that Nathan "would have to be leaning over at the waist" to reach the actuators and trim tabs below.

> A: It's an unnecessary repair that was done with an urgency the day before the boat was to go offshore. Considering the difficulty and inconvenience of removing the trim tabs, I just don't understand, with all the other things to be done, why you would get involved with that. And, the removal process is going to leave you with holes in the boat just above the waterline.
>
> Q: Let's talk, Mr. Klopman, about the use of a hole saw, a corded hole saw, in connection with the removal of the trim tabs and that process. Did you draw any conclusion on that?
>
> A: Yes. The process of removing the trim tabs would require some tools, but there's no logical reason to use a hole saw in removing that actuator. It's of absolutely no use. At the same time, once again, you're leaning over the transom with a corded tool two inches above the waterline. You're seriously risking electrocution. So I don't know what would drive someone to do a job that's unnecessary in the first place. The trim tabs don't really need to be removed. You're going offshore and you're leaving the boat with holes in the waterline. I'm at a loss.

Mirroring the underwriting VP's testimony, Klopman testified that if in the course of his work as a marine surveyor he had been aboard a boat and seen puttied transom holes near the waterline, he would have telephoned the underwriter then and there to "place the boat on port risk ashore."

The proper hole repair would have been for Nathan to use the Fiberglass Boat Repair Kit,[121] which he bought at West Marine the same time he bought the Epoxy Putty Stick, to soak the fiberglass matting with resin and place it over the holes to allow "the tenacious ability of the resin to adhere to the surface," making the holes "perfectly secure and watertight."

Klopman then addressed the bilge water in the boat as described by Nathan just prior to the sinking. Narrating his graphic diagrams of bilge water levels observed by Nathan, first halfway up the battery boxes, and within a minute later, three inches below the cockpit deck, Klopman showed that there was a difference of ten to twelve inches in water level between Nathan's two observations. Because they were only a minute apart, Klopman "would expect the water levels to be somewhat corresponding." He added, however, that "with significantly higher water level back aft, that naturally tends to suggest that the stern of the boat was sinking."

***

Naval architect Eric Greene, with a degree from MIT, added to Nathan's problems by causally connecting seawater ingress to his shoddy putty repair. Skipping over extensive technical testimony on water plane coefficients from what was not a *New York Times* bestselling book, *Wetted Surface Area of Recreational Boats*, and further skipping over weight differentials from topped-off fuel tanks and how much that weight diminished over thirteen engine hours until sinking, Greene's testimony on Liam's questioning was in essence common sense.

First, the removal of the forward bulkheads made the boat less seaworthy, increasing tortional stress and reducing buoyancy. "Short of hitting a large foreign object or a rogue wave coming over the top," Greene did not "see any way that this boat would rapidly sink by the

---

[121] Tr. Ex. 5.58.

bow. It would go down by the stern, but it's the rapidity of the sinking that I find incredulous."

Second, Greene recounted the experiment he performed before we filed suit, replicating Nathan's putty repair, which "made the boat unseaworthy."

> A: The proper way to fix the holes would have been to haul the boat and be able to inspect your work, put a solid plug that would preferably taper so it did fill the hole, and then fiberglass on the outside. So before I even did this experiment, I was convinced his was an improper way to repair the boat. This just reinforced my opinion.

Greene had drilled four half-dollar-size holes in plywood as described by Nathan in his EUO and using only three-quarters of the Epoxy Putty Stick, as Nathan had testified, Greene tried to seal those holes. "There was insufficient volume of epoxy putty to fill the holes and no way to prevent the material from going out the back of the holes as you were trying to effect repair from one side."[122]

---

[122] Tr. Ex. 38.

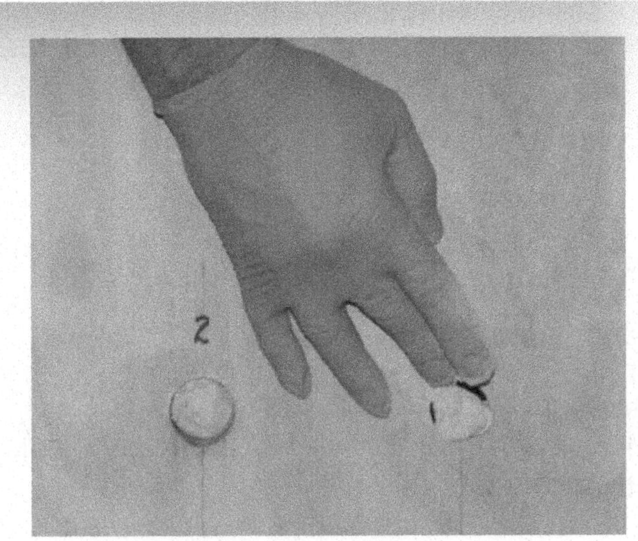

Figure 6. Attempted repair procedure in progress

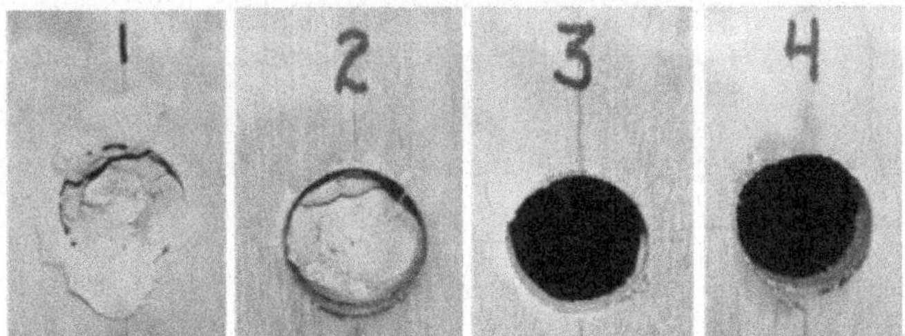

Figure 7. Results immediately after attempted repair

While the four holes would clearly be well above the water surface when the boat was on plane, due to a void of displaced water astern the transom down to the bottom of the hull, that was not the case at slow speeds.

> A: According to Mr. Carman's examination under oath, he spent approximately five hours trolling in a northerly direction. The significance of this would be that the prevailing swells at the time were from the southeasterly direction, and that would mean that he would be trolling with a

> following sea, which would make the effect of improperly repaired holes in the transom more problematic. The likelihood of water coming in those holes would be more significant with the following sea.

"Go Rams!"

Moving on from Nathan's unseaworthy alterations to the boat, Liam next put on our Block Canyon eyewitness on the day Nathan says he sank there, *Prudence* Captain Alex Aucoin. He was truly a good find. "Block Canyon's a place where I've been my entire fishing career, pretty much."

Aucoin presented stunning testimony. A University of Rhode Island grad with a degree in coastal management and fisheries, Aucoin had seventeen years of commercial fishing experience. He captained the *Prudence* on September 18, 2016, lobstering near the north end of Block Canyon that day. Convincingly, he remembered that specific day because he is "somewhat of a Down East center-console enthusiast, so I actually knew that boat personally" from Point Judith, where *Prudence* berthed at Town Dock, and he later heard the Coast Guard broadcasts that it was overdue.

Prior to testifying, Aucoin had reviewed his log for September 18. At trial, he marked on NOAA Chart 12300 where *Prudence* was working from 5:00 a.m. until heading back home that afternoon.

> A: We're an offshore lobster boat. We haul lobster trawls. So we go back and forth. The trawls are around a mile long, there's forty pots per trawl, and we haul them up and then set them back on that mile. So we go back and forth all day long.

Prudence has all the best navigational electronics including one radar that was set on a six-mile range to observe nearby vessel traffic. Aucoin testified he would have been able to visually identify Nathan's boat or its orange life raft in the clear weather had either been within three miles. He drew three- and six-mile lines bounding the two sides of *Prudence*'s two-legged west to east hauling track that morning,[123] then in the afternoon went south to north, straight through the Fishtails "between 110 to 135 fathoms right at the top of Block Canyon on the western side."

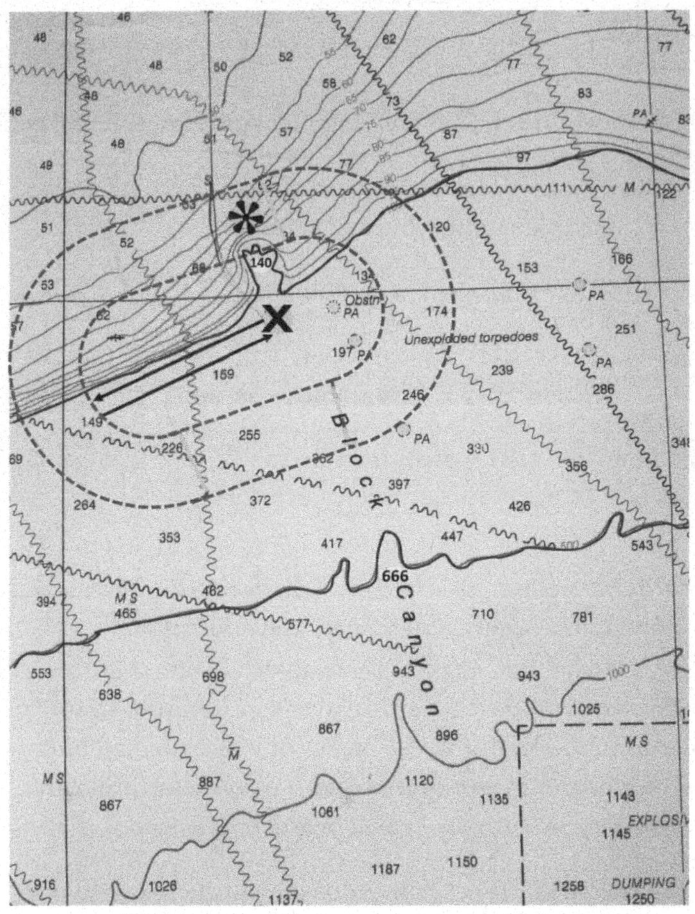

123 https://www.rid.uscourts.gov/sites/rid/files/documents/17cv38/081619/p1.2.13.pdf

Q: And on September 18th, 2016, while you were transiting Block Canyon during the day, do you recall seeing another boat?

A: No.

Q: Do you remember seeing a life raft?

A: No.

When Aucoin's testimony was completed, we knew it had gone well.

THE COURT: Mr. Aucoin, you're welcome to go. Thank you for your testimony.

THE WITNESS: Thank you.

THE COURT: We appreciate your time. Go Rams! because they clearly trained you well.

Who knew the URI mascot is a ram?

***

Liam's next witness was Martha Charlesworth, Marine Insurance Legal Counsel, our client's representative at counsel table.

When Nathan first made his insurance claim, Martha had been already assigned to oversee it. Liam started off with a simple question about her insurance claim notes, copies of which we had long ago provided to Defendant. Here's a very typical, exasperating exchange that we had to deal with on virtually every document during the trial:

THE COURT: Okay. You've identified it. Are you moving its admission?

MR. O'CONNELL: I am, Your Honor.

THE COURT: Mr. Anderson?

> MR. ANDERSON: I object on the basis of hearsay and that this witness has not laid a foundation that would bring it within a hearsay exception. I would also object on the ground that if it is a business record, and some of it may very well be, but there's also hearsay within hearsay and I would object for that hearsay within hearsay to go in for the truth of the matter asserted.

This is precisely why Liam went to Sumatra to get the *Orient Lucky* chart and log, to avoid a similar Anderson double-hearsay objection, just in case the judge saw it differently than he did here.

> THE COURT: That objection is noted, overruled, and Exhibit 17.2 is admitted in full.

Also typical when it came to any exhibit, Liam had been designated by the judge to coordinate with the courtroom clerk to make sure Martha's claim notes were properly numbered and recorded on the master exhibit list. This is a basic housekeeping tool that the older we get, the more likely we are to royally botch, as I often do. Let's follow Attorney Anderson's lead and call the courtroom clerk "Clerk Z." She was lovely and gracious and had more decades of experience than anyone else in the courtroom. Thus, Liam frequently had to right an upside-down chart or photo or renumber an exhibit.

Martha eventually, before too much time trickled by—but tick-tock it did to our detriment every time an objection was made—resumed her testimony.

> A: The call came in from Mr. Carman on a Friday afternoon, and he was confused that I knew who he was, so I just explained that I hadn't reached out to him, I was giving him time to grieve, and I just walked him through what the claims process would be. I knew there was one person presumed dead and a boat that was sunk, and per my note

Mr. Carman did say that it was not likely to be recovered because it was very far offshore.

Q: What did you do next?

A: So my next step was to do a written reservation of rights, which I emailed to Mr. Carman and I assigned your office for coverage assistance. Especially when it comes to sinkings, we always want to know if any work had been done on the boat, and we just ask for any information that the insured thinks would help us understand what was going on, to get a better picture of it.

Q: Okay. Did you receive a written account from Mr. Carman?

A: I did.

And into evidence, this time without objection from Attorney Anderson, came Nathan's one-page report to Martha—the sinking evolution ending with "I then made myself take rest."

Martha recounted her request that Nathan present himself for an examination under oath, the new information from Attorney Santos's October 12, 2016 letter to the Connecticut prosecutors, her written denial of Nathan's claim, and our filing this suit, which is what brought her to Providence to testify. She was personable and straightforward, and everything she did in handling Nathan's claim was by the book, careful, and in good faith.

"If He Were My Client..."

With Martha just about to wrap up but still on the stand, and Nathan on deck, Judge McConnell announced, "We'll take our midafternoon break," adjourning for fifteen minutes. "Can I see counsel at the bench, though?"

The judge immediately confronted Attorney Anderson.

THE COURT: David Anderson, with Mr. Carman about to testify, I need some level of assurance from you that he's been fully advised of his Fifth Amendment rights.

For instance, there could be issues of the repairs that he made to the boat that could be used against him in a potential future criminal prosecution.

I'm not claiming that any of this is true. I'm just concerned about in a civil context involving insurance coverage issues that he could be giving information that could later be used by the government against him.

Now, with that said, I would—I'm suggesting that you assure him that he can assert his Fifth Amendment right. He can assert it before he gives any further testimony.

Liam and I looked at each other and couldn't quite believe what we'd just heard. Judge McConnell was actually recommending that Nathan take the Fifth, fold his cards, and effectively drop his insurance claim.

MR. ANDERSON: He has, Your Honor, in connection with this case and lawsuit against him in New Hampshire, he has taken the Fifth Amendment with respect to answers which would incriminate him in connection with the Connecticut assault weapon ban, and he has repeatedly—

MR. FARRELL: I think that's misstated.

MR. ANDERSON. With respect to any information relating to the sinking of his boat, he has not taken the Fifth with respect to anything about—

THE COURT: Has he been fully informed of the risk involved with testifying that could have Fifth Amendment waiver violations? That's my concern.

MR. ANDERSON: In connection with this trial, the answer's no.

THE COURT: He needs to be informed of that—

MR. ANDERSON: Okay.

THE COURT: —before he testifies, and I need for you afterwards to assure me that he's been fully informed of that right and that he understands his right to assert his Fifth Amendment.

And then this bomb, its shock waves limited to counsel at the sidebar, showing even for Judge McConnell how hard it was to separate his bifurcated intentional sinking Phase II trial from this Phase I faulty repair insurance trial:

MR. ANDERSON: Okay. I would note, Your Honor, he's probably given twenty, twenty-four hours of testimony on this subject matter in every court, days and days of depositions and so forth; but I will advise him.

THE COURT: And if he were my client, he wouldn't have said a single word so far.[124]

---

124 "Nancy Gertner, a Harvard Law professor and former federal judge, also says Carman's testimony in the boat insurance trial 'could be used in the homicide case' and handed over to a prosecutor. And Carman could have avoided all of this if he backed down from the $85,000 claim. But he didn't." Susan Zalkind, "The 25-Year-Old Accused of Murdering his Mother and Grandfather is On Trial—for Boat Insurance," *Vice,* August 23, 2019. https://www.vice.com/en/article/the-25-year-old-accused-of-murdering-his-mother-and-grandfather-is-on-trialfor-boat-insurance/.

Things were looking grim for Nathan. That he might not testify after all seemed too good to be true. So naturally, I pressed.

> MR. FARRELL: Is Limeburner in play? You said earlier that Dr. Harris will not be testifying.
>
> THE COURT: Dr. Harris is the medical doctor?
>
> MR. FARRELL: Mass General Hospital, yes. But Limeburner is the Woods Hole oceanographer who talks about the reverse drift and that Mr. Carman would not have been able to sink at Block Canyon and drift to where the *Orient Lucky* picked him up.
>
> THE COURT: I could see where some of that testimony could be relevant at a minimum to his credibility, and—
>
> MR. O'CONNELL: I think it also is relevant with Aucoin's testimony.
>
> MR. FARRELL: Harris and Limeburner are fairly similar—
>
> THE COURT: Yes, I suppose—
>
> MR. FARRELL:—in their conclusions.
>
> THE COURT: Then you're probably right. You made me rethink it.

And again we couldn't quite believe our ears. Attorney Anderson was not going to object to oceanographer Limeburner's and Dr. Harris's testifying in Phase I regarding Nathan's credibility even though their testimonies substantively went to Nathan's criminally intentional, fraudulent sinking.

MR. ANDERSON: Your Honor, I do think that they have testimony which is arguably relevant, perhaps maybe even to credibility as to this claim.

THE COURT: If you're not objecting to them—

MR. ANDERSON: I'm not. I mean, if they want to put 'em on, put 'em on.

Attorney Anderson must have been 1,000 percent positive that he would blow Limeburner and Harris away on cross-exam. Was Anderson's arrogance and hubris, his personal involvement, getting in his way? Liam and I were even more confident they would both shine. But similarly, was our arrogance and hubris, our personal involvement, getting in our way? We didn't think so.

Objectively, based on the evidence obtained in our exhaustive discovery, in order for Anderson to be able to discredit Limeburner and Harris, Nathan would have to present an earth-shattering surprise during his testimony.

As I had anticipated, and as Attorney Anderson had mentioned in his opening, it had to be related to altering Nathan's solid, repeated, prior testimony about sinking at 140 fathoms in Block Canyon. It had to render Aucoin's eyewitness account of no other boat there meaningless. It meant Anderson and Nathan had their endgame in sight and were ready to go. I therefore counted on Nathan testifying in spite of Judge McConnell's admonition that he take the Fifth.

This sidebar was the yin and yang of Nathan's future—ending up cuffed and shackled as the judge warned or drifting away to freedom and fortune as his lawyer envisioned. Defendant had just upped the ante, transforming Phase I into criminality even before Nathan took the stand, ratcheting up the pressure. Depending on how I did with him on cross, Nathan would sink or swim in life.

Court adjourned early so that lawyer and client could deliberate as Judge McConnell directed. Just as Liam and I both assumed Nathan would choose to testify the next day, we also assumed Anderson would get Nathan to sign a malpractice waiver for not taking the Fifth. That evening Liam worked on preparing Limeburner and Harris and I kept refining my work on Nathan.

As an opposing party, since the Insurer was calling Nathan to the stand, I would be treating him as an adverse witness and cross-examine him with loaded questions. That would severely limit his ability to change his pretrial story. Significant changes in his prior testimony would come when Attorney Anderson had his turn to ask open-ended questions. Then I would have the chance to re-cross Nathan on testimony he gave on Attorney Anderson's questions.

***

I ran three miles at sunrise, ate a healthy breakfast, and tried to ration my coffee intake. I walked over to the courthouse early and alone, peppered by TV reporters on my way up the outside steps. "Are you calling Nathan today?" "What are you going to ask Nathan?" "You gonna ask what happened to his mother?" Over the decades you learn how to carry a big boxy trial bag in each hand, the dominant one also holding with minimal spillage a cup of coffee, which was a Dunkin' medium hot black. "Dunkin' keeps me running," I responded, like their ads, then securing the coffee cup between my teeth as I navigated my right bag under my left arm to free my right hand to open the courthouse door. Funny, right? Well, the reporters thought it was and it made it onto TV and YouTube. My only trial media statement.

The regular crowd shuffled in. Upon taking the bench, the Honorable John J. McConnell, Jr., referee and official timekeeper, commenced the day's proceedings.

> THE COURT: I have Plaintiffs with two hundred seventy minutes remaining, four and a half hours, and Defendant with three hundred minutes remaining, five hours. Mr. Farrell.
>
> MR. FARRELL: Thank you, Your Honor.

Despite Judge McConnell's strident counsel the afternoon before, Nathan at no time during our insurance trial took the Fifth. That was a big mistake.

I wanted to start with a zinger and finish up with a shoo-in (the term ought to be "shoe-in," as in horseshoes), knowing in between it would be a scrum. So after getting Nathan to confirm he was interviewed by the Coast Guard and the local Rhode Island police in Boston after *Orient Lucky* dropped him off, I asked:

> Q: And you were also met there by Attorney Trent LaLima of the Hartford law office of Hubert Santos, isn't that correct?
>
> A: If you mean met at the Coast Guard station in Boston, that is correct.
>
> Q: And you didn't ask him to be there. He showed up, and you were surprised he was present?
>
> A: That's true.

Zing. Even Hubie knew right off that Nathan had struck again. I tried going further.

> Q: You've asserted the Fifth Amendment about a dozen times or more in this case, haven't you?
>
> MR. ANDERSON: Objection, Your Honor. Relevance as to Phase I.
>
> THE COURT: Sustained.

You can do that with a judge as the trier of fact in a bench trial and not worry about getting yelled at for contaminating the jury and risking a mistrial. And it also gave me a calculated chance to see how far I could go before running afoul of Judge McConnell for trying to further turn our insurance coverage case criminal. Even after the Fifth Amendment sidebar of the afternoon before, the answer was loud and clear: Not very far. Kid gloves it was going to be for Nathan. He and I would be walking a tightrope but the judge was not going to let me turn it into a public hanging.

Laying the foundation for my navigation cross-examination was next. We had mounted the three NOAA charts Nathan had testified about during his EUO and first two depositions on posterboards and placed them on easels. From the witness box he admitted he had previously drawn his courses on them. But Attorney Anderson then objected to the charts' authenticity, which was completely frivolous and probably intended just to throw me off, with Judge McConnell quickly interjecting, "The fact that he put marks on it he just acknowledged, so I believe it would be authentic. The objection is overruled."

I then marched ahead, step-by-step, getting Nathan to compare one nautical mile's measurement on the distance scale of one of the charts with the distance on the right side as represented by one minute of latitude.

> Q: So will you agree with me that one minute of latitude equals one mile?
>
> A: Based on the demonstration you just did, that appears to be so.

Bouncing around a little, to break up Nathan's now quite familiar linear thinking (hyperlogical and/or autistic?), we then dealt with Nathan's alterations to the boat before the fateful voyage.

First alteration: Using the Feeney diagram as supplemented by Nathan's drawings of the bulkheads during his EUO.

> Q: So looking at the bird's-eye view of the vessel there, the forward bulkheads that you removed with the Sawzall are depicted here running athwartship from the fish box?
>
> A: Yes.

With time constraints, we really did not need to do a lot more on that since Nathan's removal process was already spelled out in our proposed findings of fact and conclusions of law, which Judge McConnell had already read and I knew he would reread when drafting his opinion after trial. If the assembled media didn't quite follow, that was their problem.

Second alteration: Bilge pumps. Bud Smedberg had already established that Nathan had problems with the port bilge pump.

> Q: On Friday you discovered the pump was not working, Friday the 16th of September?
>
> A: Yes.
>
> Q: And did you replace that bilge pump the following day on the 17th?
>
> A: Yes, I did.
>
> Q: But that wasn't the first time you put in a new bilge pump there, is it?
>
> A: Yes, that's the first time that I replaced the pump, to the best of my recollection.
>
> Q: You replaced it earlier in April, did you not?
>
> A: Not that I'm recalling.

Wrong. This was not Nathan misremembering. With Liam's anticipation and identification of a photo we would now need and Vanessa's nanosecond retrieval of it from our laptop exhibit files, she seamlessly displayed it on the courtroom monitors for all to see.

> Q: And so, to make the record clear, now I've shown you Exhibit 32.47, and this is a photograph, it's dated April 6, that you produced to us in discovery, correct?
>
> A: I see that, yes.

Q: And it shows a new and different bilge pump than the one Mr. Woods installed?

A: Yes, it does.

Q: So not only is there a new bilge pump in the boat as of April 2016, but you replaced that bilge pump on September 17th, 2016, as well, didn't you?

A: I did.

Coupled with Smedberg's testimony and Point Judith Marina work orders documenting ongoing fuse and electrical problems, Nathan looked like he was concealing his obvious bilge pump problems, so I pressed on.

Q: So just to make clear, this is Exhibit 1.1, which is from your December 16, 2016 examination under oath; and my question to you regarding the day that you sank, on line fourteen, "Is it fair to conclude that with the presence of all that water, that the bilge pumps were not functioning correctly?" And how did you answer it back then?

A: I see on line seventeen the answer "yes." And I can expound, like, what I mean, if you'd like.

Q: No, I think that really is an adequate answer.

Nathan got tripped up again regarding a different JC 31 "plug" that Point Judith Marina cut out of the hull to install a thru-hull water intake for the washdown pump—very much needed to wash off fish guts and blood. The washdown pump was right next to the port bilge pump. So we're not talking about the JC 31 hull as a plug here. Instead, this one-inch diameter cylindrical little plug would have been more than one-inch thick—a nice cross section of mahogany encompassed in inner and outer layers of heavy fiberglass—showing just how very solidly the

JC 31 hull was constructed. Better than an x-ray or a CT scan, this sample bore was something a boat owner would want to hold onto—unless he wanted to claim the hull was flimsy—and we had asked for it in discovery. Nathan had asked for it too.

> Q: Have you ever produced that plug in this litigation?
>
> A: No, because I—if I ever had it, I don't have it now.
>
> Q: Oh, when did you lose it?
>
> A: I don't remember ever asking for it or having it.

So Liam and Vanessa again nimbly retrieved and displayed Point Judith Marina work orders on the monitors.

> Q: So here's one of them that we're looking at on the screen, and do you see where it says, "Keep core cutout for the owner"?
>
> A: I do, yes.
>
> Q: Okay. And did you receive that core?
>
> A: I see what you're talking—what's on the screen.
>
> Q: And then it says below that, "Tim gave core to Nathan."
>
> A: I see that note.
>
> THE COURT: Why don't we take our midmorning break Mr. Farrell. We'll be back at 11:15.

Our point had registered with the only person who mattered.[125]

Third alteration: Nathan's trim tabs removal. After the break, he admitted he had not consulted with seller Brian Woods, or marine surveyor Bernie Feeney, or Point Judith Marina about removing them, and he had no fuel consumption data to suggest the trim tabs were problematic, which was the original reason he took them off.

Then I engaged in a little theatrics, always a risky thing for me, to illustrate Nathan's convoluted trim tabs removal and shoddy hole repairs. Playacting Nathan and using Klopman's transom exemplar, I followed Nathan's EUO description. Lying on my belly on the top of the transom, my feet levitating, I fully extended my arms down to the make-believe waterline, a couple of inches above the courtroom carpet.

> Q: And you did it by leaning over the transom and taking off the actuator and the trim tab which was below the water by hammering it out, and that's the process you needed to follow, correct?
>
> MR. ANDERSON: Objection, Your Honor. Compound question. There were multiple statements, which any way he answers the last question—
>
> THE COURT: I agree. But I don't want you to do that again, Mr. Farrell.
>
> MR. FARRELL: I'm in good shape.
>
> THE COURT: I'm not so sure. I'll sustain the objection.
>
> MR. FARRELL: I think I am.

[125] There was another sample bore plug, but we couldn't get our hands on it. It is visible in Bernie Feeney's photo of the JC 31 transom, sitting on the starboard trim tab. Nathan didn't want it, so Bernie took it after his survey. When he was interviewed by the FBI, he gave it to them to exemplify the hull's solid construction. The FBI would not let us use it.

THE COURT: You may well be, but your breathing caused me a little concern when you're hanging over.

Q: But the point being you had to bend right over the transom.

A: I did, yes.

Again, point registered with the only person who mattered.

We briefly covered Nathan's use of the West Marine Epoxy Putty Stick to fill the four transom holes, not in exhaustive detail because that, too, was all spelled out in our proposed findings of fact and conclusions of law. Just in case, we had some spare change in our bag of tricks in case Nathan tried to nickel and dime me—an Eisenhower silver dollar, Susan B. Anthony dollar, JFK half-dollar, George Washington quarter, Buffalo nickel, Lincoln penny, FDR dime—but I wanted to avoid spending time going down that rabbit hole when Attorney Santos's half-dollar holes were all we needed.

Q: Where did Attorney Santos get the information, if not from you, that the holes were half-dollar size, in the letter that he sent to the prosecutors?

A: I guess I can say I provided him that information, and I was trying to estimate the hole size. I now realize I confused half-dollars and silver dollars. I remember I told the Coast Guard right after the fact that it's the coin slightly larger than a quarter.

That answer sounded to me every bit as mealymouthed as when Nathan came back from lunch with Attorney Anderson during our first deposition session. And apparently that's the way it sounded to Judge McConnell too.

THE COURT: Is that your testimony or your recollection now, Mr. Carman, that it was silver dollar size?

THE WITNESS: I know it was not an inch and a half or close to an inch and a half. I was—my estimation right now is sort of convoluted from having talked about it and remembered it for so many different occasions—

THE COURT: Understood.

I took it that the only person who mattered probably now understood Nathan to have originally and most credibly testified and admitted to four half-dollar transom holes, and his trial attempt to downsize was less than credible drivel. But you can't stop and ask the judge if he got it. To make sure, I had to hammer it home.

Q: I was just asking you the size of the holes—

A: Yes, sir.

Q: —and you told me in your examination under oath the holes were the size of a half-dollar, did you not?

A: Yes. I was estimating, but I was mis—the estimate—yes, I did.

Q: And there was no backing inside the transom on the interior bilge of the boat, correct?

A: I wasn't aware of any.

Nathan then tried again to obfuscate but failed.

Q: Is it also a fact that there was one or two inches of this putty left over afterwards?

A: I know there was some putty left over. One or two inches, again, is clearly an estimate.

Q: But that's what you told me in your EUO three months after the event, right?

A: Yes.

Q: So I can rely on what you told me during the EUO?

A: To the—I was trying to provide you information to the best of my ability. To the extent that I estimated incorrectly, it was a mistake.

Again Judge McConnell jumped right in.

THE COURT: Are you saying now that you estimated incorrectly, or are you just merely pointing out that it was an estimate?

THE WITNESS: Estimating how much putty or what the diameter of the holes is an estimate.

THE COURT: But my question is that you made the estimate of one to two inches quite a while ago. You're not giving us a new estimate now; you're just pointing out that that was an estimate.

THE WITNESS: That's correct.

THE COURT: Thank you.

Good job Judge, who now had his own taste of Nathan's attempts to vacillate.

I then asked about the hole saw.

Q: And you can't deny using a hole saw in conjunction with your removal of the trim tabs, correct?

A: I did not bore a hole in my boat, period. I do not remember if I used either a drill bit or, like, the teeth of a hole saw to roughen up the edge of the existing hole, not expanding it any measurable amount. But just as the instructions in the

> fiberglass repair kit say for the resin repair, it recommends using a drill bit to roughen up the edge so that you have a clean, fresh surface to be adhering to. I may have used the teeth of a hole saw to do that, or a drill bit. I just don't remember.

That seemed defensive, contrived, and certainly contrary to Iozzi's testimony. I just left it alone.

On to the key fiberglass repair kit that Nathan failed to effectively use.

> Q: You could have taken a piece of this fiberglass mat and cut it up into a circle that would have enveloped the hole that was exposed at the actuator, correct?
>
> A: I suppose.
>
> Q: Looking at the exhibit that's on the screen, that's D-111. So just to the portside of the scupper and going up in this area of the transom is what could have been used as a tuna door, am I correct?
>
> A: I think someone had tried to make it a tuna door and then they just glassed it in so you couldn't—it would have taken a lot of work to be able to use that as a tuna door.
>
> Q: And that's the point. It was glassed in, correct?
>
> A: Yes.

Having thereby established Nathan's "incomplete, improper, or faulty repair" of the four half-dollar transom holes, it was time to go back to the chart exhibits and dig into his sinking and drift lies.

Up to this point Judge McConnell had been following along with me and pretty clearly getting it, but in this next segment I lost him.

My D = S x T foundation was like pulling teeth from a squirrelly patient. The Desperado tried to change his earlier testimony on all three variables, no real surprise. Frequent objections from Attorney Anderson, most of them sustained, had me breaking into a hot sweat amidst fears I was blowing the linchpin to our wet case. Judge McConnell interjected at one point, "Mr. Farrell, I think you're getting into argument now," warning me he was ready to shut me down.

Laboring on with all the grace of a mule, I finally got Nathan to admit departing on the fateful voyage from Ram Point Marina at 11:12 p.m. on Saturday September 17, then fishing at his so-called Striper Rock—the X southeast of Block Island that he marked on the charts—and departing from there three hours later, around 2:12 a.m. on Sunday September 18, arriving at their most southern point in Block Canyon—the Block Canyon X turnaround—five hours later or around 7:12 a.m.

Time = five hours, good = Block Island X to Block Canyon turnaround.

Nathan next tried to deny his prior testimony on Speed. While he admitted testifying in his first deposition, "My experience in general was the boat cruised, I don't know, like broadly at maybe 15, 16 knots or so," he now testified for the first time that was before his overheated diesel was replaced with 15 more horsepower, along with a faster propeller, now yielding 20 knots at 2,600 RPMs. I immediately corrected him that my deposition question had specifically asked, however, about the Block Island X to Block Canyon X leg of the fateful trip—the only time he had done it. There wasn't much more for him to say other than "Okay" after I read his deposition testimony that on that leg "It would have probably been like 15 knots."

Speed = 15 to 16 knots, good = Block Island X to Block Canyon turnaround.

Then Nathan tried to deny the last Distance variable and his New Hampshire deposition testimony that the southern terminus turnaround in Block Canyon to head north was "an additional 80 miles" south of the Block Island X. "I don't know where I got an additional 80 miles from," Nathan told the court.

But on this Distance vacillation, in addition to Nathan's prior New Hampshire deposition testimony, we had just nailed down Speed and

Time, we had his chart drawings, and we had sunrise, which triangularly boxed him in, as originally in his examination under oath testimony. Grabbing my dividers, I walked him through distance measurements on the charts in ten-mile intervals.

> Q: So, using the charts and the latitude measurement for 1 minute equals 1 mile, you'll agree with me that the location from the Block Island X that you drew just northeast of the wind farm, to the X in Block Canyon that you drew during your examination under oath, is...10, 20, 30, 40, 50, 60, 70 miles, correct?
>
> A: Yes.
>
> Q: Okay. But as I suggested to you in the EUO, and you've suggested to me today, you really went further south than the X that you drew during the EUO. You probably went, well, 10 more miles because 70 plus 10 equals 80. You went 80 miles. You went 10 more miles south of the Block Canyon X.
>
> And let me show you what 10 miles would be. I'm going off here to measure it, 10 miles. I'm taking it from your X, and I'm taking it right down in the heart of Block Canyon right north of the spot where it says 666 fathoms. Do you see that? That's 10 miles.
>
> A: I see what you're doing on the chart.

Several of the reporters snickered at my enunciated 6-6-6, suggesting they, too, thought I was crossing Damien, the Devil's son.

"No Cameras in Federal Court," Charlie Hall

Distance = 80 miles, good = Block Island X to Block Canyon 666 fathoms turnaround.

Now with the reluctant Genius, I had to try tying together the elegant D = S x T equation to the 666-fathom point where he would have started his new northward S-course curveball. I gave him a little chum, so it would look like I was giving him the benefit of the doubt (and it also made the math cleaner). Did Nathan think his speed "might have been a little faster" than 15 knots?

A: I do, yes.

Q: Let's call it 16 knots. 5 times 16 equals 80, correct?

A: Yes.

Q: All right. And what I'm saying by that is at 16 knots, traveling for 5 hours, brings you 80 miles away, correct?

A: Yes.

Q: You've also told us that it was sunrise.

A: Yeah, that's an absolute.

Q: Right. And so it was sunrise or just after sunrise, which is like 6:30 a.m. So 7:12 in the morning would have been 5 hours after you departed the Block Island X. To get you down 80 miles over a 5-hour course, it would have been a speed of 16 knots, and you'd have gotten down to that spot just at 666 in the middle of Block Canyon, correct?

MR. ANDERSON: I object. I don't think he has the knowledge to chart it that way.

THE COURT: Overruled. You have to answer, Mr. Carman.

A: Yeah, I'm not sure I understood the question.

So I broke it down.

Q: All right. Sir, your testimony is you got down to the southern terminus of your trip to Block Canyon a little after 7:00 a.m., just after sunrise?

A: That's correct, the southern terminus as it appeared on my chartplotter.

Q: Whatever that southern terminus is, where you turned around, it was about 7:00 a.m. and that's as far south as you went?

A: That's correct.

Q: We can get the location because we know that it was 80 miles south of the Block Island X, and we know it took you 5 hours to get there. So doing the math means you're traveling at a rate of 16 knots, and we can plot that location.

And I'm asking you to agree with me that using that math, 5 hours at 16 knots amounts to 80 miles and brings you 10 miles further than where you drew, and in the middle of Block Canyon it's that 666-fathom mark, correct?

A: I agree with that math, yes.

Q: As soon as you got there to your southern terminus, you turned around, you headed north, you put the rods out, your rubber squids out, and you started trolling north toward Point Judith?

A: The centerline on the chartplotter was north, and we were going in an S pattern over that centerline in a northerly direction.

Did he think I hadn't read that testimony from his New Hampshire deposition?

Q: And you trolled for about 5 hours after you started, right?

A: Right.

Q: So now we're talking about midday and it would be a little bit after noon, around then, that you sank, correct?

A: I believe so, yes.

Q: And you were trolling at a speed of, what, 4 or 5 knots?

A: Yes.

Another piece of chum:

Q: Average, what, 5 knots, 4 knots? What do you think?

A: Probably average 4 knots.

He took it. It slowed his progress north, he thought, but it also made the math for the new northbound D = S x T trolling course I was developing cleaner.

Q: 4 knots. Okay. And these S curves that you were making, you could set your autopilot to a function that allowed you to make a semicircle to the west and a semicircle to the east and then another semicircle to the west, and you would be making these looping circles north along the centerline of Block Canyon so that you would entice fish that way. They're more likely when you're making the turn to see something different with the way the squids were presented, and you're more likely to get a strike from a tuna fish or large game fish by making that sort of curving course to the north?

A: That's correct.

Great. A very compound, multiple-question question, but no Anderson objection. Nathan thus confirmed his S curve course as consisting of semicircles.

Q: And how much ground do you think you covered over that 5-hour period heading north?

A: I don't know.

Q: Let's look. I made this little drawing for you, Mr. Carman, and I think you'll see the dotted line goes up the page towards that asterisk, and that asterisk represents what you drew on Chart 12300, Exhibit 39, as a direction you were going back toward Point Judith. Correct?

A: Yes.

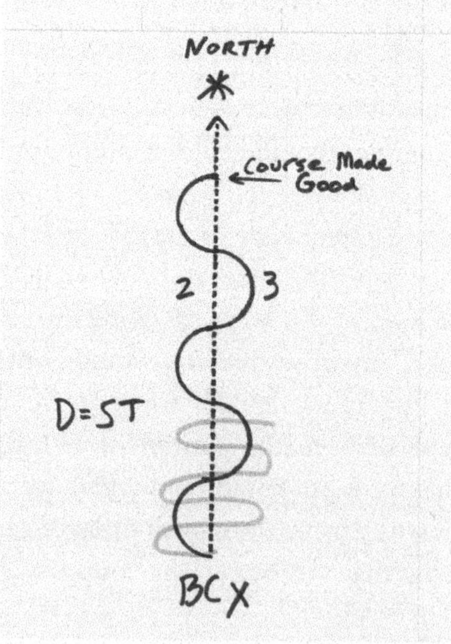

Q: So the BCx on this page represents your southern terminus where you started trolling. Okay?

A: Okay.

Q: And you started—and I've drawn these semicircles heading north; do you see that?

A: I do.

Q: Do you know the formula for the circumference of a circle as being pi times diameter?

A: I don't know what the formula for circumference of a circle is.

Q: Did you go to the Greater Hartford Magnet School for Science and Mathematics during grades ten and eleven?

A: No. I went there from—all of ninth grade and part of tenth grade.

Q: And you're a genius; right, Mr. Carman?

A: I have no idea.

Q: In your New Hampshire deposition you told the lawyers that you're a genius and you have at least a 140 IQ, did you not?

A: That's what my mom told me. I've never seen the tests.

Q: Are you going to tell me that you don't know that the circumference of a circle is figured out by taking the diameter and multiplying it by pi, which is 3.14? You don't remember learning that in school?

A: I don't have that figure memorized. If I wanted to find the circumference of a circle I would go into Google and I'd type in how do you find the circumference of a circle.

Q: Can we do that?

THE COURT: No.

Q: All right. Let's look at it this way, okay? Your testimony in your New Hampshire deposition was you made a semicircle to the left and a semicircle to the right, and that's how the autopilot was programmed for you to move north?

Having made plain I was going to crush his hanging semicircle curveball, Nathan tried to change his testimony.

A: The autopilot was programmed for us to move north on what I've described as an S pattern. I don't know if it was a semicircle or an ellipse or half an oval.

Q: A semicircle is what you said. I've drawn a semicircle. In order for you to get to the top of the half circle, you've got to travel more than the distance as the crow flies. You've got to travel the whole arc of the semicircle to get there. That's the point, correct?

A: Yes.

Q: And in order to do it to the top of the next half circle, you've got to travel all the way along the arc of the next semicircle to get there as the crow flies?

A: You do.

Q: And so what you're doing is you're traveling more distance than you're making good on your course north, correct?

A: Yes.

Q: Would you agree with me that if you were trolling as you said at 4 knots for 5 hours on a straight line, you would go 20 nautical miles?

A: Yes. That's simple arithmetic.

Q: Okay. Would you, just looking at my diagram, say that the ratio between the straight-line diameter to the half circle is about two to three?

THE COURT: Mr. Farrell, I'm going to interrupt you and tell you you're going to have to move on. You're not asking questions that are in the knowledge of this witness. These are mathematical calculations. They're potentially engineering issues. It's not something that this witness has any ability to comment on. This is your diagram, on top of it. I'm going to ask you to move on.

Arrgh! That seriously torqued me off. Although I didn't articulate anything else, it must have harmonicked with my body language too. I had moved beyond pi x Diameter eighth-grade math at His Honor's direction, got no complaints from the Genius doing "simple arithmetic," and now I was merely asking him to eyeball the ratio of diameter to semicircle arc. This was hardly "engineering." Attorney Anderson hadn't even objected. Yet a second judge was going out of his way, overly protective of poor Nathan, our worry ever since his EUO.

THE COURT: And because I just threw Mr. Farrell for a loop, we'll take a lunch break a little bit early. I have some criminal matters to handle

> during lunch, so we'll be back at 1:30. We stand adjourned.

A full courtroom can be the loneliest place in the world for a lawyer.

My cross of Nathan Carman was far from *Law and Order* terse and mesmerizing. The team was not pleased. Liam shrugged. Martha whispered the judge wasn't even paying attention at the end. Vanessa wouldn't look me in the eye.

As we exited the courtroom, the Sisters' lawyers and Mr. PR huddled with backs turned toward us and I saw the Quarterback cupping his hand over his mouth as he spoke. I could feel the media's stare on the back of my neck, like rubberneckers at a motorcycle accident.[126]

Our team glumly holed up in the sparse jury deliberation room. I ate only for energy. Everyone, except maybe Liam, who at least knew what I was trying to do, said I had to give it up, win back the judge, and move immediately to something else. They were all worried. So was I. But it was essential we sink Nathan at 140 fathoms. Without it, Liam's Sumatra trip was an utter waste. Attorney Anderson would be able to shoot Limeburner's opinion full of holes.

This wasn't my first rodeo. Time to cowboy up. Like after getting thrown by my horse in the Gila Wilderness bow hunting elk with Eddie Reid and Vietnam Airborne Silver Star Vet Jack Brow, those two the dozen toughest guys I know. Like after the close of evidence when the judge didn't get it until my closing argument in the *Biktjorn* trial for Vince. I was four-for-six over my career ignoring and challenging a judge's explicit, core-issue directive, but for one of those losses I'd snatched defeat from the jaws of victory and I sure didn't want to do that again. Yet the more I played Nathan's testimony over in my mind, the more I thought we had him on the hook.

Nathan was doing everything possible in his trial testimony to place the sinking spot well south of 140 fathoms, so he'd be closer to the Gulf Stream. To move his southern turnaround in Block Canyon farther south, he tried upping his southbound speed to 20 knots from 15 to

[126] At least one journalist got it. *See* Zalkind, "The 25-Year-Old Accused of Murdering his Mother," n. 124.

16 knots, which over 5 hours would have put him 100 miles, not just 75 to 80 miles, south of the Block Island X. From that more southern turnaround point, he reduced his EUO testimony's average trolling speed north of 4 to 6 knots down to 4 knots. And after just testifying his course north was semicircles, he then tried to flatten them into ovals or ellipses in order to further reduce his progress north over the ground.

This was all set up on the trial record already and I wasn't about to give it up, no matter what Judge McConnell had just said. Liam and I talked it all through, slowly co-opting Martha and Vanessa when they confirmed key parts of Nathan's testimony the way I remembered it. We simplified things to their essence. We could still put Nathan's alleged sinking in Block Canyon right back at 140 fathoms, which he had sworn to three prior times under oath. Where *Prudence* Captain Alex Aucoin did not see him.

It didn't matter if no one in the courtroom besides Liam, Martha, and Vanessa knew what I'd be trying to do. I was okay going toe-to-toe with Judge McConnell on this if I had to. I didn't even care if he didn't follow it now—I knew I could tie it all together for him on closing argument. And I certainly didn't care if D = S x T was a snooze for the media longing for a salacious bombshell. I simply had only one goal. Well, two. First and foremost, I was going to get it on the record that Nathan's story was indelible that he knowingly sank at 140 fathoms. And second, that would eventually get Nathan convicted of murdering his mother.

Summing up, here's where we were: Nathan's course made good over the bottom from Point A to Point B in a straight line would be much faster than if his course at the same speed followed semicircles from Point A to Point B. Over 5 hours, semicircle to the west, semicircle to the east, repeat, repeat...his S-course north would not get him as far in 5 hours as the same speed on a straight course. Stated differently, at the end of 5 hours on the S-course, he would be south of where a straight course would have put him.

How much?

Take a circle of one unit diameter, D = 1. Its circumference = pi x D, or 3.14 x 1 unit = 3.14 units. It doesn't matter what length the unit is, so long as it remains constant; it could be one big circle or scores of little circles the same size. So the arc of half a circle measures 1.57 units. Therefore, in order to go 1 unit north over the ground, Nathan would have had to travel 1.57 units around the semicircle. But Judge McConnell didn't let us get there using the pi x Diameter formula. So just rounding it off, and using nautical miles for the units, Nathan advanced only 1 mile north for every 1.5 miles he actually traveled around the semicircles. That's equivalent to only 2 miles north for every 3 semicircle miles.

Accordingly, the semicircle course reduces his forward progress to the north, in the ratio of two to three, meaning that at 4 knots over 5 hours, 20 miles straight as the crow flies must be reduced by one-third to determine how far north over the ground his semicircles course made good. That would be 13.33 miles north of 666 fathoms. And where is that location? The Block Canyon Fishtails at 140 fathoms. *Voilà.*

Court resumed after lunch.

> THE COURT: Mr. Carman, you remember you're still under oath?
>
> THE WITNESS: I do, Your Honor.
>
> THE COURT: Great. Thank you.
>
> CONTINUED DIRECT EXAMINATION BY MR. FARRELL:
>
> Q: One last point with the chart, Mr. Carman. Measuring 20 miles which would be—
>
> A: Can I go down and see what you're doing?
>
> Q: Sure.

Our team was on pins and needles to see if I could pull it off without getting humiliated by Judge McConnell, as the rest of the courtroom resigned themselves to more boredom.

Q: So I'm marking off 20 miles to represent 5 hours of trolling at 4 knots, had you been going straight ahead from that 666 point in Block Canyon, and I'm going to mark it in orange.

The orange mark would have been where you could have gotten had you gone straight and not made S curves during those 5 hours at 4 knots.

A: I didn't see you using your protractor.

I repeated it with my dividers (which is not a protractor).

Q: That's 20 nautical miles.

A: Okay.

Q: And 666 to the orange line is 20 miles?

A: If I started at the 666, then yes. I don't know that I started at the 666.

Q: Okay. That's fine. My point being if you had gone straight as the crow flies from 666 north through the heart of the canyon, you'd have ended up at that orange line?

A: I think you're asking me just straight arithmetic, and I would agree with you.

Q: Okay. And would you also agree that in that distance from 666 to the orange line, that the 140-fathom mark is about two-thirds of the way to the north from 666 to the orange line?

A: Approximately.

QED. But it was all a demonstrable lie—the sole, inescapable lie in the unwitnessed murder of his mother at sea—irrefutably false as would be shown by Woods Hole Oceanographic science and as Judge

McConnell already realized from *Prudence* Captain "Go Rams!" Aucoin's account of an otherwise vacant Fishtails on the afternoon of Sunday September 18, 2016. Besides Liam, I suspect few in the courtroom appreciated that I had just harpooned Nathan, this time for his mother.

Taking a deep breath, I momentarily made myself take rest. Then, showing Nathan that first written report of his to Martha, he admitted not telling her he'd removed the bulkheads, not telling her he had ongoing bilge pump problems, not telling her he had filled four transom holes with epoxy putty the afternoon before the sinking. And where he had written they'd first stopped to fish at "a spot southwest of Block Island"? Nathan testified, "That would be mistaken for southeast."

Three Key Omissions + Alleged Mistake = Credibility Problems, another elegant equation, which I did not need to tie together for Judge McConnell.

With Nathan estimating the whole sinking evolution taking "three to five minutes," I tried to keep the sinking cross-exam just as quick. As he had largely testified during his examination under oath, I rat-tat-tat asked and he serially admitted this chronology from the witness box:

- Seeing water halfway up the battery boxes at the forward hatch
- Shutting down the diesel
- Seeing water three inches underneath the deck at the port cockpit hatch
- Asking "Mom to please start bringing in the lines," which was "the last time that I said anything to her or that she said anything to me"
- She never asked "What's the matter?" or "Why are you shutting down the engine?" or "Why is there water in the bilge?"
- "She didn't say anything. 'What's going on Nathan?' She didn't say anything like that"
- She never said, "Give me a life preserver"
- "She didn't scream"

Then I pushed, careful not to cross the line of accusing Nathan of intentionally killing his mother.

> Q: And I just want to make sure, is the reason you didn't say anything to your mother or hear anything from your mother after you told her to reel in the lines, is that because she couldn't talk or she couldn't hear you?
>
> A: I don't understand the question.
>
> Q: I'm asking you, Was your mother even onboard at that time?
>
> A: I've told you that yes, she was onboard.

At no time did he check his transom holes repair, perceive any change in the trim fore and aft, or see any water on deck.

Three times he went into the wheelhouse to grab safety gear, "within a foot or two of where the EPIRB was mounted, correct?"

> A: That's correct.
>
> Q: And you didn't pick up the EPIRB and manually set it off, did you?
>
> A: No, I did not.
>
> Q: And the EPIRB would have sent a message to the Coast Guard to let them know that you were in distress, correct?
>
> A: That's how it's supposed to work.
>
> THE COURT: Can you hold up for one second? This may have been testified to, but I've forgotten. What is EPIRB?

I think the judge wanted to hear it from the horse's mouth.

> THE WITNESS: It stands for Emergency Position Indicating Radio Beacon, and it's a device where

if you push a button, it communicates with satellites your location.

It's important to stress that once you press that button, there's no way that I'm aware of to undo it. There are going to be helicopters there.

THE COURT: Kind of like the button under my bench here, that if I hit it here, I can't undo it, and the marshals come a-running?

THE WITNESS: Correct.

Q: And you say that there were no vessels on the horizon at any time during that day?

A: I didn't see any vessels in that time.

Q: And in contrast to when you called the Coast Guard in the Harbor of Refuge when your boat overheated, you did not call the Coast Guard when your boat was full of water, when the engine was turned off, and you were almost one hundred miles at sea in an area you've never been before. Is that correct? It's a yes or no.

A: That is correct.

Q: And you walked out to the deck, and you walked to the bow with your third bag of survival gear, and as you were approaching the bow, the boat fell out from underneath you, right?

A: It started to feel squishy under my feet, and—

Q: It went bow down, bow-first?

A: That's correct.

Again I pressed up against criminal intent, trying not to go too far and get reprimanded.

> Q: During the rest of the time you were moving the things up to the bow, is the reason your mother didn't say anything because she couldn't talk?
>
> A: I believe she could talk. I don't believe there was anything physically wrong with her at that time.
>
> Q: And you made it into the life raft, but nobody else did, correct?
>
> A: That's correct.

As we had before when questioning Nathan, because it never happened, we covered his seven days in the life raft even faster. Initially the swell was a four-foot sine wave? Yes, he replied. Really, you genius, a sine wave, yet you don't know the circumference of a circle? And of course he was soaking wet initially but he quickly changed into dry clothes. After that, "I got wet at times but wasn't saturated," and yes, "I was cold, but I wasn't hypothermic" even with seawater coming into the life raft, which he had to sponge out.

Turning to *In the Heart of the Sea* whaleboat cannibalism, Nathan admitted, "Yes, my reason for packing two weeks of food for two people was because that book influenced me." Sorely tempted, knowing the media would have loved it, but aware that Judge McConnell would not have been amused, I did not ask Nathan if he ate his mother. Besides, I never thought he did.

But why his focus on averting 1820s South Pacific gruesomeness when he had the modern-day electronics of a VHF radio and EPIRB at his fingertips? Because, "If I had known the boat was going to sink, I would have immediately set off the EPIRB. By the time the boat sank, none of those modern appliances were available to me."

Particularly since the EPIRB was wrongly mounted inside the wheelhouse.

For Dr. Harris's testimony the next day, I then in quick succession had Nathan authenticate the key photos I'd addressed in my opening statement from his *Orient Lucky* rescue—"standing up in the life raft waving a flag," swimming "a relatively short distance" to the life ring, holding onto the life ring with your left arm while "pressing off with your right hand from the hull of the ship"—and one more:

> Q: And do you see your right and left hand firmly grabbing onto the handrail there?
>
> A: I do.
>
> Q: And did you miss any steps going up that gangway?
>
> A: As I testified in my deposition, I don't recall if I missed any steps. I didn't struggle to walk up the gangway.
>
> MR. FARRELL: Thank you, Your Honor. No further questions.
>
> THE COURT: Thanks, Mr. Farrell.

***

It was now time for Attorney Anderson to try to make his client look good. Nathan did not.

A large portion of Nathan's testimony on direct examination by Attorney Anderson, which lasted most of the afternoon, dealt with photographs of boat parts and equipment, with Nathan identifying in some detail technical features of the engine, transmission, shaft, stuffing box, propeller, exhaust; the three fuel tanks which held 380 gallons of diesel; the boat's thru-hull fittings and pumps, transducers, and bilge water overboard-discharge piping; and his personal installation of state-of-the-art electronic navigation equipment and his use of the touchscreen, chartplotter, and integrated AIS display. His testimony was articulate and informative, the boat's components shipshape and grease-free, demonstrating the overall seaworthiness of the boat's systems and his capable, technological knowledge of using them.

Which stood in glaring contrast to his kindergarten Play-Doh repair of his four half-dollar holes.

Oh so smart yet oh so stupid. But why? It was becoming more and more clear all the time.

Nathan's testimony wound up that first day with his claim that the new engine was heavier and more powerful than the one he had overheated. This he claimed made the boat bow-heavy. Photos were shown of the boat in its slip, with a small rainwater puddle on deck amidship not draining out the scuppers. That explains why the bow sank first, he said. And Nathan reiterated, as he had to me in the morning for the very first time in the long travel of this case, that the new engine gave him a twenty-knot cruising speed. He also reiterated his semicircles trolling north were not semicircles after all but flatter ellipses, which he drew with highlighter on my diagram.

None of these points were at all convincing. Klopman's diagrams of ten to twelve inches more water aft had knocked out any bow-first sinking as physically impossible, and Nathan's repeated prior speed testimony of fifteen to sixteen knots on the fateful voyage discredited his brand-new claim of twenty knots, just as his prior testimony on semicircles discredited his new ellipses geometry.

***

Nathan was still on the stand when court adjourned for the day. The Sisters' team swooped in like terns working a school of stripers. Michael Connolly buttonholed me at counsel table and told me that I had to do more to eviscerate Nathan. That during the sinking-sequence testimony, "you could hear a pin drop in the courtroom," but I needed a more in-his-face, aggressive attack to break Nathan down. I countered that it was better that I stay surgical and let Nathan do himself in, but Michael wanted me to be sensational. The stage was set: CGIS Special Agent Eric Gempp was in attendance and with the media aching for a good story, the Sisters would get their wish for criminal prosecution—if only I would go for the jugular.

But Judge McConnell had gone out of his way to keep this insurance trial from convicting Nathan. We were giving the judge all the evidence he needed to deny insurance coverage and I was not about to jeopardize the Insurer's case for the wishes of the marginally cooperative Sisters who, for financial reasons, would not testify Linda was dead and would not agree with the Insurer to waive wrongful death claims.

Bill Michael joined in to doubleteam me. In not so many words they said I was missing the chance of a lifetime to draw and quarter a ghoul and my cross-exam could be so much more flashy. Actually, they were crediting me more than I deserved because it's not a style I ever confidently developed. Both former Assistant US Attorneys (AUSAs), they possess a full array of courtroom and jury skills far exceeding mine. But they didn't have my admiralty bench trial experience. While I completely understood that all the courtroom observers wanted blood, I was resolute in remaining a stiff. Liam and I had an audience of one who did not want a murder case on his hands.

After a second quick run of the day to clear my head, Liam reported the Sisters' team was now inviting us to dinner for more pep talk. Not much interested, more and more convinced we were getting just what we needed from Nathan to win our insurance case, I reluctantly agreed to hear them out.

A nice dinner at McCormick & Schmick's failed to resurrect any Johnnie Cochran in me, so we collectively developed Plan B, which Liam quickly renamed the "Nuclear Option." To illustrate Nathan's total lack of credibility, we'd display the Shooters Outpost records of Nathan's Sig Sauer purchase, assured he would take the Fifth again, and then we'd display his videoed police interviews after the Chakalos murder denying firearm ownership and any purchases other than a shotgun. For maximum impact the Sisters' team wanted me to spring it on Nathan without warning, with flair.

I stodgily would not commit, and made myself take rest.

***

The next morning, Attorney Anderson resumed questioning Nathan.

Despite Nathan's describing his relationship with Martha Charlesworth as "professional and pleasant," Attorney Anderson tried to show that the Insurer beat up on his poor client and took advantage of him throughout. That was going nowhere, as Judge McConnell signaled.

> THE COURT: Mr. Anderson, you can—I said this from the beginning. You all can try this case any way you want, but you have less than two hours left, and I understand you have other witnesses and whatnot.
>
> MR. ANDERSON: I'll move it.
>
> THE COURT: Good.

They moved to the trim tabs removal. Nathan testified:

> THE WITNESS: There was no metal pipe as Brian Woods testified or at least initially testified that he used. There was no pipe like that. It was just the black flexible nylon tubing that was screwed directly into the back of the actuator head.
>
> THE COURT: And is it your testimony that that did not require you to increase the size of the hole in order to remove it?
>
> THE WITNESS: That's correct. It did not require me to increase the size of the hole.

Referring to the Klopman transom exemplar, Judge McConnell asked Nathan:

> THE COURT: So the hole that you see in that example now, is that the size of the hole that you attempted to fill, approximately?
>
> THE WITNESS: It may be. I—

THE COURT: How about a little better than that?

THE WITNESS: Sitting here right now, I cannot recall seeing the hole. I recall having recalled it so many times.

This testimony rang even more hollow than the gaping half-dollar holes from Attorney Santos's early letter. Ultimately, I still contend it did not matter whether Woods had used a bronze connection or had simply connected the flexible tubing straight to the actuator. It didn't even truly matter whether Nathan had drilled larger holes with his hole saw.

What mattered was that Nathan was stuck with his cross-exam admissions and pretrial testimony of exposing four half-dollar-size holes with no inboard backing at the transom waterline and puttying them shoddily without fiberglass. I submit he thereby established, as was his goal, a simple explanation for the boat's sinking the very next day, as much as he would not admit it. This was the Genius/Play-Doh dialectic, the Desperado playing head games, certain we would take it hook, line, and sinker. But we were ahead of him, and he was still over his head.

Attorney Anderson's attempts to fog up Nathan's navigation testimony from my cross-exam fell short. Nathan for the first time claimed the mounted charts used at trial, in his depositions, and going back to his EUO were different than what was displayed on his chartplotter. Attorney Anderson asked:

Q: Do you know what the background was on your chartplotter, like what map or chart was used?

A: No, I don't.

Q: Did it look similar to where you told your autopilot to go?

MR. FARRELL: Objection. That's garbled and unintelligible.

THE WITNESS: I agree.

MR. ANDERSON: I'll rephrase it.

Q: Did the chart on your plotter have a place that said Block Canyon?

A: Yes.

Q: And when you told it—relative to the words "Block Canyon," where did you tell the autopilot on your plotter to go to? And I'm saying B-L-O-C-K Canyon.

MR. FARRELL: Objection, Your Honor. Telling the autopilot, it's vague and ambiguous.

THE COURT: Can you answer, Mr. Carman?

THE WITNESS: I think I can, yes.

THE COURT: Overruled.

A: The words "Block Canyon" ran essentially north to south or south to north, and I selected the southern end of where those words appeared. And the center of what looked like—of bathygraphic lines looked like they were a canyon.

Q: Okay. Was it close to the word "canyon" on your plotter, if you know?

A: I don't remember what—

THE COURT: Mr. Anderson, I'm not sure how this is relevant—

MR. ANDERSON: I'll move on.

THE COURT: —if we don't have the underlying map to give us some reference.

Couldn't have said it much better myself. Checked that off as something I did not have to deal with on re-cross.

Judge McConnell continued to interrupt Attorney Anderson throughout his direct exam. At one point, as Nathan was describing getting into the life raft and his claimed seven-day drift, during which he described up to twelve-foot seas, Judge McConnell jumped in:

> THE COURT: Mr. Carman, when the boat sank, what was the condition of the ocean at that time? You may have answered this. I apologize.

Again, from the horse's mouth:

> THE WITNESS: Sure. It was relatively flat, but there was a swell with like a four-foot swell, not breaking waves but sort of a smooth sine wave.
>
> THE COURT: And this may be difficult, but one thing that has stuck in my mind is that I haven't heard you describe a search for your mother, that is, I realized you talked about the boat going down and it being dramatic and immediate. Did you search for your mother?
>
> THE WITNESS: Yes.
>
> THE COURT: Tell me how you searched for your mother once—once you knew the boat was going down.
>
> THE WITNESS: So I didn't know the boat was going down until I was in the water.
>
> I honestly don't remember if right then I yelled out to her. I know once I got into the life raft, I was yelling out, "Mom, mom," making sure to pause so if she was responding I'd be able to hear

her. And, like, I was standing up in the raft looking around trying to see her on the surface.

THE COURT: Did you ever dive into the water to look for her to see if she was being held down by anything?

THE WITNESS: No, I did not. Standing up, I have a greater field of view, and that was the best way to be looking rather than being underwater.

THE COURT: No, I meant when you were in the water, did you dive down and look for her?

THE WITNESS: No, I did not dive down.

THE COURT: Go ahead, Mr. Anderson.

With Judge McConnell's suspicions further whetted, things went from bad to much worse for Nathan. Attorney Anderson resumed:

Q: Why were you bringing those things forward if you weren't thinking you're probably going to sink?

A: Because I felt that was the prudent thing to do. I knew there was a potential that, to me, seemed remote but present, and I knew that short of activating the EPIRB and causing helicopters to show up, we needed to rely on ourselves.

I thought the prudent thing at that time was to be prepared for worst-case scenario and then try to diagnose and fix the problem.

Q: And these—

THE COURT: Hold on. But you didn't shout out to your mother to get prepared?

THE WITNESS: I was asking her to prepare in the sense of part of what had to happen was bringing in the fishing lines because we were stopped at this point and they would get tangled. They would—they could tangle the prop. Slack lines around a boat are bad, so they had to come in.

And my mom was—when we were on the boat, I was the one who knew what we were doing. I viewed my mom more like a passenger in the sense that, I don't like this term, but she was more kind of part of the problem rather than the solution in that if I told her there's water in the bilge, I'm concerned, she was going to panic and make things worse.

MR. ANDERSON: Are you done, Your Honor?

THE COURT: Yes. Thanks.

Nathan, too, was done. This was the type of headline testimony the Sisters wanted and it best came voluntarily from Nathan on questioning by the judge. That his mom was "part of the problem rather than the solution" hung like fog in the courtroom that would not lift. Repeated on the TV news that night and in the papers the next day, it was no leap for the media to suggest Nathan's mom was the "problem" he had to get rid of in order to get his "millions of dollars of inheritance."[127]

When Attorney Anderson wrapped up his direct exam of Nathan, re-cross was next, which I planned to keep very brief. But first we would deploy the Nuclear Option, in a way Liam and I decided was reasonable and short of blowing things sky-high without warning.

---

[127] Katie Mulvaney, "Carman: As boat foundered, mom became 'problem,'" *The Providence Journal*, August 23, 2019. https://www.providencejournal.com/story/news/courts/2019/08/23/nathan-carman-as-boat-took-on-water-mom-was-more-of-problem-than-solution/986618007/.

MR. FARRELL: Your Honor, Plaintiffs request a sidebar.

THE COURT: We're going to stand adjourned until after lunch. Why don't you come up. You want this on the record?

MR. FARRELL: Yes, please…

Up to the bench we three trial counsel walked.

MR. FARRELL: Out of deference to the Court, I want to advise you of what we plan to do on re-cross of Mr. Carman, and that is we want to show him to be a liar, and we have—

THE COURT: We call that challenging his credibility.

MR. FARRELL: We want to challenge his credibility quite seriously by showing two lies that he made to the Windsor Police Department regarding guns and his ownership of guns subsequent to his purchase of a gun in New Hampshire.

We are not looking in any way to put this toward the murder of the grandfather.

THE COURT: Then how do you intend to prove that's a lie?

MR. O'CONNELL: We have a certified copy of the invoice and all of the records from the firearms store.

THE COURT: In essence, you're claiming that he told the police that he didn't own or purchase guns or a gun?

MR. O'CONNELL: Any firearms.

THE COURT: Any guns. And you have proof that he actually had?

MR. O'CONNELL: One hundred percent.

THE COURT: If your point—if your true point is to give me evidence that when suspected of committing another crime, Mr. Carman lied and, therefore, I can and should assume that he may be lying now when there's questions about his actions, the point will be well taken.

MR. ANDERSON: Your Honor, they're just trying to force him to take the Fifth in this case and on an issue that's completely unrelated.

THE COURT: Hold on. If they ask these questions, does he intend to take the Fifth?

MR. ANDERSON: If—and I haven't spoken to him, but—

THE COURT: Right. There's much that turns in this case on the credibility of a variety of witnesses, obviously first and foremost Mr. Carman. And so I'm going to double-check and reread the rules over the lunch, but I'm pretty sure it comes in for that purpose.

MR. ANDERSON: Okay. So I am going to—first of all, Your Honor, to be clear, I object to, on evidentiary grounds specifically, that they're trying to introduce evidence of a false statement, which was not one under oath or in a deposition or at trial but simply a false statement, like lying to your girlfriend.

THE COURT: It's a little different than lying to your girlfriend. The question that I don't know, that I'm going to struggle with, is whether a lie under the circumstances described, I won't repeat them, three years ago is relevant to his current credibility. I'm going to figure that out.

MR. ANDERSON: May I just say one thing? It was not three years ago. It was in the year 2014. Five years ago, about two and a half before the time the boat sank. So we're talking five years ago.

THE COURT: I'll let you know when we come back.

"Arguing," Charlie Hall

Attorney Anderson had just done an excellent job, fast on his feet, scrapping for his client after Liam and I had made it clear to Judge McConnell that we had video evidence ready to go of Nathan lying to the police on something way more serious than lying to your girlfriend. Better, we had done it without a public spectacle that almost certainly would have irritated the Court.

On reconvening, Judge McConnell announced his ruling, but also in private, at a sidebar.

> THE COURT: Could I see counsel, please…
>
> I'm going to sustain the Defendant's objection and not allow the evidence under Rule 608. The statement wasn't under oath. It was four to five years ago, it was a single incident, and it's unrelated to the issues that are being tried. Everyone's objection is noted.

But this was definitely no setback for the Insurers. Here's where a bench trial is so different from a jury trial. Jurors would never have heard the sidebar discussion. But with this bench trial, Judge McConnell both got to hear what our evidence was and ruled against us. Very hard, even for a judge, to unhear what we had just presented. So by ruling against us, he thereby protected his record on appeal, while also suggesting he did not need that evidence on top of what he already had to conclude Nathan lacked credibility. Judge McConnell's boss, the First Circuit Court of Appeals, would be unable to reverse a finding against Nathan on his argument that lies to the police at age seventeen should not have been admitted.

I smiled for the public, assuring Liam as we walked back to counsel table that this was a good sign.

For my re-cross, all I wanted to do was quickly convert two points. First point:

> Q: You never produced the invoice for your West Marine purchase in Middletown, Rhode Island, to us in discovery, did you?

A: I don't know what was produced by my attorney in discovery, but I thought that was produced.

Q: No. I found it.

Vanessa then showed on the monitors the Middletown store's invoice I had obtained and then matching West Marine catalogue photos of Nathan's purchase of two harnesses, normally used by competitive sailors when hiking out in a race. But only one of the harnesses had a built-in, inflatable personal floatation device.

THE COURT: Mr. Farrell, remind me, what's the date of these purchases?

MR. FARRELL: September 17th, 2016.

THE COURT: Saturday?

MR. FARRELL: Saturday, yes.

THE COURT: Okay.

The same day as the final voyage. Point made. And the final point:

Q: And you happened to have an AIS receiver hooked up on your boat, did you not?

A: It was an integral part of the last radio, the last VHF radio that I installed.

Q: So you could monitor the comings and goings of large vessels from your vessel because you received that information?

A; That's correct.

Q: However, you didn't transpond or transmit your position, so you weren't telling other ships your position by way of the AIS?

A: To be clear, I would have had to not just hook it up, but I would have to buy a whole separate set. The VHF radio had a receiver. It did not have a transponder that could have been hooked up.

So, Nathan could see other vessels' locations by AIS but other vessels could not see him by AIS. Pretty stealthy if you wanted to play hide-and-seek. And eventually get found.

Q: Now, when the *Orient Lucky* passed by, it passed by you within thirty yards, isn't that right? When you were yelling at the crew, that's how they noticed you?

A: It's my feeling, from what I observed, that they heard me yelling.

Q: The ship was thirty yards away from you at that time?

A: That's a rough estimate, yeah.

Q: Did you ever see the movie *Cast Away*?

A: Not that I recall.

MR. FARRELL: No further questions, Your Honor.

THE COURT: Thanks, Mr. Farrell.

TB 12

The time had come for Liam to establish himself as a preeminent maritime trial lawyer of his generation. He called Dr. Harris from the Massachusetts General Hospital and Harvard Medical School.

Dr. Harris recited his qualifications, including editing *Auerbach's Wilderness Medicine*; his "extensive background in out-of-doors and marine environments, cold weather environments"; and his routine care of patients suffering hypothermia from outdoor accidents, "sometimes because they're undomiciled, sometimes because of substance abuse."

Utilizing the US Coast Guard's hypothermia assessment protocol, Dr. Harris input Nathan's 6'3" height, 185 pound weight, estimated 18.75 percent body fat, and clothing during his alleged drift and gave him conservative, benefit-of-the-doubt environmental inputs of 69°F air and 73°F water temperatures, 40 percent relative humidity, and two- to three-foot seas for the first five days followed by six- to ten-foot seas the last two days. He recognized Nathan was not fully immersed in the water but he was wet and cold, continuously sponging up seawater, as he had testified by deposition.

> THE WITNESS: Evaporative losses are significant if you're outside the water. Radiative losses are significant.
>
> Essentially we're very good when we're at about ninety-eight degrees. You get down just a couple of degrees, we vigorously fight to maintain that core temperature, so you have shivering.
>
> You get down to ninety-six, ninety-five degrees, you can't control it, you're profoundly shivering, and that's where hypothermia really has its origin.
>
> And very quickly from there, by the time you get down even a couple of degrees lower than that, ninety-three, you're physically incapacitated. If you are out under those conditions for seven days you would be profoundly hypothermic, if not dead.

Dr. Harris then narrated how the *Orient Lucky* rescue photos[128] reflected that Nathan was not at all hypothermic. "Just standing up" in the life raft, let alone "vigorously waving" a flag, was "remarkable."

---

128 Tr. Ex. 53; Tr. Ex. 32.4, https://www.rid.uscourts.gov/sites/rid/files/documents/17cv38/082319/P32.4.pdf.

Noting that "our bodies, when we get cold, we shunt blood from the extremities, from our fingers and toes, toward our core, and the fine motor function, the ability to do things with your fingers, your toes, is very rapidly lost." Anyone out on a very cold winter day skating or skiing a little too long knows this. Thus, Dr. Harris found "some of the most interesting photographs" depicted Nathan using his hands. Amazingly, swimming with his clothes and boots on, "his right hand tightly grasping the rope of the life ring says 'Wow, this guy is extraordinarily high-functioning; he's not hypothermic anywhere to the degree consistent with seven days of the physical conditions reported'" by weather records and Nathan's depositions.

The photo of Nathan against the *Orient Lucky* hull shows "he's not only using his shoulder to fend off the side of the ship, he's using his fingertips."

The video and photo showing Nathan's climb up the gangway said it all.

> The physical act for any one of us to climb ten meters, thirty to thirty-three feet, vertical to get up on the main deck is a vigorous act. You can see him very rapidly ascending the stairs. You can see him pretty easily

> grabbing the railing.[129] Again, fine motor functions completely intact. He's got exquisite muscle tone and ability that speak to a normal core temperature that, again, is in no way consistent with that length of exposure given those conditions.

Dr. Harris also spoke with the *Orient Lucky* captain through a translator. "He was struck by how normal Mr. Carman was operating."

Attorney Anderson could do nothing with Dr. Harris on cross-exam, trying to discredit everything, such as his estimate from afar of Nathan's low fat percentage, or minimal insulation from the cold. So Liam decided on re-direct to have some fun, making himself the brunt of a joke, showing how at home he is in the courtroom and the good rapport he'd developed with the judge.

> Q: And I'll finish up, and quite frankly, I can't believe I'm going to do this. But, Dr. Harris, looking at me—
>
> A: Yes, sir.
>
> Q: —and the press pool, please be kind, what do you think my fat percentage is?
>
> MR. ANDERSON: Objection, Your Honor. Beyond the scope of cross.
>
> THE COURT: I'm going to save Mr. O'Connell from himself and sustain that objection.
>
> Dr. Harris, you can step down. Thank you, sir. Much appreciated.
>
> THE WITNESS: Thank you very much.
>
> THE COURT: Mr. O'Connell, your next witness.

---

[129] Tr. Ex. 32.14. https://www.rid.uscourts.gov/sites/rid/files/documents/17cv38/082319/P32.14.pdf.

MR. O'CONNELL: Richard Limeburner, Your Honor.

The linchpin of our wet murder case, which nevertheless made its way into Phase I, came off in convincing fashion.

Limeburner described himself as a "physical oceanographer. I study circulation and currents. I've worked at Woods Hole Oceanographic Institution for forty-five years." He does "a lot of work with satellite-tracked surface drifting buoys, hundreds of them on Georges Bank, and they basically drift west through the area" where Nathan testified that the boat sank and where *Orient Lucky* found his life raft. During his testimony he narrated photos and images from a PowerPoint presentation.[130]

Reverse drift techniques Limeburner developed over the years "which predict the path from where drifting pieces came, by combining the windage on the objects, the currents on the objects" were fruitful in three well-known recoveries. First, he backtracked pieces of helicopter wreckage found three weeks after a crash to the site where three bodies were found with the rest of the helicopter off Block Island. Second, for one hundred years, people had been looking for the *Portland*, which sank in an 1898 northeaster with the loss of 230 souls. Backtracking bodies that came ashore on Cape Cod, he found the wreck on Stellwagen Bank. Third, most famously, and as earlier mentioned, he found Air France 447 two miles deep in the equatorial Atlantic Ocean.

None of those prior finds of his had real-time wind and current data available from a Woods Hole Oceanographic buoy. "There's two sets of data that I'm interested in, the near-surface wind data and the near-surface ocean current," all provided by this Offshore Surface Mooring (OSSM) buoy, and supplemented by several others on the Shelf Break "frontal array" located right in between the 140-fathom mark in Block Canyon and the *Orient Lucky* rescue seven days later.

Utilizing US Coast Guard and Norwegian Coast Guard studies which included the "specifications of the life raft that Mr. Carman was in," Limeburner was able to factor in coefficients for the effect of wind

[130] Tr. Ex. 55.

on its surface area above the water and for the effect of current on its surface area underwater, with the drogue "parachute" sea anchor both deployed and not deployed during the seven days.

Limeburner's analysis started by summarizing scientific studies documenting that generally there is an east (to west) current along the Shelf Break south of the New England coast. He also described the other New England-area currents, showing the Gulf Stream sixty miles south of the Shelf Break.

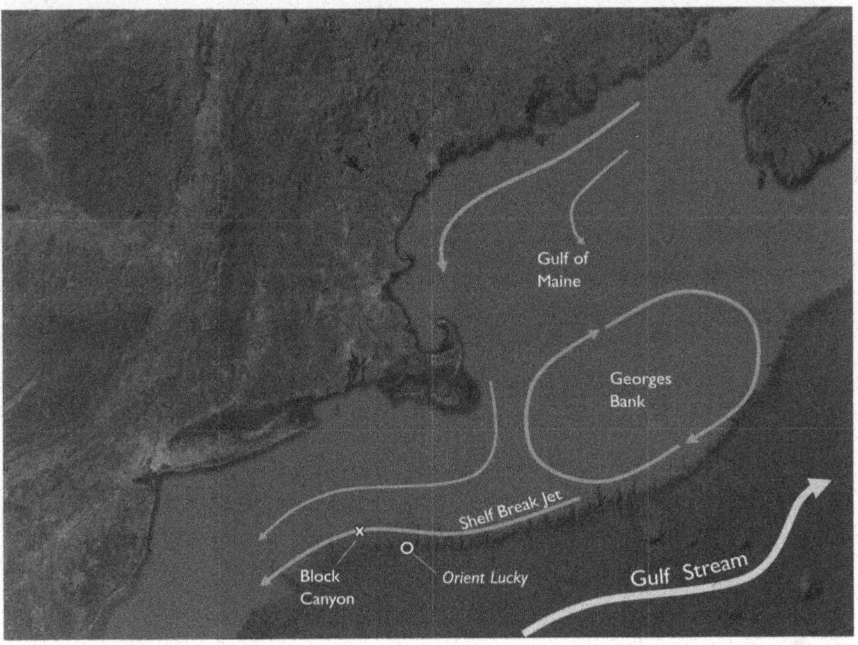

He recognized that the Gulf Stream can sometimes meander north, with large eddies spinning off, resulting in west (to east) current near the Shelf Break, as he depicted on June 13, 1997. But he showed there was nothing like that happening with the Gulf Stream during September 2016.

The data from the OSSM buoy, which Limeburner's computer organized into one-hour average intervals and vectors over Nathan's alleged seven-day drift, generally showed "the currents were going towards the west" and also "the winds were blowing towards the west." Limeburner explained:

> What this tells me is since the winds and the currents are all going westward, that the life raft had to have started at a location much farther to the east to have ended up at the *Orient Lucky* location.

He then displayed from the "really accurate measurements at the OSSM buoy," predicted courses for Nathan's life raft, with and without the drogue anchor deployed. Limeburner's reverse drift, where the life raft would necessarily have started in order to drift to the *Orient Lucky* seven days later, put Nathan's sinking spot about 40 miles to the east and south. "So then I said, 'Let's go to where Mr. Carman said the boat sank'" in Block Canyon at 140 fathoms. "And I plotted forward in time seven days where he would have drifted to," and "he would have ended up much further to the west because that's the direction of the wind and the current."

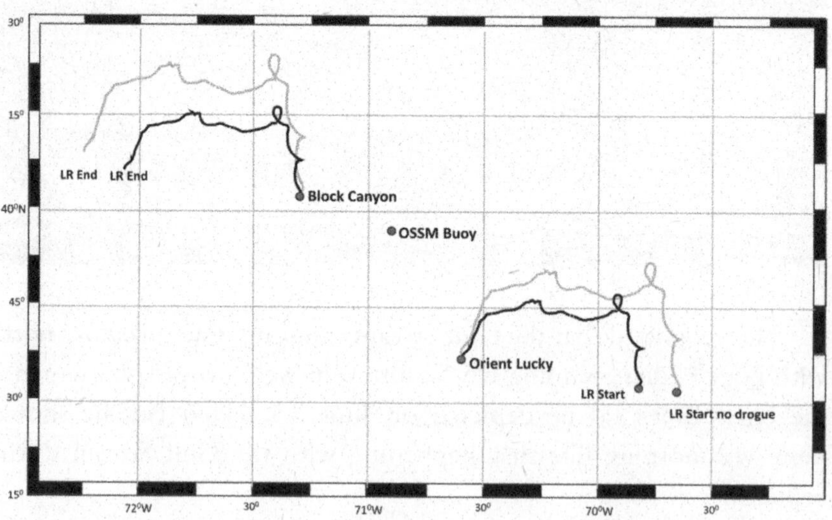

Limeburner drove home his point in the simplest of terms.

> If you take a helium balloon and you release it in the air, it goes downwind; it doesn't go upwind. If I take a tennis ball and I go to New Orleans and I throw it into the Mississippi River, it goes out to the Gulf of Mexico; it doesn't go to St. Louis.
>
> I don't see how a drifting life raft could go from Block Canyon upwind, upcurrent to the *Orient Lucky* position over that period.

It got better. Limeburner overlaid his predicted reverse and forward drifts on other sets of data. Coast Guard flight patterns show a September 19 flight to Block Canyon was almost directly over the life raft's drift if the JC 31 had sunk there. The Coast Guard would have seen him from the air, not to mention the Coast Guard cutters that were crisscrossing the area.

Neither, as he testified, did Alex Aucoin see Nathan, further demonstrated by Limeburner's plot of *Prudence* AIS data depicting its course on September 18. The two boats would have been on top of each other at the alleged noon sinking, and *Prudence* would have been "within one or two nautical miles of the drifting life raft at five in the afternoon."

Limeburner summed it up:

> And so, in my opinion, the location where Mr. Carman was found conflicts with my estimates of his drift path. My estimates were from real-time observations. I usually don't have real observations of the wind. I usually have to use satellite-computed winds or I have to use historical data. This is real-time data from a scientific mooring twenty miles away.

On cross, Attorney Anderson was fast running out of time and there was bickering between client and lawyer, with both of them visibly melting down. Anderson tried desperately to place Nathan in the Gulf Stream to ride it northeast, but the Woods Hole oceanographer emeritus would have none of it.

Q: And if Mr. Carman were down around the end in Block Canyon, he would be between the Shelf Break and the Gulf Stream, is that correct?

A: The Gulf Stream would be much further offshore, and he would still be in the region that the current observations predict a westward flow.

Liam did not bother with any re-direct, a show of confidence and strength, and with that, the Plaintiff Insurer rested.

***

With less than five minutes remaining on Judge McConnell's clock for Defendant's case, Attorney Anderson called Roth Sr., advising the Court, "Let me go get him. He's waiting out in the hall." Roth Sr. came through the swinging door, accompanied by Roth Jr., who got hit by it, and then took a seat at the very back, slumping, eye sockets sagging, so sadly strung out.

Roth Sr. claimed the old plug "oozed pigment or water from the rotten wood." When he drilled the holes for the trim tabs installation, "water came out."

THE COURT: Mr. Anderson—

MR. ANDERSON: I'm out of time?

THE COURT: —you want to wrap it up.

MR. ANDERSON: I'll reserve my two minutes for redirect.

THE COURT: You're four minutes over.

MR. ANDERSON: One minute for redirect?

Defendant had just demonstrated abysmal clock management. We were about to see the opposite—a perfectly timed cross-examination, based on Roth Sr.'s pre-trial deposition wounds.

THE COURT: Mr. O'Connell.

Q: Mr. Roth, you testified that you drilled the holes in the transom of the boat for the trim tabs.

A: I did.

Q: How many holes?

A: Two.

Q: So 2009 was the last time you worked on that boat?

A: Correct.

Q: You testified today that it wasn't a boat, is that correct?

A: That is correct.

Q: So today, August 23rd, 2019, you're stating under oath that it was not a boat, it was never underway as a boat before Mr. Woods got it?

A: No, not to my recollection.

THE COURT: Mr. O'Connell, you want to be wrapping it up, please.

For New England Patriots fans reading along, TB 12 went to work in the red zone with a hurry-up offense, firing a touchdown pass with no time remaining.

Q: Mr. Roth, if you were to take your two holes that you say you drilled into the transom of the *Chicken Pox*, and before you got underway you have to repair those holes, how would you do it?

A: Before? If they were just exposed holes?

Q: Yes.

A: Above or below the waterline?

Q: Above.

A: I mean, duct tape would do it.

Q: Duct tape would do it? Hmm.

MR. O'CONNELL: This is the last point, Judge.

Q: I'm showing you your deposition, and on page thirty-seven, line eleven, you finish up your answer by saying, "I mean, the old days they would use a wooden plug."

A: Correct.

Q: And then you were asked, "Tapered down?"

And you said, "A tiny bit, yeah."

Then the question was, "And then pounded in there?"

And you said, "Yup."

And then you were asked, "And then what would you do?"

And your answer was, "Leave it if you want, or you could sand it down flush."

And then you were asked, "You could sand it off. You could cut it off?"

And your answer was, "Yeah, you could do a lot of things."

Question: "You might then fiberglass over that?"

> Answer: "Yes, yeah."
>
> Question: "But would that be the preferred way to do it?"
>
> Answer: "Yeah. I mean if I was going to do it, yeah, I would have glassed over it. I mean I just would have glassed over it, thrown a patch over it and in an hour it would have been dry and been fine."
>
> But today your testimony is that you would have duct-taped it?
>
> A: I didn't say I would have duct-taped it. I said basically anything you could put in the hole to keep the water from coming in if it's above the waterline would work. The old days, yeah, used to put a wooden plug in, is what they used to do.
>
> MR. O'CONNELL: Nothing further, Your Honor.

Time on the clock expired as the only defense witness besides Nathan gave idiotic duct tape testimony. Once again, we see that water always seeks its own level. But even Roth Sr. said Nathan should have fiberglassed the holes.

> THE COURT: You can step down, Mr. Roth. Thank you, sir. Appreciate it.
>
> Counsel, evidence is now over. As I've told you earlier privately, we will schedule closing arguments for sometime after Labor Day and then I'll issue findings of fact and opinion at some point after that.
>
> We'll stand adjourned.

Right afterward, outside the courthouse, TV crews caught up with Brian Woods, who had attended every day of trial. He finally had a chance to say something about Nathan that he could not while testifying in Phase I. "It was an excellent boat. The survey proved excellent. He used it for many months before he had this problem. He altered the boat. I mean, ultimately, he sank the boat."[131]

Clean Sweep

At closing argument on September 4, TV and print reporters filled the courtroom, texting dispatches.

As Plaintiff, we went first and I wrapped up the Insurer's case in seventeen minutes, making three points.

First, Nathan's description of his faulty hole repairs contributed to the sinking, voiding insurance policy coverage. Four putty-filled half-dollar-size or even quarter-size holes at the transom waterline lacking interior backing and lacking exterior fiberglass seals were bound to fail. With Nathan's oft-described four-foot sine wave from the southeast as the boat travelled slowly north on its semicircle trolling route, the boat's rolling and rocking over five hours incrementally took on water through the holes, slowly filling the bilge even toward the bow due to the removed bulkheads, with down-flooding eventually progressing as the breaches in the hull dropped below the surface, yielding a stern-first sinking.

Second, I presented Judge McConnell a duplicate set of my dividers so he could play with the D = S x T testimony and chart Nathan's course and semicircles himself in the privacy of his chambers. "Much appreciated," said the judge. I then summarized the navigation, using my dividers and the charts, addressing the semicircle course while trolling:

> And I asked him, "If you started out at 666, which is what all the math and all the formulas say, and you went north at 4 knots as you were trolling for 5 hours until midday, if it was a straight line, you'd cover 20 nautical miles." But we know he didn't cover twenty nautical miles. He covered two-thirds of that on his course made

[131] https://turnto10.com/news/local/closing-arguments-set-in-nathan-carman-insurance-trial.

> good to the north, which is thirteen miles. And where does thirteen miles bring us from 666? Smack-dab at the 140-fathom mark.

We then displayed slides superimposing the *Prudence* course through the Fishtails as reflected by AIS data, which coincided with the same time on September 18, 2016 when Nathan claims he sank and the beginning of his life raft drift. Which further confirmed *Prudence* Captain Alex Aucoin's eyewitness testimony that he saw nothing there, and coupled with oceanographer Limeburner's and Dr. Harris's testimony, destroyed Nathan's seven-day-drift fantasy. Every single day "adrift" a lie.

Third, addressing the sinking and "not a word from his mother during this calamitous event," instead of telling her to bring in the lines, what Nathan should have said was:

> "Mother, we have a big problem here. We've got a lot of water in the boat. Here's a life jacket. Don't bother reeling in the lines. Pick them up out of the rod holders and throw them overboard and meet me in the pilot-house. I'm going to try and radio somebody, and if I can't raise anyone, grab the EPIRB that you bought for this very purpose and set it off so we can have helicopters come to get us, and we'll be home for dinner."

I concluded:

> In sum, while focusing on shoddy, puttied, self-inflicted holes and other predeparture alterations to his boat, it is appropriate for the Court to also look at Mr. Carman's deep-rooted credibility problems, I'll say lies, regarding his boat's sinking evolution and his navigation in getting to that spot.
>
> And, accordingly, we ask that the Court grant our Complaint for Declaratory Judgment.
>
> Thank you, Your Honor.

THE COURT: Thanks, Mr. Farrell.

Whether that was truly a good sign or not, which it sincerely seemed to be as I looked in his eye, would have to await Judge McConnell's reaction to Defendant's closing argument.

As Attorney Anderson stood up to close, Nathan turned and eerily nodded to engage Brian Woods, part seething, part smirking at him, putting Woods on notice that he was about to be torn apart. Not a good move by Nathan in front of a watchful federal judge. And Woods survived just fine. Anderson rambled for an hour on how the plug was never intended to be a boat and was somehow unseaworthy when Woods sold it. But Anderson could point to no evidentiary backup other than Roth Sr., contending it was impossible to know why it sank. Judge McConnell eventually interrupted, "Are you getting close to finishing?" which was a good sign, and Anderson shortly did.

Judge McConnell then announced he would issue his decision in a few weeks, and adjourned.

This is when Nathan addressed the media throng on the federal courthouse steps, recited as this book opened.[132] Liam tugged my arm, I turned, and we moved closer to watch. Anderson got a kick out of his client. Carman called me out. I decided it was time to get a license to carry.

***

Acknowledging that our team lacks psychological training and had no opportunity to review Nathan's medical or psychiatric records, it was clear to us that whatever his diagnosis, Nathan was able to turn it on, and off, at will. His spunky courthouse steps speech in a business suit was latitudes from his peculiar "then I made myself take rest" and his meek "I can be given to speaking softly" meows when we first met his scruffy self three years earlier.

Perhaps Nathan Carman was just manipulative, perhaps he was not on the spectrum at all, perhaps psychopath is the proper term.

---

[132] *See* n. 1 and text.

These are just some of the weighty questions along with dissected trial scenes analyzed by our team as we tried to unwind with a liquid lunch that turned into dinner, also liquid, at the Capital Grille. This required one more Hilton overnight. Then back home to slog through our transcript submissions for the judge to read, highlighting Nathan's pretrial testimony in support of the factual assertions and citations contained in our proposed findings of fact and conclusions of law.

Longer than any jury deliberations, weeks went by with the trial incessantly replayed in my brain as Liam and I focused on other cases.

But always, in the front of my mind a knot cinched up tighter and tighter, into the bilge of my gut. Should I have been flashier? Made Nathan whimper like in Brattleboro? Was that even possible when Phase I came down to an "incomplete, improper or faulty repair" clause in an insurance policy? How did it all look to our jury of one, who judiciously did not want a murder trial? And with 140 fathoms indelible now, weren't we a long way toward winning a Phase II intentional sinking if we had to? Rationally, I at least, came up with little we should have done differently.

Curiously, Attorney Anderson must have felt the same way. He and I unavoidably crossed paths, waiting around for a hearing in another case in Boston's gloomy Suffolk County Superior Court, his client a drunk fisherman who fell off a pier in January, spent nine days in the hospital detoxing, and actually had hypothermia. Anderson flashed a victor's smile at me, dripping with disdain, which had zero to do with his hypothermic drunk and everything to do with his double murderer. It surprised me more than anything. Never count your chickens before they've hatched. And the wait dragged on.

Exactly two months after closing argument the written opinion came down—a clean sweep for the Insurer. Judge McConnell held that Mr. Carman had violated Exclusion D in his All Risk marine insurance policy because he "made improper and faulty repairs to his boat that contributed to its sinking," and therefore the policy "does not cover Mr. Carman's loss."[133]

Consistent with Phase I and II bifurcation, although "[t]his litigation brought to light certain facts about Mr. Carman, his family, his boat, and the events leading up to and after the boat sank," the decision made clear "the Court is making no determination of whether Mr. Carman intended to sink his boat or to harm his mother. Those allegations are not a part of the counts the Court heard during the trial of this civil case."

Nevertheless, for Defendant Nathan Carman, the decision's findings of fact were scathing. By removing the bulkheads, and by reducing the boat's structural integrity, buoyancy, and seaworthiness, "the boat sank faster." There were continuing electrical problems with the port bilge pump, with neither it nor the stern bilge pump "functioning properly." Mr. Carman used an electric power drill to enlarge Woods's ½ inch holes, "leaving four half-dollar-size holes in the transom." Mr. Carman did not use "fiberglass mat fabric…to seal the holes. Simply putting epoxy into the holes without backing meant that the epoxy could get pushed through the holes" and "more likely than not this improper repair at least indirectly caused water to fill up the bilge, causing the boat to sink."

The judge's opinion summarized our key witnesses' testimony, concluding after each that Woods, Feeney, Klopman, Greene, the underwriting VP, and Charlesworth were "credible." In contrast, although Roth Sr. "conceded" Mr. Carman's repair was "incomplete because he did not seal the exterior of the holes with fiberglass," otherwise Roth Sr.'s "testimony was not credible." The opinion was thus well immunized from appeal.

The opinion also explained that while insurance coverage might have been denied due to Mr. Carman's *uberrimae fidei* failure to disclose his boat alterations to the Insurer, or since he knew the boat was unseaworthy when departing Ram Point Marina, there was no need for the

[133] 419 F.Supp.3d 336, 2019 AMC 2986 (D. R.I. 2019). https://ecf.rid.uscourts.gov/cgi-bin/show_public_doc?2017cv0038-177. It is an honor, albeit a sad one, to note that this was the last case ever published by the illustrious, almost one-hundred-year-old *American Maritime Cases.*

Court to go beyond his breach of the "incomplete, improper or faulty repair" clause, which "resolves the entire case."

Because the Insurer "appropriately denied coverage" and was "fair and transparent" and "never misrepresented" the policy throughout its dealings with Mr. Carman, his counterclaims were all dismissed as lacking merit.

Consistent with the judicial wisdom and restraint he demonstrated throughout trial, Judge McConnell did not comment directly on Nathan's lack of credibility or the science fiction of his drift story, leaving that to an unmentioned future criminal jury, as contemplated during the Fifth Amendment sidebar. Thus, Aucoin, Harris, and Limeburner did not make their way into the written opinion despite their compelling testimonies because Judge McConnell's crediting them would have been tantamount to finding Nathan's sinking story incredible and fraudulent. Which it was. But not at 140 fathoms in Block Canyon. The judge did not need to say any of that to support his implicit conclusion that Nathan lacked credibility, which our Nuclear Option probably helped.

Attorney Anderson perfunctorily moved for a new trial, which Judge McConnell quickly denied. Then, as leverage, Liam prepared a bill of costs, a trial victor's routine filing to recover certain expenses (not attorneys' fees) like deposition transcript copies and subpoena fees, which totaled around $11,000. Nathan was broke, and Anderson agreed by email with Liam not to appeal if we didn't chase Nathan for the money.

The thirty-day appeal period passed.

Case closed.

From the beginning of his involvement, Judge McConnell did not want a civil bench trial, where the standard of proof is "more likely than not," to prejudice or perhaps usurp poor Nathan's criminal due process with a jury, where conviction requires a steeper burden of "beyond a reasonable doubt." The judge had enunciated his concerns about Nathan's incriminating himself in the Fifth Amendment sidebar and offered him a way out.

It is well known, however, that you can lead a horse to water but you can't make it drink. Like his beloved Cruise, was Nathan now headed to the knackerman?

2020–2023

25
"NOT GUILTY!"

The US Attorney's Office in Vermont had no interest in harboring a double murderer in Vernon.

I received a grand jury subpoena for the Insurer's file and all of the testimony and evidence we had assembled. Right before COVID shut down the world, I loaded up my truck and with My Dear Amelia, we delivered the goods in Burlington, Vermont during her February 2020 school vacation week.

Over the next couple of years Liam and I responded to Vermont US Attorney Nikolas Kerest's various inquiries. He went to Williams College and had Block Island boating experience, so we hit it off.

This all cinematically culminated May 10, 2022 when my successor as Maritime Law Association President, Barbara Holland, and I had just strolled under Admiralty Arch in London, on our way to dinner at Winston Churchill's favorite club with Admiral Fred Kenney, USCG (Ret.), Legal Counsel for the UN International Maritime Organization. A short and sweet email from AUSA Paul Van de Graaf "Re: Nathan Carman" on my phone stopped me midstride. "Was arrested this morning. The federal indictment has been unsealed. We will be seeking detention."

Despite his shackled scream of "Not guilty!" while led by US Marshals to a courthouse back door for his arraignment, as seen on TV that day, Nathan Carman, a Defendant once again, was thereafter detained in a Keene, New Hampshire county jail cell rented by the feds. Too ironic: It was just down the road from his West Chesterfield fire truck, false address, and grandfather's Christmas light show.

Nathan's federal public defenders put together a motion for his release "on conditions pending trial."[134] They submitted several supportive letters, including one from the pastors of the Vernon Advent Christian Church, who wrote, "Nathan seems to be stable and does not pose a threat to the community."[135] The public defenders also wrote, "Nathan was diagnosed with Asperger Syndrome" at age five. At age seventeen, after Cruise died, he was hospitalized for a week, where Linda assaulted John, but "Asperger's was still the only concrete 'diagnosis'" for Nathan.

The government's position was that Nathan should be denied bail, period. He had "severed his ties with his remaining family" and lacked "any meaningful community ties." Available medical records indicated Carman was on psychiatric medications between ages seven and seventeen but then refused to take them. During his post-Cruise week in the hospital, "Carman was diagnosed with potential mood and psychotic disorders," and he had "a history of hostility and aggression." Since his indicted offenses involved "deceit, deception and subterfuge" in the killing of his mother and grandfather, "nothing is off the table" and "witnesses would be at risk" if he were to be bailed. "He has little or no empathy for others," the government warned.[136] One of his Vermont neighbors saw Carman throwing "human excrement," and following his arrest, an FBI search found $10,000 cash hidden in his house and "maggots in his refrigerator."[137]

---

[134] *United States v. Nathan Carman*, D. Vt. Case No. 5:22-cr-49-gwc, Document 27 (hereafter cited by Doc. number).

[135] Doc. 27–4.

[136] Doc. 8.

[137] Doc. 30.

Letters were also submitted by father Clark Carman, asserting that Nathan "is a good person,"[138] and in contrast, by his Aunts Elaine and Charlene, stating that "shortly Nathan will have a non-discretionary distribution made to him from a family trust[139] that would allow him significant ability to flee the jurisdiction of the court and allow him sufficient funds to carry out further acts of violence to the family."[140]

After a hearing, District of Vermont Chief Judge Geoffrey W. Crawford denied the public defenders' motion, ordering that Nathan "remain detained pending further proceedings."[141]

The criminal Indictment[142] in *United States of America v. Nathan Carman* seemed to generally follow along with our fraud affirmative defense and our proposed findings of fact in the Rhode Island insurance case.[143] As part of his scheme, the Indictment alleged, "On December 20, 2013, Nathan Carman murdered his grandfather." But there was no murder charge for that one in the Indictment. This was not so much because there was no smoking—or soaking wet—gun, but because there was no federal jurisdiction over the Connecticut state law crime of murder. Federal maritime jurisdiction, even in the Green Mountain State of Vermont, was available, however. Count Seven alleged:

> On or about September 17–18, 2016, within the special maritime and territorial jurisdiction of the United

---

[138] Doc. 36–1.

[139] This probably refers to the September 17, 2023, seven-year anniversary of Linda Carman's disappearance and her legal death date, more than a year in the future, when Nathan would become a multimillionaire.

[140] Doc. 33–1.

[141] Doc. 35.

[142] Doc. 1.

[143] "The insurance case tied all the evidence together and may have spurred a new effort to charge Carman, current and former investigators said. The insurers' lawyers laid out a case accusing Carman of plotting both killings and covering them up, using police investigation findings and information they obtained themselves." Dave Collins and Denise Lavoie, "How investigators say 'murder on the high seas' case came together against Nathan Carman," Associated Press, May 26, 2022. https://www.wmur.com/article/nathan-carman-case-52622/40114218.

> States, defendant Nathan Carman unlawfully killed Linda Carman with malice aforethought. Moreover, Nathan Carman killed Linda Carman willfully, deliberately, maliciously, and with premeditation.

He "planned how he would report the sinking…and his mother's disappearance at sea as accidents." In our insurance case, "both in discovery and at trial, Nathan Carman maintained his false narratives, misrepresenting what happened to Linda Carman" and what occurred on the boat, just as he did in the Sisters' Slayer Suit, with Nathan's "scheme to defraud and obtain money," both his $85,000 insurance policy proceeds and what was now a $7 million Chakalos Family Dynasty Trust inheritance.

There were three specific mail fraud counts, and three specific wire fraud counts, all occuring in Vermont, and all falling within federal jurisdiction, charging Nathan with a double-murder scheme and transmitting false narratives when he sent out false discovery responses while he was representing himself pro se in the Sisters' Slayer Suit.

As later briefed by the government, "Put simply, the charged scheme involves money, murder, and misrepresentations."[144] The Indictment's final Count Eight alleged federal wire fraud in the false narrative emailed from Vermont about the voyage Nathan "provided to the insurance company at the initiation of his fraudulent insurance claim"—the October 19, 2016 "then I made myself take rest" description for Martha Charlesworth.

Over the next year we continued to cooperate with the US Attorney and AUSAs, answering a variety of questions and providing Martha for an interview. She and many of our witnesses were going to be testifying for the government and we learned of others.

ATF Special Agent Kellie Senecal was looking forward to testifying. She had been pushing the Connecticut and New Hampshire US Attorney's Offices for years to go after Nathan for misrepresenting his address to Shooters Outpost and for then losing the Sig Sauer. She

---

[144] Doc. 66.

was completely baffled by the feds' lack of interest after the State of Connecticut failed to charge Nathan for John Chakalos's murder, and she was continually amazed at state and federal infighting and interoffice politics getting in the way. So when Nathan did it again, she had crowed, "I told you so."

Brian Woods, along with Jonathan Klopman, finally had an opportunity to inspect the trim tab components Nathan had removed to his truck, which the South Kingstown PD would not let us inspect for our case. Because ⅜ inch bronze tubes still screwed into the actuators had thin rings of 5200 adhesive around the outside circumferences—altogether ½ half inch in diameter—that evidenced conclusively the thru-transom holes originally drilled by Woods were indeed ½ half inch, as called for by the Bennett template.

Jonathan Klopman's graphic demonstration of Nathan's unbelievable bow-first sinking and N. Stuart Harris, MD's physiological opinions on Nathan's lack of hypothermia would be key evidence in the government's case.

The government decided not to use Richard Limeburner, however, opting instead for in-house USCG oceanographer Arthur Allen, whose opinion was consistent. Normally, a party can only use one expert per discipline. Allen had access to all the Coast Guard's search and rescue records and precise search patterns. He also had developed the Coast Guard's reverse drift analysis program. Allen could opine as a Coast Guard insider that Nathan's life raft would have been found during the SAR effort if he had been in the sixty-two-thousand-square-mile search area, and further, that his drift story was so totally refuted by wind and current conditions as to remove any reasonable doubt that it was all a lie.

I was beyond curious to watch how the trial scheduled for October 2023 in Rutland, Vermont would unfold and booked a Hampton Inn room there early on, knowing that the trial, combined with leaf-peeping season, would exhaust local accommodations.

But I ended up cancelling my reservation.

On the road again, I was in Montreal on June 15, 2023 for a meeting of the Comité Maritime International, an assembly of maritime lawyers from around the world. Nathan had truly been a resident of

New Hampshire for about one year at that point, when I got a morning voicemail from AUSA Nate Burris asking that I call him. Nate reported Nathan Carman had just been found dead in his cell.

Neither Liam nor I was shocked, knowing from taking twenty hours of testimony that Nathan was a most perplexing soul. Vince and I had also discussed Nathan as not having the tools to survive long-term incarceration and we all predicted that eventually either Nathan would do himself in or somebody else in the big house would.

The official press release from the Cheshire County Department of Corrections states that Nathan Carman, age twenty-nine, "was found unresponsive overnight in his cell on one of the routine inside rounds completed by Correctional Staff. Mr. Carman was the sole occupant of the cell." The Keene Police Department Incident Report reflects that CPR was performed for forty minutes and at 3:18 a.m. "he was pronounced deceased." On his desk was a stack of files and a notebook.

> The notebook was labeled "Attorney-client privilage [*sic*]. All content are legal notes subject to Attorney-client privilage [*sic*] Nathan Carman." This cover of this notebook was photographed but, after consultation with the Attorney General's Office, none of the contents of this notebook or the legal files on the desk were examined or read. These documents were seized as found and secured for safekeeping.

The death was deemed "not suspicious" by the State of New Hampshire.[145] But what about the specific cause? Douglas L. Iosue, Superintendent of the Cheshire County Department of Corrections, told me even he never received a copy of the New Hampshire medical examiner's report on the cause of death. My request for a copy under the

[145] "Death of Vermont man charged with killing mom at sea was not suspicious, autopsy shows," NBC 10 Boston, June 28, 2023. https://www.nbcboston.com/news/local/death-of-vermont-man-charged-with-killing-mom-at-sea-was-not-suspicious-autopsy-shows/3078223/.

New Hampshire Right-to-Know Law, RSA Chapter 91-A, was denied and the US Attorney's Office would not provide any specifics.

Iosue told me by phone that he is 99 percent sure Nathan's death was suicide. I followed up with his higher-ups and can confirm that a well-placed New Hampshire law enforcement official told me off the record that it was indeed suicide, they just wouldn't say so. Perhaps that is in reaction to recent high-profile jailhouse suicides, like those of former New England Patriots henchman/tight end Aaron Hernandez in a Massachusetts state jail; Jeffrey Epstein, while in federal custody; and also Whitey Bulger after his prison transfer, which wasn't a suicide but was tantamount to a death sentence. I obtained more specifics from Bill Michael, learning that Nathan used shoelaces to choke himself.

Connecticut Attorneys David X. Sullivan and Martin J. Minnella had taken over Nathan's criminal defense from the Office of the Federal Public Defender. Attorney Sullivan (then in private practice, before his appointment as US Attorney for the District of Connecticut) told me since they no longer had a client, even they did not get access to the autopsy report. But there was communication from Nathan to his attorneys about what to do in his absence (perhaps in his notebook or on a confidential thumb drive Iosue told me was used to exchange information between prisoner and lawyer), perhaps further showing that what he did to himself in jail had its intended effect.

Attorney Sullivan also told me he is convinced, of course, that Nathan would have been acquitted. I tried several times subsequently to engage Attorneys Sullivan and Minnella, to no avail. But I must seriously question how these inlanders could defend our overwhelming nautical evidence.

AUSA Paul Van de Graaf told me, in contrast, that he is convinced a jury would have found Nathan guilty beyond a reasonable doubt of murdering his mother at sea. In answer to my biggest curiosities, no, the FBI did not recover spent shells for ballistic testing from Vernon or West Chesterfield search warrants. No, they did not find the JC 31 wreck. No, they did not have satellite photos of the JC 31 outside the Coast Guard's sixty-two-thousand-square-mile SAR area. No, they did not have any major evidence that we did not know about, although they did have more evidence from the Sisters on Nathan's financials, or actually, the lack thereof, at the time of the final voyage. Essentially though, what the US Attorney's Office had against Nathan was lie upon lie upon lie upon lie…

Was it only a coincidence that I had been subpoenaed as a trial witness just ten days before Nathan took his own life? Within a few days Nathan's lawyers would have received a copy of my trial subpoena and would have updated Nathan thereafter. Attorney Sullivan told Shelley Murphy of *The Boston Globe* that on Nathan's final night they had a "very productive and proactive" phone call and "he was in excellent spirits." But as I told Shelley, Nathan Carman must have felt "more trapped than when he was with a sinking boat."[146] Trapped at 140 fathoms.

It was at Nathan's sparsely attended funeral that Attorney Minnella, who paid for it, eulogized, "The real story of Nathan Carman may never be told."[147] But the story would not die. Netflix produced a documentary featuring home movies of Nathan as a child; there was another ACS News *20/20* episode, "Family Lies";[148] three other books; and several podcasts.

The indicted "innocent until proven guilty" who dies before criminal conviction is finalized gets a clean slate, the charges formally dismissed. Other studies might emphasize that to build suspense and reasonable doubt for poor Nathan. But in my mind, based on the evidence fairly presented herein, and as demonstrated by his last act, Nathan Carman brutally, heartlessly murdered both his grandfather and mother for family money. Beyond reasonable doubt.

---

[146] Shelley Murphy, "Nathan Carman, accused of killing his mother at sea, found dead in his cell at N.H. jail," *Boston Globe*, June 15, 2023. https://www.bostonglobe.com/2023/06/15/metro/nathan-carman-dies/.

[147] Shelley Murphy, "'The real story of Nathan Carman may never be told,' lawyer says at funeral," *Boston Globe*, June 22, 2023. https://www.bostonglobe.com/2023/06/22/metro/nathan-carman-funeral/.

[148] "Family Lies," ABC News *20/20* video, April 4, 2025. https://abc.com/episode/405bde80-f336-4436-a3d8-ce200d485148.

BITTER ENDS

Our voyage complete, it is now time to whip loose, or bitter, ends.[149]

Regarding a couple of macro issues, first and foremost, let Nathan Carman's tragic saga stand as an example that maritime crime does not pay. Linda was declared dead by a Connecticut probate court on September 17, 2023. Despite all his efforts to accelerate his receipt of one-quarter of the Chakalos Family Dynasty Trust, Nathan ironically predeceased her by three months. Did that let the Sisters off the hook on the announced plan to donate his "blood money" quarter share to charity? We don't know.

Something this book does not deeply explore, because Attorney Anderson and Nathan made his medical and psychological records irrelevant in our marine insurance case, is his mental health. We only got a confirmed Asperger's diagnosis from the criminal pleadings. But Nathan must have had some other affliction(s) too.

Whatever his issues, did they stem from birth, vaccinations, an absent father, a single mother with a gambling problem? Can a seventeen-year-old be forced to take medication? A twenty-two-year-old? Do pharmaceuticals even help, or make it all worse?

---

[149] *See Knight's Modern Seamanship*, "Knotting and Splicing," 662–63, n. 34, and *Chapman Piloting & Seamanship*, "Marlinspike Seamanship," 795, n. 35. Whipping prevents the fraying of loose or bitter ends.

Was he just plain evil, or more scientifically, possessed by a criminal gene?

What was his poor mother to do? Let him live in an RV in her driveway so she could keep an eye on him, while he drove her crazy? Or let him move away, not knowing what he was up to, while he drove her crazy? Loving him so much that she knowingly risked her life fishing with him, texting Sharon Hartstein, just in case?

Unstopped, a family tragedy struck twice.

And Nathan is not alone. With the other two under-thirty young men in this book, Ms. Y's deceased young boyfriend and Roth Jr., both ravaged by drugs, we have a random threesome slipping through the very big cracks of our mental health/criminal justice interface.

Add another one, too, a Nathan predecessor, Sandy Hook's Adam Lanza. It is a stretch to call it a silver lining, but an expansive Connecticut assault weapons ban resulted, effective April 4, 2013.

So Nathan went from Connecticut to New Hampshire, gave a false address, and purchased his Sig Sauer on November 11, 2013, putting on a convincing show of sanity for Shooters Outpost salesman Jed Warner.

Thus, state and federal gun-control and background checks are broadly implicated in this sorry tale too. But opponents say guns don't kill people, people do—or boats do. And so on.

So what?

***

Now, turning to micro issues which still need to be addressed. As our team had determined by December 2017, Nathan Carman's at-sea escapade gives rise to two very different stories, one a known fiction, one a known unknown.

The fictional story is based on Nathan's navigation testimony, as first sworn in his December 2016 examination under oath, consistent with his January 2018 deposition in our case, consistent with his August 2018 New Hampshire deposition in the Sisters' Slayer Suit, and consistent with his August 2019 insurance trial testimony. That story, in short, has mother and son stopping to fish southeast of Block Island at imaginary Striper Rock, then heading south for five hours to 666 fathoms in Block Canyon, where they turned around and trolled north in semicircles, sinking at 140 fathoms in Block Canyon's Fishtails. We mathematically held him to that navigation story, which he swore to multiple times, although he tried to squirm out of it at trial. And it sinks him.

Because we know the JC 31 did not sink there or how he described it. Aucoin on *Prudence* saw nothing. It is unadulterated fiction that the boat sank bow-first and Nathan then drifted over the next seven days in his life raft from the Fishtails to the *Orient Lucky*. Each of those seven days in a life raft is utter fiction too. Our experts from Woods Hole and Mass General were beyond reproach.

The remaining interstitial known unknowns in Nathan Carman's actual time at sea can now be brought into better focus. How did he get to *Orient Lucky*, undetected by Coast Guard SAR efforts? What happened to Linda? What happened to his boat? What size and how many transom holes were there?

Maybe none, to answer that last question. There are no known witnesses who actually saw any new hole drilled through the transom at Ram Point Marina, even Mike Iozzi who was sitting right there watching Nathan use a hole saw. How many holes? What size? No one knows.

Except Nathan. And what he said, soon after his rescue, as reported in Attorney Santos's letter to the Connecticut prosecutors, was that there were four half-dollar-size holes, which he then inadequately sealed. That was testimony from Nathan himself that Judge McConnell used to deny his insurance claim.

But what if Nathan had in fact used the fiberglass repair kit he also bought at West Marine that day and applied resin-saturated patches over the puttied holes? Or what if he did not drill any new holes in the transom and just fiberglassed Woods's four ½ inch diameter holes shut? Done right—Nathan was certainly smart enough—Woods's solidly constructed sea boat could have stayed afloat indefinitely. Until scuttled.

Whether Nathan and Linda went east or west of Block Island (either is plausible), did they actually go to Block Canyon? Probably, because it is far and away the closest canyon to Block Island, due south. Talking Linda into making that trip offshore, skipping fruitless fishing at non-existent Striper Rock, they could have arrived at the Fishtails well before sunrise, in time for first light, the best time for hungry big fish on the prowl. Using his vision, radar, and AIS receiver, Nathan could confirm the JC 31 was all alone then, even before *Prudence* arrived ten miles to the west to begin lobstering. This gave Nathan a couple of hours to work with, and Linda wasn't even planning to report back to Sharon Hartstein until 9:00 a.m.

But Nathan then had seven days to kill. Not Linda—that happened quickly. Seven days during which he was not enjoying leisurely brunches adrift, not wet and shivering, not beaten by up to twelve-foot seas in his Bouncy Castle. Seven days he was not spotted by Coast Guard ships, helicopters, fixed-wing assets, or any other vessels.

The JC 31 must have been totally operational during that week it was missing with him aboard. Did he head south to Virginia, where he had sought refuge when Cruise somehow died? Or did he hide out on off-limits Nomans Land, just south of Martha's Vineyard? No friggin' way. Coast Guard broadcasts and press releases described the boat as distinctive, as was its owner. Someone would have seen and said something, especially after news reports came out about Nathan's miraculous rescue.

He must have stayed well outside the Coast Guard search and rescue area, say, more than one hundred miles south of Nantucket, in the warm Gulf Stream, confident of its northeast current (but his major failure was not doing his homework on the Shelf Break's west current). He had plenty of fuel. And thirty days' provisions. And at least $1,000 cash. But there was very little vessel traffic in those environs and all the while he would be listening on his upgraded radio and surreptitiously watching AIS transmissions of vessel comings and goings to make sure they did not detect his presence.

No doubt, the Desperado hid out—until the Coast Guard posse called off the search. Then Nathan got himself in his boat to where he would be incredibly (repeat, incredibly) rescued on Sunday, a week after the alleged sinking.

But, you ask, could Nathan and Captain Zhao have been in cahoots? Could that explain Nathan's nice handwritten thank you note? On a dark and stormy night, could Nathan have slunk to a Providence pier during an earlier *Orient Lucky* call? Could he then have given the good captain a nice briefcase full of cash as a down payment, with Nathan's final $1,000 due upon successful rescue at a to-be-arranged time and place on Captain Zhao's next voyage here? Now that's fiction. As earlier postulated, Nathan was humanly incapable of conspiring with others. Adding a language barrier and the always-changing schedule for trampers like *Orient Lucky*, any "another vessel must have been in on it too" theory is so full of baseless, refutable speculation that it must be ruled out.

Yet a known known is that the *Orient Lucky* log and emails to the Coast Guard make no mention, besides the life raft, of any other proximate vessel in the rescue evolution. How did Nathan in his life raft get so close without the *Orient Lucky* observing the JC 31 beforehand?

Working just by himself, per usual, the Genius would have known from his VHF radio and AIS receiver and integrated courseplotter screen that *Orient Lucky* had headed south that morning out of Providence and that it turned sharply east at 5:45 a.m., following the Ambrose-to-Nantucket shipping lane. Then, at 9:00 a.m., *Orient Lucky* turned sharply south, at fourteen knots, to change ballast water south of the Shelf Break.

Getting the JC 31 into position, this time Nathan really did prepare to abandon ship. He plugged the fuel vents so there would be no spill and securely tied down anything floatable so there would be no flotsam. He readied the life raft, stocking it with supplies in case it was ever found, or in case he miscalculated and truly drifted away. Using the washdown pump, he quickly flooded the bilge. Perhaps he used a hammer to punch open any week-old fiberglassed transom holes. And he may, or may not, have loosened the hose clamps on the engine's saltwater cooling pump (which Attorney Anderson asked Jonathan Klopman about during his deposition). Unlike his Harbor of Refuge gig, this time Nathan made sure the seacock stayed open.

Into the life raft jumped Nathan. Diesel perhaps still running, cooling water keeping it from overheating and giving off telltale steam, his—well, no longer his—*Flying Dutchman* sailed eastward on autopilot, filling with water until it sank stern first, quickly without forward floatation voids, and down with it went the aluminum wheelhouse swallowing the EPIRB. If that happened only one mile horizontally away from the *Orient Lucky* course line, it would be that much harder to find the JC 31 wreck one and one-half miles down.[150] Which the Sisters' sonar efforts failed to do.

Independent of Liam and me, that is what Brian Woods also concluded on how Nathan scuttled his solid-as-a-rock boat.

CGIS Special Agent Eric Gempp (now retired from the Coast Guard), who led the federal criminal investigation and interviewed the *Orient Lucky* crew in Boston, generally agrees with our conclusion, with one exception. He believes Nathan to have been so extraordinarily controlling (we certainly concur) that he would not have taken any chance that the JC 31 wouldn't sink, so he must have made sure it went down before letting the life raft drift away to intersect *Orient Lucky's* southbound course.[151]

Either way, all of us assume Nathan watched from his boat while *Orient Lucky* kept heading south, and while it was still several miles to the north, he timed things just right and jumped into the life raft for his brief ride, praying, in his way, that the ship would not alter its straight-line course.

---

[150] Let's just hypothesize the JC 31 sank where Limeburner says Nathan must have started his life raft drift in order to arrive seven days later at the *Orient Lucky* rescue location. Could Nathan have gotten to thirteen miles south of that beginning drift spot to turn around and head north in his semicircles by a little after sunrise around 7:12 a.m. on Sunday, September 18, 2016? No way. That turnaround location would be over 160 miles from Nathan's Block Island X at his "Striper Rock" southeast of Block Island. At sixteen knots, it would have taken him ten hours to get there, which would have been high noon. But as Nathan agreed with me at trial, it was an "absolute" that he was constrained by sunrise as the time he started trolling from his southern terminus.

[151] Concurring with us that Nathan's bow-first sinking story was hogwash, Gempp also doubts his Block Canyon story that the life raft was on the surface when Nathan got his bearings, since its automatic hydrostatic release is designed not to work until it was submerged 1.5 to 4 meters. But Nathan wouldn't have known that since he released the life raft himself before sinking the boat as *Orient Lucky* bore down.

And whereas Nathan picked a terrible place to concoct an outrageous drift story southeastward from 140 fathoms, so near Limeburner's Woods Hole oceanographic buoy, Nathan was lucky to have a perfect day to be found so near there by the *Orient Lucky*.

We all conclude that the watch standers on the *Orient Lucky* bridge simply failed to see the JC 31 by either radar or eyesight—and quite understandably given the sea conditions depicted in the *Orient Lucky* rescue photos of Nathan waving his red flag.

In the best of conditions fiberglass boats yield notoriously poor radar images, the radar waves bending around their smooth curves and not bouncing back crisply to the sending vessel's rotating radar antennae. Three-dimensional metallic perpendicular planes, mounted as high as practicable, provide the clearest radar image.[152] The JC 31 had none. Even its aluminum wheelhouse's flat sides had rounded edges. As any recreational boater using radar knows, it is not a panacea.

That day, moreover, to the extent the eight-foot ocean waves physically obstructed the radar waves from fully reaching the rolling JC 31, its radar image would appear less distinct than in calm conditions.

Furthermore, with *Orient Lucky*'s radars set for longer-range scanning in the open ocean combined with that day's choppy waters creating unwanted sea clutter on the radar screens, it would be harder still to differentiate small contacts,[153] a problem compounded by adjusting the controls to suppress sea clutter because "echoes from small close contacts may be suppressed also."[154] Even if *Orient Lucky's* computerized ARPA (automatic radar plotting aid), which is normally used in congested waters, was operating at sea that day absent vessel traffic,

---

152 *See*, e.g., *Chapman Piloting & Seamanship*, 593, n. 35; "Safety Alert: Improving small vessel detectability," *Professional Mariner*, August 22, 2023. https://professionalmariner.com/safety-alert-improving-small-vessel-detectability-to-reduce-collisions/?mc cid=6315e15f1d&mc eid=4864ab7375 (NTSB Safety Alert SA-087/June 2023).

153 *Radar Navigation Manual* (Defense Mapping Agency, 1985), 25.

154 Richard A. Block, *Radar Observer Manual* (Marine Education Textbooks, 1987), 18.

contact acquisition and automatic plotting of the JC 31 would have the same problems.

The *Orient Lucky* watch standers, heading south and looking straight into the bright noontime fall equinox sun, understandably failed to make visual contact too. Well south of the Shelf Break, where no fishing occurs, a recreational boat would be entirely unexpected. Its white hull and aluminum flashes would easily blend in with the heavy whitecaps, and just like radar, the JC 31 in the troughs would be partly obscured by cresting waves. Even the bright-orange life raft went undetected, until 12:40 p.m., as recorded in the *Orient Lucky* log, when Nathan yelled at the deck crew from thirty yards away—or so he incredulously said at trial.

Ever covering his tracks, before he entered the water to swim to the life ring, Nathan also cut a hole in the life raft, which soon sank.[155]

Bravo Zulu (Navy-speak for "well done") to Nathan for pulling off the JC 31's final day undetected before scuttling it, timing his short little life raft ride just right. And while a precise re-creation is admittedly challenging (can anyone come up with a better explanation?[156]), it absolutely remains a big fat lie that Nathan drifted for seven days in his life raft from 140 fathoms to the *Orient Lucky*.

That brings us to the $7–$11 million question. Did the $44 million trust shrink to $28 million due to back Connecticut income tax payments and penalties after New Hampshire booted John Chakalos's

---

[155] *Orient Lucky* photos show the life raft deflating as soon as Nathan abandoned it. Gempp, also on the case before Nathan was found, quickly sent a fixed-wing asset to find the life raft, and it did. But by the time a Coast Guard vessel got there to retrieve it, it was long gone.

[156] Actually, we probably do have the technology. Liam and I tried early on to get commercial satellite images but had no luck. But we always assumed military satellites would have seen the JC 31, and the Navy's submarine acoustical sensors would have heard the sinking, as when the *Titan* beer can imploded on its descent to the *Titanic*. But those tools were off-limits even for CGIS, Gempp told me. And he confirmed that commercial satellite images were extremely scanty inside or around the sixty-two-thousand-square-mile SAR area, and what little there was near shore revealed nothing.

residency claim? We don't know. But more importantly, how exactly did Linda disappear at sea?

Mother "was part of the problem," Nathan forthrightly testified at trial. What was his optimal "solution"? Certainly not stashing her body in the fish hold. What if the boat was ever found?

Wrapping her with a newly purchased West Marine harness without floatation and anchor chain for permanence around an anchor and dropping her somewhere off the continental shelf? Sure, certainly conceivable, but not Nathan's kind of solution. It would preserve too much physical evidence for too long.

This is the guy who less than three years before picked up his spent shells, discarded his destroyed computer hard drive and truck GPS, and meticulously disappeared his brand-new $2,099.99 assault rifle. And as we learned on the April 4, 2025, *20/20* "Family Lies" episode, Nathan had left a hateful letter about his mother in his Vermont home before the fateful voyage. But no computer—yet another chilling parallel with the murder of his grandfather.

No, it was imperative for Nathan that there be zero evidence of his next victim, no cuts or bruises, no traces of blood on the boat, in case the Coast Guard were to find them, or her, or just him, and he knew they would start looking soon. Getting rid of his mother ASAP was his only way to go.

Granted, there is no one who can tell us what happened. But out of the blue, this time from the pulpit, I was going to stick Nathan a third time if we tried Phase II, and I urged this "solution" on the AUSAs.

The clues are in Nathan's December 16, 2016 EUO testimony about the two-by-two-by-five-foot cooler containing iced bait he says his mother brought along and in his October 19, 2016 written statement to Martha Charlesworth describing the "brown slick on the surface of the water that was the color of engine oil" and lasted "an hour" when his mother disappeared.

But he misdescribed "the color of engine oil" as "brown" and never mentioned any rainbow-colored, purplish sheen we all know from refined petroleum products.

In fact, Nathan was describing a chum slick, not a brown crude oil spill from the *Exxon Valdez* or the *Deepwater Horizon*. Add that to his *20/20* "Lost at Sea" TV assertion "I did not cause my mother's death" for his chosen "solution" to his "problem."

Predawn Sunday, September 18, 2016, while pretending to get ready for trolling, something like a simple "excuse me, Mom" and elbowing Linda overboard got things going. Then, as with the Sig Sauer, Nathan put his warped faith in the sea.

Like a wiggling whiting, Linda became the centerpiece of his "mackerel, squid, and maybe some bunker" smorgasbord, fresh from her big cooler. Overly generous with his chum offerings, chunks submerging, fish oil and gurry with bilirubin spread a greasy brownish slick over the surface. With nutrient-rich waters upwelling from the depths into the 140-fathom honey hole, here came the resident sharks, following the breakfast trail,[157] soon electrified by Linda's increasingly panicked treading water, spawning a feeding frenzy.

"Help me, Big Guy, help me," she pleaded and pleaded. But he would not. And with his sin of omission, Nathan watched his mother's body disappear at sea. Piece by piece, like his Sig.

No wonder, as Nathan wrote Martha, "then I made myself take rest."

---

[157] The "oily nature" of mackerel makes it "a homing beacon for sharks." Captain John Galvin, "Fishing the Northeast Canyons," FishTrack, 2021. https://www.fishtrack.com/article/fishing-the-northeast-canyons.

ACKNOWLEDGMENTS

It surprised me that so many volunteered to read drafts of this book and I am grateful for their thoughtful insights, often urging me to curb my snarkiest comments. In rough chronological order, many thanks to Walter Mullin, Cory Hott, Shea Farrell, Eddie Reid, Eric Biss, Sam Farrell, Corelle Rokicki, Liam Potter, my agent Tina Wainscott, Amelia Rokicki, Derek Burritt, Dotty Shelton, Martha Cusick, Fred Goldsmith, Kate Mullin, Sarah Cusick, Colleen O'Connor, Julie Lynch, and Denny O'Neil. Thanks also to Jonathan Klopman, beyond his fine work on this case, for his help with the graphics.

Yours for a fair tide, DJF

ABOUT THE AUTHOR

Photo Credit:
Christopher Seufert Photography

David J. Farrell, Jr. received his primary maritime education and initial Coast Guard licensing in Chatham, Massachusetts. He graduated from Belmont Hill School, Williams College, Columbia University, and Duke Law School.

For forty years Attorney Farrell has been a maritime casualty trial lawyer, eight years in Seattle and afterwards on Cape Cod. A past president of The Maritime Law Association of the United States, he received the U.S. Coast Guard Commandant's Distinguished Public Service Award. A titulary member of the Comité Maritime International, he served as a legal advisor to the U.S. State Department and U.S. Coast Guard at UN International Maritime Organization meetings.

A frequent speaker and author on maritime law and public policy issues, Attorney Farrell has written hundreds of nonfiction briefs during his career. *Dead in the Water: The Real Story of Nathan Carman* is his first nonfiction book.

To see more *Carman* case photos and exhibits, visit davidjfarrelljr.com.